W9-BSZ-976

SEX BEHIND BARS

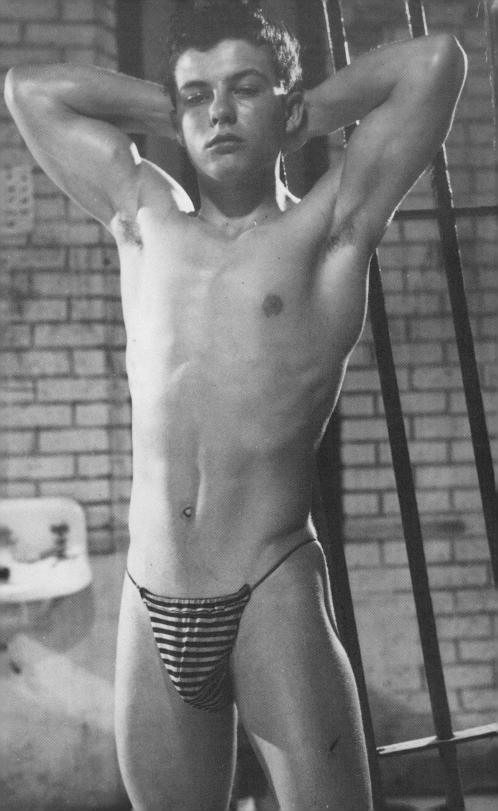

SEX BEHIND BARS

A Novella, Short Stories
and
True Accounts

Robert N. Boyd

Gay Sunshine Press
San Francisco

Copyright © 1984 by Robert N. Boyd.
1st edition. 3rd printing, 1995
Frontispiece & cover photos by A.M.G.

All rights reserved. Except for brief passages quoted in a newspaper, magazine, radio, or television review, no part of this book may be reproduced
in any form or by any means, electronic or mechanical, including
photocopying and recording, or by any information storage and retrieval
system, without permission in writing from the publisher.

The author would like to express his deepest appreciation to the following
persons, without whose assistance or encouragement this book would never
have become a reality: Marvin Bevans, John Calendo, Dean Drury, Donald
Hanover III, Brandon Judell, Winston Leyland, Henry Mach, Sam Staggs,
Darryl Towles, Irving Waldorf, Jim Yousling.

ACKNOWLEDGEMENTS

"Life Behind Bars" first appeared in *Mandate* (Sept. 1983); "Prison Slang"
first appeared in *In Touch* (Feb. 1983); "Sex Behind Bars" first appeared
(as "Sex in Prison") in *In Touch* (March 1981); "Prison Sex" first appeared
in *First Hand* Magazine (Part I: "Rape," Feb. 1983; Part II: "Turn-Outs,"
April 1983; Part III: "Joint Sissies," June 1983; Part IV: "Prison Guards,"
Fall 1982); "Slippery Sex" first appeared in *First Hand* (Aug. 1983); "Butch
Virgins" first appeared in *First Hand* (Sept. 1983); "Tank Boss" first
appeared in *Blueboy* (Aug. & Sept. 1980); "Prisoners" first appeared in
Blueboy (July 1981); "The Hole" first appeared (as "The Lock-Up") in
Honcho (Oct. 1983); "Going Home" first appeared in *Numbers* (July 1982).

Library of Congress Cataloging in Publication Data:

Boyd, Robert N.
  Sex behind bars.

   1. Homosexuality, Male—Fiction.   2. Prisoners—Sexual behavior—
Fiction. 3. Homsexuality, Male—United States. 4. Prisoners—United
States—Sexual behavior. I. Title.
PS3552.08787S4 1984   813'.54   83-20687
ISBN 0-917342-34-8 (lim. ed.)
ISBN 0-917342-37-2 (pbk.)

Gay Sunshine Press
P.O. Box 410690
San Francisco, CA 94141

CONTENTS

INTRODUCTION

T HE LINE OF DISTINCTION between fact and fiction is a fine one, often unnoticeable, often imperceptible, especially when the fiction is contemporary (as opposed to historical or science fiction). The many stories in this collection are a combination of my imagination and my observations of what actually goes on in a prison setting.

The publisher and I agree to include fiction and non-fiction side by side, because the whole picture of male-male sex behind bars cannot be fully painted by just one or the other of those two literary avenues. Most anthologies are devoted to either fiction exclusively or to non-fiction; so the reader may well ask himself why this one is a combination. While reading, he may wonder where the truth leaves off and imagination takes over.

A snitch gets stabbed to death in the middle of the exercise yard. Fact or fiction?

A young man is raped then hangs himself because he cannot deal with it emotionally. True or false?

Two young jocks share the same cell; do they, or do they not, succumb to basic urgings, even though neither of them is gay?

I've often told friends and critics alike that there is as much truth in my fiction pieces as there is in my factual articles. In fact, most of my fiction has been based on actual events which I have personally witnessed (at least knew to be a fact). The story, "Prisoners," is a fictionalized account of an actual murder which occurred in a joint where I was doing time. The characters arc thinly disguised and there is enough fiction to detract from the reality of the situation (so as to avoid libel suits!); but rest assured: those things did happen.

In my factual articles, I have frequently softened the descriptive impact, where possible, in order to avoid sensationalism. The several-part article, "Prison Sex," which appeared in *First Hand* magazine, is an excellent example of this. There was no way I could describe in full the brutality of rape nor the torment suffered by the turn-out, when restricted to a repertorial format.

Close analysis will reveal that I've used both fiction and non-fiction, hand-in-hand, to give the reader an accurate view of sex behind bars. The story "Tank Boss" is pure fiction—I am not the main character described in that story, even though I used the first person singular viewpoint. Nonetheless, I have indeed, at one time or another, enjoyed the types of experiences recounted therein. The "twins" (in real life) were two brothers who, although one year apart in age, looked amazingly alike; the "villain" of the piece was drawn from a character I actually met in prison, who tried to interfere with my sex life by intimidating certain young men who would come to me for sexual favors. The four-way at the end of the story was nothing more than a fantasy when I wrote it; it became a reality, with three different participants, at a later time.

"The Hole" was written in January of 1983 and was nothing more than a figment of my imagination. In April of that year, I found myself living the reality—I got caught in the act, almost exactly as I had described it three months earlier!

Perhaps the only thing missing from the many views presented in this book is the kinkier aspects of sex. I'm sure that "water sports" are practiced behind bars, just as they are in the free world; but I've never participated nor have I known any guys who did. This anthology cannot be described as a definitive work on the topic; but taken as a whole, it gives as accurate a view of prison sex as can conceivably be compiled in a book of this nature.

Fiction alone, or non-fiction alone, could not succeed in giving the overall picture; so we've included a generous selection of each. Some of these stories and articles have appeared in print, separately, as noted on the copyright page; others are original, written specifically for inclusion in this anthology. The publisher and I hope that by being presented with a collection of fiction and nonfiction, the reader will come away satisfied that he has gained a true perspective on all facets of gay life in prison.

LIFE BEHIND BARS

U NTIL I WAS THIRTY, I was a successful young businessman, an up-and-coming junior executive, with the world at my feet. Coming home from a party one night, I was suddenly pulled over by a police car. I figured that perhaps I had failed to signal for a turn a few blocks back; but to my utter amazement, I was abruptly arrested. You would have thought that I was Public Enemy Number One: I was surrounded by what seemed like eighteen cops with shotguns, rifles, and handguns. Later I was informed that I was being arrested for attempted robbery and was taken to the scene of the crime, where (to my further amazement and uncomprehending disbelief) I was *positively* identified as the culprit.

In the blinking of an eye, my world disintegrated in front of me. Because the witnesses were positive I was the criminal, and because I couldn't prove that I wasn't, I was convicted by jury. I spent eight months in county jail. For a well-educated, well-to-do young man, it was an unreal nightmare. The most hideous crime I had ever committed was to drive while under the influence of alcohol (and even so, I had never been caught at it).

When I got out of jail, I found that I was unable to convince anyone of my innocence. I had lost my job as cost estimator and contract negotiator, and my employer wasn't interested in hearing my side of the story. Over the years, I've given up trying to convince anyone that I really didn't do it. But how does one refute three eyewitnesses when one's only alibi is that he was driving home from a gay party?

As a convicted felon, finding a job was difficult in the extreme. I even found it hard to get a job washing dishes, because an employer simply didn't want a felon working for him! And if I failed to mention the conviction, they wondered what a man like me was doing wanting a job as a dishwasher. Eventually, I found a job as a busboy.

Making ends meet was rough going, and eventually I over-extended my checking account. Most of us have played the old "try to beat the check to the bank" game with our personal checking accounts; most of us do *not* realize that it can be a felony if any check (or any number of them) exceeds $100. I found out the hard way and was arrested for felony non-sufficient funds checks. Upon my plea of guilty, the judge sentenced me to prison.

*   *

Looking back across eleven years of time, that first day in prison is a blur of images; everything was new, strange, alien, foreboding, and unreal. Perhaps the most vivid impression remaining with me is that the relationship between guards and inmates was much more casual than I would have imagined. In movies, guards are either sadistically brutal or they're the "good-guys" You rarely ever see the true picture: most of them are simply doing their jobs. They don't see themselves as cops or the upholders of justice; they're just average guys making a living. There are, of course, exceptions. I have personally known a few guards who would have been right at home at Auschwitz, Buchenwald, or Belsen, with chains, whips, and nutcrackers! Even so, I learned real quick to keep a respectable distance. It's okay to socialize with guards on your assignment or in the course of daily routine; but it is definitely taboo to become too friendly. Other cons distrust a man who talks too much to a guard— who knows for sure what the conversation is about? To a con, the lowest thing on earth is a snitch. A guy who spends too much time with a guard, no matter how innocent the talk, is subject to being labelled a snitch. The label is called a "jacket" in prison slang—it's something you wear—and a snitch jacket, even if unfounded, will be a man's undoing in prison.

A *fish* (a new arrival) undergoes a battery of tests: educational, medical, psychological.... He is interviewed by several people (counselors, doctors, psychologists, etc.) and eventually is trans-ferred to a prison which the staff feels is appropriate for the individual. Prisons range from the maximum security types (like San Quentin) to the "country club" types (like Chino), with everything in between: firefighting camps for good security risks, the "gladiator" schools for young, tough, hoodlum types, and the tinderboxes of violence.

In some states, out-front homosexuals are segregated; in other states, they mix in with the general population of the prison. I was in California. In that state, they segregate the flamboyant, effeminate homosexuals, but other types of gays are simply integrated into the prison population. As scared as I was, I played it straight. Only after I had been there for a long time did I slowly come out of my closet. I am no longer afraid. However, I still wait until I get to know what a new prison is like and what the attitudes towards gays are before I come out of the closet.

During the past eleven years, I've been in seven different prisons as the result of five felony convictions (four were check-related beefs, and one was the original attempted robbery which I didn't do. By the way, I'm not snivelling; I am, indeed, guilty of the four check beefs.) There is no adequate way to tell an outsider what prison is really like, because in the first place no two of them are the same. Even different prisons in the same state are different from each other.

As I write this, I am in a prison in Nevada. There are four prisons for men here, and one for women. I am in the Southern Nevada Correctional Center, about 20 miles west of Las Vegas; it is as different from the Maximum Security Prison near Carson City, where I spent more than two years, as night is different from day. At "Max," there are no movies for the inmate population. Here at SNCC, we not only get several movies per week (actually, they are video tapes of movies played on a closed-circuit channel at the prison), but sometimes the movies are X-rated!

Once they showed *Eruption,* with John Holmes. I wasn't here at the time, but my friend Randy tells me that after the movie, he and the other gays on the yard were propositioned by dozens of men, as if sex were going out of style the next day. Even *during* the movie, there were surreptitious knocks on his cell door. The showers were kept busy, both during and after the movie, and not always one at a time. Someone might wonder whether there was any group sex in the viewing room. The answer is no. But there were an awful lot of guys who couldn't keep their hands off their own crotches, according to Randy's report. For the gays, it was a night to reap the harvest.

Certain guys who ordinarily wouldn't "fuck around" decided to give in to the temptation to let a "sissy" take care of their sexual needs.

Perhaps the biggest question in the minds of most readers is: Does the lack of women make straight guys turn gay or do things they usually wouldn't do? Yes and no. Unless a straight guy is raped, he ordinarily won't perform a homosexual act as a "bottom" man. Some men will not, under any circumstances, get involved with a gay convict; other will go so far as to fuck a "sissy" in the ass or allow one to give them head, although they will not reciprocate. Some men feel that their macho image suffers if they "fuck around" in any manner; others feel that it is *not* unmanly to be a top man. It all depends on the man himself, and sometimes on the peer pressures to which he, individually, is subjected. But I personally have never heard of two straight guys getting it on together. And let's face it, if they do, one or both is probably gay anyway.

Each prison differs in almost every aspect. Take food, for example. At Max, the food was good at all three meals; here at SNCC, only the evening meal is worth eating. At Chino, in California, all the meals were good, but it was the same thing from week to week—the cooking showed no imagination. Food preparation on a large scale will never be as good as Mom's, but some joints have better food than others. Right now, because the State of Nevada is almost bankrupt, the food gets worse from one day to the next. We eat an awful lot of USDA "commodity" items (free cheese, and such things) and frequent pasta dishes such as casseroles and spaghetti. There was a time when milk was served at all three meals; now it is served only at breakfast. Coffee substitutes have replaced real coffee, fresh fruit is becoming scarcer, and hot dogs and turkey roll are served much more often than beef or chicken.

Most joints have a "canteen," or inmate store, where one can buy everything from cigarettes to shampoo. Here, too, the items available will differ from one joint to the other. At Max, there was a time when you couldn't buy food stuffs; here at SNCC, you can buy bread, tuna, potato chips, bean spread, and all sorts of snack items.

But money is the problem. The state has abolished inmate pay. Now, if you have a job, all you get is time off your sentence (up to ten days per month). Most men are dependent on friends and relatives to send them money occasionally. I myself have no one who can send me money; so I've managed to keep myself in spending money by writing articles and stories; my education wasn't totally wasted.

There was a time when sex-oriented magazines, like *Playboy, Mandate,* and *Honcho,* were not allowed inside a prison. Over the years, however, staff attitudes have relaxed and court decisions have played key roles, so that now many prisons do allow sex-oriented material. Here in Nevada, however, I recently had to fight a battle with staff to be allowed to have my Greystone Calendar (all male nudes). Luckily, they knew I was in the right and did not make me pursue it to the courts. Now I am able to receive any and all gay publications.

Women guards have become an established fact in men's prisons. At Max, a female guard commented to me one day, when handing out the mail, "You know, Mr. Boyd, I like it when you get your magazine subscriptions! I enjoy browsing through *Mandate* much more than I do *Penthouse!*" (All mail is opened and inspected for contraband; the only time they actually censor mail is when they have reason to suspect that the correspondence might contain details of criminal activity. Thus, that female guard was within her rights to open the envelope and to inspect its contents).

Female guards, however, were the ones who talked the warden into discontinuing X-rated movies here at SNCC; the men had become so aroused that the female guards feared for their own safety. All of our complaints (namely that if they can't handle the heat, they've got no business working in a men's prison) met with no success. We no longer get X-rated movies.

An inmate's biggest enemy is not the guards or even the other cons, it is boredom. There are not enough jobs to keep every man occupied, and even if there were, the evening hours need to be filled, too. Some men (like myself) do not allow boredom to set in. I am very active all of the time: I play chess, bridge, and other games; I write articles and stories; I suck as many cocks as I can get my mouth on; I spend a lot of time with my fellow gays. We have our own team for sports: volleyball, baseball, and football. I also enjoy reading and listening to music.

At several prisons an inmate may have his own portable TV. Since I personally do not like TV, I'm not hurting. Some guys spend all their time in front of the boob-tube. You might be surprised to learn that some of the men in prison can tell you more about soap operas than the average suburban housewife can.

Most prisons, if they have nothing else, will have a gym. A lot of guys who had never before considered weight-lifting take it up once they come to prison. Not only is it something to do, but in the predatory environment of prison, a muscular body is usually enough of a deterrent against aggressive individuals. Aside from pumping iron, there is basketball, volleyball, and perhaps even a pool table. Here at SNCC, they recently installed a video arcade. The gym often becomes the most popular place in the prison. The athletic field, though, is also fairly popular during warm weather. At SNCC there is a baseball diamond only; some joints also have tennis courts, racquet ball courts, handball courts, or even a golf course (Chino has a nine-hole course). Walking around the athletic field is also a common pastime. We gays find that it is a neat way to cruise.

Prisons are, for the most part, autonomous entities; they make their own rules and answer to no one. The public doesn't give a damn what goes on inside prisons, unless one of the "good-guys" is hurt in a riot. Because of public apathy, excesses by prison staffs usually go unchecked, and a warden can play the game as he wants to play it. That's why some prisons allow gay publications and why other prisons do not. Technically, by law, an inmate cannot be deprived of his constitutional rights (and *access* to knowledge and information is as much a part of freedom of the press as is the actual printing itself). Even so, if the warden decrees No Gay Magazines, it's pretty hard for the gay inmate to get around that dictate, because nude male photos can be classified as "obscene" in some areas and the Supreme Court has seen fit, like Pilate, to wash its hands of the issue. No one ever bothers to question whether pictures of nude females should be allowed inside a men's prison.

Rules and regulations apply *only* to convicts. By way of example: in 1979 I was given a "write-up" for a rule infraction. By the time they got around to taking me to a Disciplinary Hearing, the prison Staff had violated fourteen of their own rules regarding the handling of disciplinaries. When I took those matters up on appeal to the Director of Prisons, it was deemed that those fourteen violations were minor and technical in nature. Yet just last month, I spent five days in Punitive Segregation ("the hole") for such a trivial matter as borrowing a friend's radio for a few hours!

A guard can call an inmate every derogatory name in the book, but let the inmate simply say, "Fuck you!" and he gets five days in the hole for using abusive language. He can call me a "cocksucker," but let me call him a "cuntlicker," and *I* go to the hole. The intelligent inmate will recognize the fact that he's in a "no win" situation and will flow with the tide.

To the outsider, prison rape and violence generate the most curiosity. I personally have never suffered the indignity of rape, nor have I ever been forced into doing something with another inmate that I didn't want to do. But I've seen it happen to others. It is usually the young, the pretty, the defenceless who are the victims of rape and they are usually set upon by more than one man.

Rape, however, is not always generated by purely sexual motives. I knew one unattractive guy who was raped by a gang in order to degrade him. The guy was a snitch and a liar; he was raped in an open dormitory setting, where the number of witnesses (who were *not* snitches) would guarantee that word spread fast about him getting butt-fucked. Just beating the guy up would not have had the same impact. A guy can live down being "rat-packed," but he'll never outlive the "jacket" of being a "punk" or a "turnout."

My own first sexual experience in prison was a disappointment. "On the streets" we are accustomed to mutual sex. If a guy in a bar shows an interest in you, you go home with him and you get a nut, right? I was new in prison and had gone a long time without another man in my bed. When a friend told me that a guy named Curt was interested in me, I was delighted. Curt was fairly attractive and lived in the same housing unit (a tier of single cells). One night after the eleven o'clock "count" (or bed-check, if you prefer), I went down the corridor to his cell. We drank some coffee, smoked a joint, and talked a little. When it came time for sex, he stripped. I stripped, too. He told me that I didn't have to get naked. He lay back on his bunk and I gave him a blowjob. When it was over, he got up and put his pants back on. I had learned, brusquely, that most sex in prison is not reciprocal.

Since that time I have come to enjoy one-sided sex for the many pleasures it has to offer. I naturally still prefer mutual sex; when my partner happens to reciprocate, I like it very much. However, since those times are rare, I satisfy myself just by being the bottom. The gay man in prison who won't have sex unless it's reciprocal might go for years without getting to feel another man's body or the irresistible sensation of a hot, pulsating cock in his mouth or his ass.

There is more to prison, of course, than sex and violence. I just mentioned having smoked a joint. Well, grass and drugs are very definitely against the rules; but where there's a will there's a way, and convicts find ways of smuggling drugs into prisons. Don't ask me to reveal what those ways are. When you want to buy some, you pay a high price. Just one prescription-type pill can run as high as ten dollars. One ounce of grass (at, say, $80 "on the streets") costs over $600 inside. The average size joint out there will provide over ten joints in here. And the price of one of these "pin" joints is three dollars.

Most prisons have various types of clubs, ranging from a chess club to a bridge club to the JayCees to Toastmasters or even Alcoholics Anonymous. Many of these activities allow outside visitors to come into the prison occasionally. But perhaps the most common way to meet outsiders is through the various religious groups.

Religion, of course, cannot be suppressed inside prison. All denominations, sects, and beliefs are allowed freedom of religious expression (except for Satanists, Voodoo-ists, and other so-called "black arts" religions). Sometimes the chaplain is an ordained minister or priest; other times, he is nothing more than a uniformed staff member who devotes his time to religious inmates. At Max the Catholic chaplain was an ordained priest, but during a riot he carried a shotgun along with the other uniformed staff members. Here at SNCC, the chaplain doubles as the laundry supervisor. Since I personally practise no religion, I know very little else about the religious aspects of life in prison.

Living conditions also vary. At SNCC, we have two-man cells. Depending on how populous the prison is at a given time, a man may or may not have a cellmate. Max is the same way, but at the Northern Nevada Correctional Center (NNCC, near Carson City), there are large dormitories. At Chino, there were both types of living arrangements: dorms and single cells. At Tehachapi, they have huge dorms with up to 116 men in the same living area.

Almost to a man, inmates will tell you that they prefer single cells. There is little or no privacy in prison; a single cell allows at least the chance to get away from the teeming masses. Money, however, is the problem. The United States of America sends more men per capita to prison than any other country on earth, and the numbers keep growing. Prison crowding is a volatile problem all across this country, but the public only wants to lock up criminals, not pay to build more space for them. As more and more bed space is needed, single cells are converted into double cells and ten-man dorms are converted into twenty-man dorms, and so on.

Despite overcrowding, loneliness can be an acute problem. I myself have numerous friends and acquaintances; but I find myself so lonely at times that it's hard to fight off depression. A gay man needs a lover just as much as straight men need their wives or mistresses. And all of us need our families. So even though I am surrounded by six hundred men, I still get very lonely.

People "out there" cannot begin to realize how terribly important a letter can become: they can't begin to understand what it's like sometimes not to know where your next cigarette will come from; they might never have had to go for a year or two without a bottle of shampoo; nor can they appreciate the fact that sometimes a twenty-cent stamp is as unobtainable as a Rolls Royce.

I do not mean to suggest that the plight of prisoners is such that they deserve all of your pity and concern. On the contrary; I firmly believe that most prisoners deserve what they get. But we inmates, too, are human beings. We've committed crimes and must pay for them. However, there are many fine human beings behind bars who deserve better than what they get.

I make no excuses for myself. I'm here because I wrote bad checks; so I try to make the best of a bad situation. I can only hope that those who read this book will never find themselves behind bars. Despite the fact that there are hundreds of gorgeous men in here, it really is nicer out there.

PRISON SLANG

That headhunter is going fishing, trying to book a roscoe from the fresh meat. She's got l-o-n-g priors for scoping loggerheads. Won't give up the backs, though! A booty bandit can't cop a play. I jammed her a week ago; offered a dime green. She just won't bone down. Man! Scope out those cakes!"

No, that's not an excerpt from *A Clockwork Orange;* that's everyday slang behind prison walls. Convict slang tends to focalize on three main topics: crime, drugs, and sex. There are slangs for other subjects, but they are not nearly as extensive or imaginative. A guard is called *bull, cop, police, the man, turnkey, dick-licker* (not to be confused with *cock-sucker,* by the way), *screw* and other colorful terms. Home-made (or prison-made) wine is called *pruno*—it was originally made from a mixture of sugar, yeast, and prunes. Junk foods (chips, cokes, sweets, etc.) are collectively called *zu-zu's and wam-wams.*

If you're going to *jam some T's* (inject Talwin directly into the bloodstream with a *rig,* a syringe) or *neck some ludes* (swallow Quaaludes) or *fire up a doobie* (smoke marijuana) or *get wasted on pruno* (get drunk on prison-made wine), you had better have someone *stand point* (act as a lookout). Without a *point,* you might get *jacked-up* by a *screw* (get caught).

A list of slang words for drugs or drug abuse might be lengthy, but it won't compare to the list of slangs which refer to homosexuality. For example, at a conservative estimate, there are at least twenty words which mean "homosexual," [see list in glossary], more than eighteen which refer to the penis, just as many phrases to depict oral intercourse (and so many of them are interchangeable that the actual number of words or phrases for a blow-job could number into the thousands!) and so on.

The world behind bars is essentially a world without women. If there are nurses or female guards (*cows, bitches, cunts* or *dykes*) they are usually untouchable—in most cases; but of course, there are exceptions. As a result, homosexuality is, if not rampant, at least widespread and out in the open; and a large part of convict slang tends to concentrate on this subject.

Many slangs overlap or have more than one meaning. For example: *jam* can also mean "ask" or "proposition" (*I'm gonna jam that headhunter for some face* would mean "I'm gonna ask that homosexual for a blow-job"); *neck* still means "swallow" (loosely) when used to refer to oral intercourse (*Gimme some neck* means "Give me a blow-job"); *cop* is not only a guard, it also means "to get" (*cop a loggerhead*): get (suck) someone's cock); etc.

Convict slang is not only colorful, it is inventive. When one headhunter was asked why he liked to *scope* (to observe) the showers, he replied: "If I get jacked-up for copping a whammer, I want it to be Grand Larceny, not Petty Theft!"

Overheard outside the chow hall: "What's for chow, homie?" "Cellmates," came the one-word reply. Form a mental image of two naked wieners lying side-by-side on a tray and you can see why hot dogs are called cellmates.

Rhyming things seems to be a popular pastime: *Gimme some face, Ace. Gimme a knob-job, Bob. Get on the rod, Claude. Suck my dick, Slick. Gimme some head, Fred. It's all about Trouser Trout.*

A favorite rhyme is this one: *I'll bet I can flip ya and dick ya before you can throw me and blow me.*

Most cons don't know what the word "alliteration" means ("What's that? A guy who can't read?"), but they have a great fondness for its use: *Gobble a goober!; If you'll flip, you'll flop; Booty Bandit; Whip a Whammer; Butter Buns; Skillful Screaming Skull;* etc.

However, talk about sex isn't always coarse and vulgar. It's not uncommon to hear a jock ask a sissy, quite simply: "Why don't you come see me tonight?" or "Do you mind if I stop by?" The meaning is always clear to both of them.

Many words have no sexual connotation at first, but they take on special meaning when used in sentences. For instance: the word *long* rarely describes length or distance, it usually means "an abundance of" or "lots of." *Long ducats* means "a lot of money." *Long priors* means "a lot of prior convictions." The word *priors* refers to a man's criminal record, but it is also used to indicate that a man is well-known for something: *I got long priors for getting shit on my dick* implies that the speaker fucks around a helluva lot. *She's got priors for giving long skull;* in this case, *long* means "good": "It is well-known that she gives a damn good blow-job."

A *fish tank* is a reception center. The term comes from the booking areas of most County Jails where a man is placed in a cell (or tank) enclosed by windows or plexiglass on at least two sides. In some jails, it's also known as the *fish bowl.* Thus, new arrivals in jail or prison are known as *fish.* After a period of time in the fish tank, the fish *hit the yard* (that is, they are placed in the general population). In some joints, this happens only one day a week and is called *fish day.* It's common to see both booty bandits and homosexuals *going fishing* for *fresh meat* on *fish day.*

A fish who is young and good-looking might be faced with a very unpleasant alternative. *Shit on my dick or blood on my stick* is an ultimatum which means "either give up the booty or get shanked." *Pick it up or drop 'em* means essentially the same thing, except that in this case the booty bandit is offering the fish a chance to pick up the shank which he has tossed onto the bunk (but closer to himself than to the intended victim).

After the fish has been *turned-out* (forced into sex acts), he can lock-up or continue to be used sexually. If he locks-up, he will be placed in *P.C.* (Protective Custody). *P.C.* is used both as a noun and a verb: *The P.C.'s in P.C. had to P.C. in order to keep from getting boned.*

Often, there will be several slangs which say the same thing. *To book* something means to get or obtain or acquire or get ahold of; *to score* means the same thing; so does *to cop. To book a whammer* means to *cop a loggerhead* which means to *score a roscoe;* all of which conveys the information that someone has *turned a trick.*

On the other hand, sometimes the same phrase can have very different meanings. A perfect example is: *Pack your shit.*

1. I'd like to pack your shit tonight: I'd like to fuck you tonight.

2. Pack your shit, somethin' might be comin' down: Start carrying your shank because something's in the air.

3. Pack your shit, you're hittin' the streets: Pack up all of your personal property, you're going home.

The word *shit* is used for almost everything! *It wasn't shit:* "It wasn't anything." *Don't give me no shit:* "Don't give me a bad time." *I got that shit you wanted:* "I got the stuff you wanted." The list goes on and on.

A *mother-fucker* is tall, short, skinny, stocky, good, bad, smart, stupid, handsome, ugly, hard-working, lazy, and on and on and on. *He's as sharp as a m-f; it's as dull as a m-f; that screw's as chickenshit as a m-f; that sonuvabitch is as bad as a m-f; she's got cakes finer than a mother-fucker,* etc.

Some words defy definition, only mental images can convey the full meaning. *I'm a pitcher not a catcher* does not refer to the South Block Baseball Team; it means that the speaker is asserting his masculine, dominant role and assuring the listener that he neither cops loggerheads nor gives up the keyster. *What goes around comes around* is a way of saying "you get what you give"; it's an inverted, reversed, doubled-back-upon paraphrase of the Golden Rule: "What you do unto others will probably be done unto you." In the same general vein, *If you'll flip, you'll flop* is a not-necessarily-true maxim which suggests that if you'll play the dominant role right now, you'll play the submissive role later (reminds me of the saying of the late 50's—early 60's: "Today's trade is tomorrow's competition.") *If you'll pitch, you'll catch* says the same thing.

Clean time is an example of con inventiveness. The phrase is used, mostly, to refer to the amount of time a person has been free from disciplinary action (write-ups). When a screw asks a con, "How much clean time you got?" he wants to know how long it has been since you've had a write-up. When a con asks a *log-jumper* that same question, he's wondering how long it has been since the sissy booked a roscoe. Got it? (Example: A pole-climber says to a jock, "Gimme a drink of your coke." The jock asks, "Before you drink out of my cup, how much clean time have you got?")

Numbers are fun. Two of anything is *a deuce*, five of anything is a *nickel;* and ten of anything is *a dime.* Two jocks looking for a three-way might ask a homosexual if he wants to *cop a deuce* (i.e. take on both of them). If you were sentenced to five years, you *copped a nickel* (got five). When looking for someone who's selling a radio, try not to pay more than *a dime green* (ten dollars in cash, green money); you might *book a TV for a quarter* (pay only twenty-five dollars for it).

The whole nine yards means "everything" or "all of it." One sissy to another: "I booked the whole nine yards with my old man," means that she and her jock flip-flopped (they did everything together). A *mule* is a guy who packs drugs into the prison. A mule might tell his connection that he scored *the whole nine yards* (he got everything he expected to get). It can sometimes be used to confirm something: "Does Jim really have 8½ inches?" "The whole nine yards!"

Gay magazines are called *fag mags*. The centerfolds are called *dick flicks* or *roscoe shots*. Anyone (straight or gay) who gets caught scoping *trouser trout* is called a *peter gazer*. The list goes on indefinitely.

Now that all you headhunters have finished scoping this fag mag, hit the streets and book a roscoe. Jam some fish; turn someone out; burn some coal; cop a deuce—or hit the baths and cop a dime! If you've got long priors for scoping loggerheads in T-rooms, try scoring some cakes in a disco. Fuck a bunch of clean time; go for the whole nine yards. Spend some ducats and get wasted. Eat some fresh meat; it's good for you. If you score some trouser trout and bring it home, make sure you've got long zu-zu's and wam-wam's

Go do it, headhunters! And whip a whammer for me, all you J/O freaks!

GLOSSARY

Most of the definitions which follow are listed alphabetically by slang-term. There are, however, so many expressions for the most basic words (*homosexual, heterosexual, ass, cock,* etc.) that we have grouped them together at the beginning.

HOMOSEXUAL: Bitch, Brownie Queen, Catcher, Cocksucker, Cum Guzzler, Faggot, Girl, Headhunter, Homo, Kid, Lady, Old Lady, Pole-climber, Punk (derogatory), Pussy, Queen, Queer, Sissy, Turn-out (derogatory).

HETEROSEXUAL (WHO MESSES AROUND): Booty Bandit, Daddy, Hemorrhoid Packer, Jock, Old Man, Pile Driver, Pitcher, Shit Packer, Sugar Daddy.

THE ASS, ASSHOLE OR BUTTOCKS: Backdoor, Backs, Booty, Browneye, Buns, Cakes, Hole, Keyster, Poop Chute, Pussy, Shitter.

THE PENIS: Bone, Boner, Cock, Dick, Goober, Handle, Hardon, Knob, Loggerhead, Peter, Pole, Rod, Root, Roscoe, Shaft, Tool, Trouser Trout, Whammer.

ANAL INTERCOURSE: Bone, Bone Down, Book a Roscoe (or Cock, etc.), Cop a Rod (or Cock, etc.), Drive Piles, Get Down, Get Some Booty (or Pussy, etc.), Jump Into the Shower (with someone), Pack Shit, Shit On a Dick, Slide Down a Pole, Strap It On.

ORAL INTERCOURSE: Blowjob, Book a Roscoe (or Cock, etc.), Cop a Dick (or Cock, etc.), Face, Get Down, Get On the Loggerhead, Gobble a Goober, Head, Hum Job, Jump Into the Shower, Knob Job, Screaming Skull, Sleep In a Warm Mouth, Slide Down a Pole, Strap It On, Throat, Whistle On a Whammer.

BOOK (v.): To acquire, to get. *To book a roscoe* means to turn a trick.

BULL (n.): A correctional officer, or prison guard.

BURN COAL (v.): To have sex with an Afro-American.

BUTTER BUNS (n.): Anyone with large or attractive buttocks.

CELLMATES (n.): Two (or more) convicts who share the same cell or room. Also: Two (or more) wieners or frankfurters served at chow.

CHECK-OUT RIGHTS (n): A time-honored tradition which allows convicts to punch with closed fists on a convict who is either leaving on parole or being transferred to another prison.

CLEAN TIME (n): That period of time during which an inmate has been free of disciplinary actions or write-ups. Also: that period of time during which a homosexual has refrained from sex.

COOK CHOCOLATE (v.): See *BURN COAL.*

COP (n): See *BULL.*

COP (v.): See *BOOK.*

COP SHOP (n): Congregating area, or muster room, for guards. Administration. Control. Custody (or Security) Office.

DEUCE (n): Two of anything. *I caught a deuce* could mean "I was sentenced to 2 years," or "I got 2 (of something);" or *Make that a deuce* could mean "Do it twice," or "Get 2 (of something)"; etc.

DICK-LICKER (n): In some prisons, this term is used to mean guard or officer. Could also refer to a homosexual.

DIME (n): Ten of anything. *He hit me with a dime:* "The judge sentenced me to 10 years."

DRIVE UP (v.): To arrive. *I didn't drive up just yesterday!:* "I'm not a fish (q.v.), I've been here for a while."

DUCATS (n): A money substitute; anything which replaces or acts instead of cash. A general reference to money. *He's got long (q.v.) ducats:* "He's got lots of money."

FIRE UP (v.): To strike a match to. *Let's fire up a doobie:* "Let's light up a joint." Also: To hit or beat on. *I fired him up:* "I beat him up."

FISH (n): A new arrival.

FISH TANK (n): Reception Center.

FLIP-FLOP (v): To reciprocate (usually with sexual connotations), as in *Those two flip-flop:* "They both do each other." *If you'll flip, you'll flop:* "If you'll get your dick sucked, you'll suck dick"—a not-necessarily-true maxim usually propagated by those who *don't* mess around (q.v.)

FOOL AROUND (v.): To participate in a homosexual act. *Does he fool around?:* "Is he fair game?" or "Can he be had?"

FRESH MEAT (n): New face(s). Not to be confused with *FISH.* A fish is always *fresh meat;* but even a man who has been in for six years is considered fresh meat at a new prison.

FUCK AROUND (v.): See *FOOL AROUND.*

GET WASTED (v.): To become intoxicated with either alcohol or narcotics.

GIVE A PLAY (v.): To confer sexual favors upon. *Will that sissy give a guy a play?:* "Will she suck a guy's rod? or "Will she let a guy fuck her?"

GIVE IT UP (v.): Participate in sexual activity. *Give up some booty, girl!:* "Let me fuck you!"

GO FISHING (v.): To cruise the new arrivals.

GREEN (n. or *adj.):* Money, specifically cash. *I scored a balloon for twenty green:* "I bought a balloon of marijuana for twenty dollars in cash money."

HIT THE STREETS (v.): To leave prison (on parole or expiration of sentence). *I'll play that shit in here, but I'll cut it loose when I hit the streets:* "I'll engage in homosexual acts in here, but not when I get out."

HIT THE YARD (v): To emerge from the Reception Center and enter general population. *Tuesday is fish day; all that fresh meat hits the yard:* "On Tuesdays, the new arrivals come into general population."

JAM (v.): Inject intravenously, by syringe. *Jam some T's:* "Shoot Talwin into the bloodstream." Also: Ask, proposition. *I'm gonna jam that sissy for some cakes:* "I'm going to ask that sissy to let me fuck her."

KID (n): Generally a young convict who is supported or protected by an older or stronger con, usually for sexual favors. The *KID* may be either a sissy or a turn-out *(q.v.).*

LAME (n): A person of limited intelligence; sometimes used to connote limited power or influence. *My former old man was a lame:* "My former old man *(q.v.)* was an incompetent moron!"

LONG (adj.): An abundance of; lots of; a larger than normal share of. *He's got long ducats:* "He has lots of money." *She's got long priors for booking whammers:* "She has an abundant record of sexual conduct."

LOP (n): Similar to *LAME.*

MAN (n): See *BULL.*

MESS AROUND (v.): See *FOOL AROUND.*

NECK (n.): Oral Intercourse. *Gimme some neck:* "Give me a blow-job." *She gives long neck:* "She gives great blow-jobs."

NECK (v): To take pills or narcotics by mouth; to ingest. *Did you jam 'em? No, I necked 'em:* "Did you shoot those pills? "No, I swallowed them."

NICKEL (n): Five of anything. *FIVE GREEN* or *A NICKEL GREEN:* Five dollars in cash.

ON THE BOOKS (adv.): Referring to money deposited in one's Trust Account. *I ain't got shit on the books:* "I have no money in my account."

ONE-WAY STREET (n): Sexual activity wherein only one partner is active; the other is passive.

POLICE (n): See *BULL.*

P.C. (n): A person in Protective Custody.

P.C. (v.): To seek protective custody. *If you're scared, P.C.:* "If you're afraid, seek protective custody."

P.C. (n): Protective Custody. *My friend went to P.C.:* "My friend went into the protective custody unit."

PITCH AND CATCH (v.): AC/DC; To go both ways, to enjoy mutually reciprocal sexual activity.

PLAY THAT SHIT (v.): See *FOOL AROUND.* (More commonly used in the negative. *I don't play that shit:* "I don't indulge in sexual activities with another man.")

PRIORS (n): A previous record or history. *I got booty bandit priors:* "I have been known for fucking homosexuals."

PRUNO (n): A prison-made alcoholic drink. (Orig: a potent brew made from prunes).

RABBIT (n.): A desire to escape. *I've got long rabbit in me:* "Give me half a chance and I'll escape." *He made like a rabbit:* "He escaped."

SCOPE (v.): To observe, to cruise. *Did you scope on the size of that bulge?:* "Did you see his crotch?" *I know that jock was scoping me!:* "That player was cruising me!"

SCORE (v.): Similar to *BOOK,* but usually as the result of extra effort. *I scored some doobies:* "I managed to acquire some marijuana."

SCREW (n.): See *BULL.*

SHANK (n.): A knife or similar stabbing instrument.

SHANK (v.): To stab someone with a shank.

SHIT (n.): Anything! *Get your shit together:* "Clean up your act";

Pack your shit: "Pack up all of your personal property"; *Did you get the shit?:* "Did you get it (whatever it was)?"; etc.

STAND POINT (v.): To stand guard, to be a lookout. *Stand point for me while I book this roscoe:* "Keep an eye out while I do this guy."

STORE (n.): Merchandise purchased from the Inmate Canteen or Commissary, especially as distinguished from cash. *Do you want green or store?:* "Do you want cash or items from the commissary?"; *I'm selling my radio for a dime store:* "I want ten dollars worth of items from the canteen for my radio."

STREETS (n.): Anywhere outside of prison walls. *I've got an old man on the streets:* "I've got a lover waiting for me outside."

TURN-KEY (n.): See *BULL.*

TURN-OUT (n.): A convict who has been forced or coerced into sexual acts; usually a young, straight guy.

TURN-OUT (v.): To force or coerce someone into sex acts. *Were you gay on the streets, or were you turned-out?:* "Were you gay before you came to prison, or were you forced into it? (A *TURN-OUT* is scorned and derided; he is looked down upon as a weak person.)

SEX BEHIND BARS

P RISON CANNOT BE DESCRIBED as pleasant for anyone. Depending on the size of the facility, a man is surrounded by 300 to 3,000 convicts, whose crimes range from petty-theft to robbery, rape, murder, or worse. (Yes, *worse:* I was in a prison where there were two men who had kidnapped a twelve-year-old boy, taken him to a remote spot, and there dismembered his body—while the boy was still alive! A few days later, one of them returned to the shallow grave and fucked the corpse! How would you like one of these men for your cellmate?) Many inmates have multiple charges, with sentences exceeding several lifetimes. They have no hope for getting out and nothing further to lose as a consequence of their actions. Hostilities and frustrations simmer just below the surface until suddenly, unexpectedly, they erupt into acts of barbaric savagery—look at the recent riots in the prison at Santa Fe, New Mexico.

If prison, at best, is difficult for the ordinary convict, it is difficult in the extreme for the gay convict. The attitudes of the staff range from mild disgust to overt hostility. Even in so-called country–club prisons (those which come closest to the paradisical setting so many of us fantasize about), gays get the brunt of administrative disapproval. At some prisons, effeminate homosexuals are considered a threat to prison security and are segregated into special housing units where they are allowed little or no contact with the general population.

The attitude toward gays varies with the *type* of prison. One rule remains constant: The attitude of the inmates is inversely proportional to that of the staff. If the staff hates gays, the inmates think you're O.K. And vice versa. Thus, at a maximum security prison (high brick wall, gun towers, cell blocks—the typical setting for a James Cagney movie), a homosexual suffers heavier problems from his fellow inmates; staff tends to ignore him and his problems. Conversely, at a minimum security prison (country club joints), the gay convict has less to fear from the inmates than from the staff.

The key words to life in prison are "adjust" and "adapt." How well a gay convict does this will determine the heaven or hellishness of his stay. There are six basic sexual arrangements which enable you to get by. Readers who have done time may want to add to the number of categories, but my experience has shown that these six fairly well cover the broadest range of circumstances that the gay con finds himself in:

1. Whore and Pimp
2. Tip Bitch
3. Jock and Sissy
4. Old Man and Kid
5. Man and Wife
6. Freelancer

WHORE AND PIMP

Desiree is the gay monicker of one of my dearest friends on the inside. It was his first time in prison, although he had been in county jails on two occasions. The prison we were in was old and depressing; the atmosphere was oppressive. Pent-up anger lay heavily on the air. This particular prison suffered from a cycle of violent eruptions every two years. Feelings were running high that summer, and staff had taken the usual precautionary measure of locking up known trouble-makers, which only served to fan the embers of resentment. With such a tense, volatile atmosphere pervading the cell block, Desiree moved onto my tier. (A tier is a row of cells, usually twenty or thirty, with a common walkway running its length.)

I knew who Desiree was by her reputation. When our cell doors came open for evening unlock, I paid her a visit and introduced myself. She told me that on the tier she had come from, her Old Man turned out to be a lop.

"He wanted to rent me out," she said, "which I didn't mind. But, my dear, when he brought two niggers with him, that was just *too* much!"

(I apologize to all my black readers, but I want to be accurate. In prison, racism is still extremely prevalent. It is suicide for a white queen to get down with a black con. If Desiree had turned those two black tricks, her Old Man might not have done anything, but the white racists in the joint wouldn't have stopped until they killed her.)

She continued, "Later, the two niggers came back by themselves. One of them had a shank. Well, my dear, let me tell you! I knew right then and there my Old Man was a lame. I told the niggers they'd have to use that thing because I wasn't puttin' out!"

She had managed to extricate herself by making enough of a racket to attract attention. The blacks left before a race riot broke out. That same night, Desiree moved off that tier. After three days in segregated housing ("the hole"), Staff moved her to my tier.

While we were getting to know each other, McIleny walked into her cell. We were sitting on the bunk.

"I'm Mack," he announced, towering over us. "I hear you'll be needing a new Old Man. You'd be better off with me; I got a lotta power and a lotta friends."

Mack was tall, puffed-up from pumping iron and handsome in a rugged sort of way. He was not a man to fool with. "I heard what happened. You were right not to get down with niggers. Me and my friends will be taking care of that punk, Shaeffler."

I was told to leave while Mack and Desiree worked out the details of the arrangement. Later we resumed our conversation.

Before coming to prison, she had heard that she would have to get herself an Old Man. Shaeffler was the first to approach her. "How was I supposed to know he was such a wimpy lop?"

An ironic punishment was planned for Shaeffler. He was taken over and made the "property" of some of Mack's friends. They went about it slowly, and each day we received fresh reports via the grapevine about new humiliations being heaped upon him. They hooked him by having him do small favors at first (bringing a cup of coffee, helping to wring out the laundry, etc.). Soon he was doing complete laundries, making bunks, cleaning cells. In no time at all, he was "turned out" (a straight forced into sex acts). There is a distinction between a "turn out" and a rape. In a rape, a man is physically assaulted—usually by more than one person—and weapons are used to overpower the victim. In a turn out, nothing is used but fear. He is coerced into giving "just a hand-job, that's all."

Once he has humiliated himself by fondling another man's cock,

.there is no way out for the turn-out. He could seek protective custody (P.C.), but there is no guarantee of safety even in P.C.

After being turned out, Shaeffler was soon rented out. After he had been fucked by all the whites on his tier, he was sold to the blacks! A few months later, he committed suicide.

In the meantime, Desiree was being taken care of. If anyone wanted a play, they had to clear it first through Mack, who in turn asked Desiree if she wanted to do the guy. In the case of three or four of Mack's friends, she wasn't given any choice. But for others, she was allowed to say yes or no. She was, of course, given 50% of whatever Mack decided to charge the individual.

The arrangement worked well. Mack, himself, was a gorgeous hunk of manhood ("with meat for days!", according to Desiree). She liked older men and was quite happy. She was protected from any undesirables, and when problems came up, Mack took care of them.

One thing I should make clear: Although the arrangement turned out well, Desiree did not have much of an alternative. If she had stood up against him, life would have been miserable. All of her personal possessions would have been stolen. There would have been no protection from blacks (which in itself would have been tantamount to murder), and she would have been subjected to physical and mental cruelties. That's just the way things are in a maximum security joint.

FREELANCER

I am in my thirties, and although I'm no Robert Redford, I'm not unattractive. Also I am not the effeminate type, so I'm not as sought after as many of my "sisters." Yet even we older, hairy-chest types are subjected to pressures.

The fifth prison I did time in was a medium security joint. Here restrictions are more relaxed than at a maximum security joint. There are barbed-wire fences instead of high brick walls, observation towers instead of gun towers, and large dormitories instead of single cells. What you lose in privacy, from a sexual point of view, you gain in mobility.

This prison was divided into dormitories. The 12-man dorms used to have small day rooms adjacent to them, but the day rooms had long ago been converted into 5-man dorms. New arrivals went into the larger dorms; later they could move into the smaller, more intimate rooms if a vacancy occurred and if the occupants had no objection.

My first day there, I was lying on my bunk doing some heavy thinking. In the county jail I had come from, it was known that I was gay, and the word was already out here. In the halls, in the chowhall, in the dorm, I was aware of whispers and derisive remarks. I knew if I were given half a chance, people would come to like me. But would I be given that half a chance?

I looked up as someone walked into the dorm. He was absolutely beautiful! Small delicate features, pretty eyes, olive complexion, thick curly hair. (I later learned he was only 17 years old.) He stopped at the foot of my bunk and made a motion to come with him. "Robot wants to see you."

He led me to one of the 5-man day rooms. In contrast to the starkly bare dorm I had been put in, the day room was sumptuously decorated. There were tapestries and posters on the walls; bedspreads, throw rugs, macrame plant hangers and two color TVs.

Robot told Joey, the 17-year-old, to give me a chair. I was made to wait for five minutes while Robot conducted a business deal for some marijuana.

When Robot joined us, there was a tall blond about 24, who sat on the bed to my right. Robot sat on the bed to my left. Joey stood behind the chair I was sitting in.

Robot was attractive, maybe 28, and shirtless. He had a slender, hairless body. He came straight to the point. "Are you a homosexual?"

"Yes, I am," I replied.

"This your first time in the joint?"

"No. My fifth."

He offered me a cigarette. "Then you know what it's all about. Some joints got a lotta tips. We got just one." (A "tip" is prison slang for a club or gang.) "A lot of our guys fuck around; some don't. I'll tell you right now, there's a lot of guys on the yard what don't like queers—excuse me, I mean homosexuals. I'm making you a deal. You take care of us, we'll take care of you."

He lay back on his bed, propping himself up on an elbow. With his right hand, he rubbed his crotch. "This ain't no pressure thing. You don't gotta do nothing. I'm just sayin' that I'm in a position to see that you don't get no hassle from no one. Nobody fucks with the tip. If you go for the deal, anyone gives you any shit, come to me, I'll take care of it. You don't go for the deal, that's that. But we won't be responsible for anything that might come down."

There was a threat there, thinly veiled. If I didn't go for the arrangement, the only troubles I would have would come from tip members. I knew I had to assert myself at this point or I would never again have the chance.

"I've done time in five different joints and six county jails," I said. "But I never had to service a whole tip. I'd be willing to get down with some of the guys, but I've got to have the right to say no 'cause I won't be a whore on call."

We discussed the minor details, and to my relief, he agreed to my stipulations. He lit up a joint; the four of us smoked it, symbolic of having sealed the agreement.

"What name do you go by?" Robot asked.

"My own," I answered. "Robert, or Bob, or Bobby . . ."

"Joey," he said, standing up, "make sure everyone knows Bobby is awright. If he wants to get down with somebody, he can. If he don't want to, he don't have to. And no one gets on his case. Got it?"

"Got it," came Joey's youthful voice from behind me.

After that, things went smoothly. I only had two problems come up; Robot quietly took care of them.

Joey and I became quite close. He was hot and horny all the time, and I loved it. There were times when I was invited to the day room to get down with Robot, Joey, Mike (the tall blond), Grant (a short, but very muscular and extremely handsome 20-year-old) and Dean (a rather uninteresting man of about 25). Of the lot, Joey was the most spectacular in every way, and he was not content to get down just occasionally—we were in the shower every night. The whole arrangement was worth it, just to feel the silky smooth, hairless body of that demi-god.

This was a case where the arrangement allowed for an easy adjustment to an environment that could have been hostile. There were very few admittedly gay people at that joint (I'm sure many simply remained in the closet). In prison, a gay is not seen as an individual. Far too many inmates feel that gays are in prison for one reason only: to suck and fuck. Most cons feel they have a "right" to use a gay inmate for sexual release. They feel it's a queen's "duty" to service the men in prison. They cannot, or do not, understand that a homosexual might have likes and dislikes. And no man likes to think of himself as undesirable. So the gay is hit on by anyone and everyone.

In maintaining my individuality, gay pride and self-respect, I find I have no qualms in saying no. Nonetheless I do so with diplomacy and tact; it is not wise to antagonize someone you do not know—he could be a mild, white-collar criminal, then again, he could be a psychotic murderer.

A minimum security prison will seldom have any hard-core dangerous types. The inmates are either nearing the end of a moderately long sentence or they had short ones to begin with. Incidents of violence are rare; in fact, fights between inmates seldom occur, and gays find little, if any, overt pressure tactics applied to gain their favors.

My friend, Allen, will recognize himself (if he sees this article) when I call him by his name, "Mary." Mary could deep-throat a 12-inch hotdog and not bat an eyelid! I had first met Mary several years before and although I hated to see her back in prison, it was good to have her company.

The prison had a swimming pool, as an adjunct to the Vocational Divers Training program, offered by the prison to young, healthy studs who could qualify for the rigorous underwater training. Mary and I spent many a leisure hour at poolside, scheming over the gorgeous, muscular bodies.

Now, *that* was paradise!

We lived in a large housing unit which had over 200 single cells. Each inmate had his own lock and key, and even though there were rules against cell visiting after 11 p.m., the rules were neither enforced nor observed. The officers rarely stirred from their office, except for their regularly scheduled bed checks. Many were the nights Mary and I passed each other in the halls, after the midnight bedcheck, going to, or coming from, our assignations with hunky studs.

TIP BITCH

There were several small tips at that prison, usually ranging from six to fifteen men. Mary was approached by three different tip leaders, but each time she declined their offers. To become a Tip

Bitch meant to have one's activities confined to the members of that particular tip. Neither Mary nor I wanted such restrictions on our sex lives. The advantages, however, were great: The tip would supply all the dope, grass, and "canteen" that a sissy could ever want. The tips took good care of their bitches, and if a gay wants to enjoy living like a queen with just a few men—well, it's the only way to fly! However, if a Tip Bitch gets caught with any man outside the tip, she had better P.C. (protective custody), because it won't be safe to walk the yard . . . *even in a minimum security prison!*

In many ways, the Tip Bitch has the best deal. This is especially true in joints where there are more tips than queens (closet queens don't count, obviously). There a queen can literally sell herself to the highest bidder, and once she becomes a Tip Bitch, she will have very few problems. The only drawback I can see is the restriction against outsiders. In one joint, I was asked to become a Tip Bitch for a tip of bikers. That particular prison was like an orchard of ripe peach trees, and I couldn't see limiting myself to one tree. So despite the fact that four of the nine members were positively beautiful, I declined. Later, my friend "Babs" became their Tip Bitch. Within a short time she had a locker full of canteen, her own TV and drugs enough to get stoned on a regular basis. For Babs, the arrangement was ideal. As a Tip Bitch, she had settled into a little haven for herself.

JOCK AND SISSY

The Jock-and-Sissy arrangement is similar to the Whore-and-Pimp, but more open and liberal. Ingrid had been a Freelancer before meeting Todd, a handsome body-builder. The two of them hit it off and Todd was soon her Jock. They shared everything. They borrowed from and for one another, and they took care of each other's business. Even so, they placed very few restrictions on their relationship. Ingrid continued to get down with other guys (although her promiscuity lessened appreciably), but no money or commodities changed hands and Todd's approval was not necessary. By contrast, Desiree could turn no trick without the okay of her pimp, Mack, and there was always a fee for her services.

In some Jock-and-Sissy situations, the Jock will curb promiscuity; but in most cases this is impractical—there just aren't enough Sissies to go around. Ratios of straights to gays may run as high as 100 to 1.

Where such curbs are imposed, it is usually in the Man-and-Wife case.

MAN AND WIFE

Sexual liberality is fairly common behind bars. Thus, a one-to-one affair is the rarest relationship. Don and Margie had one of the purest Man-and-Wife relationships I've ever seen (inside or out). Don was tall, slender, good-looking, his neat appearance, glasses, and quiet manner gave him a scholarly look. It was my first time in prison, and Don was one of the first men I was immediately attracted to. I had begun to scheme on how to get him into my cell or into the shower when I learned that Margie was not just another queen—she was his Wife. Neither of them fooled around with anyone else. They were devoted to each other in a mutual bond which transcended mere sexuality.

Perhaps the biggest distinction is that in the Man-and-Wife relationship, sex is mutual. Most queens must be satisfied with one-way streets in the joint. Only rarely will a straight con reciprocate. Ingrid told me that before she met Todd, one con went down on her before she had the chance to go down on him. Desiree tells similar stories, and I myself was surprised when a handsome young man (whom I thought was straight) asked me to fuck him. Reciprocation is the sharp line that divides the Man-and-Wife relationship from the Jock-and-Sissy relationship.

OLD MAN AND KID

The most tragic situations are the turn-outs and rape victims. In some cases (as with Shaeffler), a man is raped solely to debase his manhood. Frankly, 90% of these men deserve what happens to them: A man either adjusts to and abides by the unwritten rules of the Convict Code, or he is begging for problems.

In the majority of cases, however, the reason for rape is simply sexual. The victim is young, pretty, and defenseless. Derek was all three of these. When I first saw him, a handsome young blond, I desperately wanted to take him to bed, but he resisted all my overtures. We celled next to each other and became close friends, despite the fact that he wouldn't give me a play.

He spent a lot of time in my cell during evening unlock. But I began to notice that every time Sonny sent for him, Derek's mood changed. He would immediately get up and leave, even in the middle of a chess game. Eventually, he confided that Sonny had walked into his cell one evening, thrown a shank on the bunk, and told Derek to either defend himself or submit to being fucked. Derek tried to talk his way out of the ultimatum. Talk was no good. Sonny, by sheer size alone, overpowered the slender young blond. A few fists to the solar plexus, then to the kidneys, and Derek was powerless. After that, he "belonged" to Sonny.

Eventually, Derek P.C.'d. P.C. is the absolute last resort in prison. When a man P.C.'s, he loses all chances of earning worktime credits, loses all privileges, is labeled a snitch (even if, as in Derek's case, he has never snitched on someone) and suffers a myriad of indignities. Derek had not wanted to P.C., but he had suffered from being fucked every day and couldn't stand it any longer.

The turn-out is called sometimes a "Kid," a "punk," or a "little girl." In some joints, the Kid is protected by the Old Man who turned him out; in other joints, he becomes fair game to just about anyone who wants him. If a young turn-out has a short sentence, he may eventually get over the traumatic experience. If he has a lot of time to do, he will probably be scarred for life.

In some prisons, the intended turn-out need do no more than put up a good fight ("show heart," as we call it) and nothing worse than a black-eye or a few bruises will result. In other cases, depending on the degree of psychosis in the attacker, no amount of heart will deter the rape. One kid put up a helluva fight and came very close to defeating his attacker but was brutally raped anyway.

The only situation I have not covered is the closet queen. I can't say too much on the subject because my own feeling is that if a man is gay, he should be proud of it. The closet queen in prison is missing a lot of good times. He might also be saving himself a lot of grief, but that's not what I call living.

Prison can be hell. There are many terrible things that happen to men caged away from an uncaring society. Suffice it to say that prison, at best, is a bad dream from which we hope to awaken one day.

Prison can also be a paradise. Remember Joey? We spent a lot of time together in a Jock-and-Sissy relationship. Our cells were on the same tier and not a day went by that we didn't get down. I got down with other guys, too, but more and more I found myself interested in teenage Joey and two of his friends of the same age. I'm in a different prison now. I still hate prison and wish I were free again, but people like Joey have made my life livable.

Like any situation in life, prison is mostly what the individual makes of it. The homosexual is surrounded by nothing but men; it's up to him to turn hell into heaven.

PRISON SEX

True Accounts

I am a convict serving time and what I have to say about sexual activity in prison is based on my personal involvement with the young men whose stories I'm telling. As a well-known gay (or "joint sissy," as I'm called here), I've had my share of problems but have known how to handle them—I'm mature and experienced in the ways of prison life. What I narrate is not hearsay or prison gossip, but what was confided in me as a friend and ally, as an understanding and compassionate listener.

For someone who's never been in prison, it's nearly impossible to understand the mentality of the average con. The only law inside prison is dictated by force and strength—the weak quickly falling prey to the strong. Being neither weak nor strong myself, I walk a precarious tightrope, delicately balancing myself between a pit of hungry wolves on one side (the cons), and a pit of snakes on the other side (the prison staff). I've managed a lot better than most and have friends in both categories: weak and strong.

The guys you're going to meet were my friends. I became quite fond of some of them, and some of their stories are all the more poignant to me. The four true accounts that follow concern (1) the brutality of rape; (2) the sad (and equally brutal) experiences of young men coerced into sex; (3) the other side of the coin—sex by mutual consent; (4) sexual encounters with prison guards. These four aspects of sex in prison coexist, and sometimes overlap; all of them should be understood.

*   *

39

I. RAPE

RICKY

I've seen a lot of "pretty kids" come and go; without a doubt, Ricky was one of the prettiest. His naturally long eyelashes would be the envy of women everywhere; his eyes were a beautiful blue-grey; his hair was jet black, thick and wavy; and he had delicate features, with a turned-up nose and real dimples. There was only peach fuzz on his smooth, adolescent body and his baby face.

I could never understand how a judge could be so inhuman as to send a seventeen-year-old boy to this men's prison—especially a boy so obviously attractive. The judge might just as well have added these words to the sentence: "It is the order of this court that you suffer assault and sexual abuse at the hands of your fellow convicts." That was bound to become part of Ricky's prison sentence.

I make it a point to get to know all the good looking guys who arrive; with Ricky, I charged in like a bulldozer. He made friends with other guys his age, and I already knew that crowd. Once Ricky saw that most of his friends had no qualms about getting blowjobs from the few "out-front sissies" around, he became one of my regular tricks.

One of the first things a man learns in prison is that there is safety in numbers. Since prison "wolves" (also known as "vultures," "coyotes," or even "booty-bandits") are much like their counterparts in nature, moving with the pack, preying on the weak, and seldom attacking until they've managed to separate a victim from the herd, Ricky remained safe from them for a long time.

He and I grew quite close. We talked for long hours at a time, I taught him to play chess and pinochle, and he learned that all gay men are not flamboyant and effeminate. Of all the sexy guys in his crowd, Ricky was the most likeable, always laughing, natural, and outgoing. The judge gave him a nickel (five years), but chances were he'd do eighteen months and then go out on parole. He might even have escaped that extra, unspoken sentence, if he hadn't gotten caught with some marijuana.

Shakedowns always come unexpectedly. The prison staff has the authority to search living areas or persons anytime, anywhere.

There's no such thing as "probable cause." The Search and Investigation Team (which we fondly refer to as "The Goon Squad") pulled a blitzkrieg-type shakedown of our twelve man dorm at three o'clock one Sunday morning. Rudely awakened, we were herded into the adjoining restroom to a "come as you are party"—no one was allowed to take anything with him. If you slept nude, that's the way you went to the restroom area. As we waited there, there were a lot of naked bodies milling around.

Joints were found in the areas of three men. They were handcuffed and taken to the Search and Investigation office just as they were— Ricky and Mark were naked, Jack had on a pair of white boxer shorts. They were all just as bare when they were put in lock-down.

As a law clerk, I had access to the men in the lock-down unit. I was appointed to act as Ricky's inmate counsel, but it was Thursday before I got to see him and spend several hours talking to him. Something more than the pending charges was bothering him. It took a long time to coax the information out of him, and when he finally told me what had happened I wasn't surprised.

He had blankets in his cell, but they didn't bring him any clothes at all until Wednesday afternoon. Guards, tired of listening to the gripes, moans, and complaints that they are essentially unable (or unwilling) to do anything about, avoid contact with the cons in lock-down as much as possible. The porter, or tier runner, serves as liaison between the inmates and the staff.

Dusty, the unit porter, was responsible for telling the guards which cells to open at which time. Cells were opened two at a time for a half hour each day so that the men could shower, and sweep, and mop their cells.

Ricky was still asleep when his cell was unlocked on Monday. Dusty had the cell of one of his coyote friends, Fitz, opened at the same time. Ricky was awakened suddenly when the two of them pulled the blanket from his naked body, and Dusty said, "See, Fitz, I told you he was pretty!"

Ricky struggled with all the strength he could muster, but the two hardened cons were able to overpower him with ease. He showed me where his body was bruised from the beating he took. They hadn't hit his face (they rarely do, since facial bruises are too visible), but the two wolves had subdued him with several immobilizing blows to the solar plexus and kidneys, after which they arranged his naked body on the bunk—face down, legs spread apart.

At first Ricky's story was disjointed and he couldn't bring himself to describe the assault in detail. But once he opened up, I was able to piece it all together and even managed to get his reactions to the physical aspects of the rape.

To Ricky, a virgin, Fitz's cock had seemed unbelievably huge, and the pain of that first penetration was excruciating. He said it felt like a knife with sixteen razor-sharp edges was being forced into his rectum. By the time he regained his breath, he was crying. All he could do was mutter, over and over again, "Don't. Please don't!" But it seemed as if Fitz enjoyed hearing his moans, so Ricky fell silent.

When Fitz had finished fucking Ricky's ass, Dusty took his turn. Now the two men turned the kid over, onto his back. Dusty lifted Ricky's legs and held them in the air as he crawled on top and shoved his cock into Ricky's ass. With no concern for the intense pain that the youth was experiencing, Dusty sadistically pulled his cock all the way out, and then brutally rammed it in again. To Ricky, it seemed like an eternity before it was over.

Ricky told me it had seemed so unreal to him; he knew it was happening, but he couldn't believe it. The two animals who had attacked him threatened to kill him if he snitched on them.

On Tuesday, Dusty saw to it that the cell of yet another of his coyote friends was opened when Ricky's was. Ricky was still sore from Monday's beating, and still stark naked in the cell. He was instructed to do as he was told, or simply get beaten until it happened anyway. He tried pleading with them, but his pleas were cut short by a swift blow to the gut. All the fight had been taken out of him, and he was fucked once again.

On Wednesday, he passively allowed Dusty and still another guy to do what they wanted. On Thursday morning, he was finally allowed to get into the shower, but as soon as he was there he was joined under the running water by a huge man whose nickname, appropriately enough, was "Moose." By this time, Ricky was expected to submit.

He begged me to do something—anything—to get him out of the ugly situation. Because the charge of possession of marijuana was considered so severe, he would remain in lock-down for a very long time. His only alternative was P.C. (protective custody).

It was a ticklish situation. Ricky wasn't a snitch and didn't want to snitch on any of the men who had raped him, but he simply couldn't tolerate it any longer. By asking me to intercede, he placed me in a precarious position; I had to get him moved to P.C. without becoming a snitch myself. Luckily, having once been the program administrator's clerk, I was on good terms with him. The P.A. was sensitive to the pressures a con like Ricky was under, so he accepted my insistence on the necessity of moving Ricky to P.C., with no questions asked.

Ricky's problem was alleviated when he was removed to P.C., but the other young guy who was busted that same night for grass, Mark, became the next target of the vultures in lock-down. Eventually, I managed to get Mark moved to P.C., but not until he had already suffered the same fate as Ricky.

"GANGSTER"

Nicknames are popular in most joints. I've been known variously as "Bouncin' Bob," "The Bobber," and even as "Mrs. Roper" (in honor of a TV sitcom character who never seemed to get enough cock). A young guy of eighteen, whose real name was Orrin, went by the name of "Gangster." He was one of those guys who thought that the only way to survive in prison was to put on a tough guy image. What he failed to understand is that false fronts are quickly stripped away, and that the worst thing a young con can do is to try to be something he isn't. While the intelligence level in prison may not be high, cons are not stupid.

Gangster was of average height, but the skinniest kid I've ever seen. If he hadn't been so skinny, he could have been attractive; but he looked like a half-starved refugee. If he hadn't brought attention to himself by playing the role of the tough guy, and if he hadn't used that inappropriate nickname, he could have remained a *virgo intacta*. Frankly, booty-bandits are interested in a pretty face and a pretty body. *Orrin* would have gone unnoticed; *Gangster* was inviting trouble.

Gangster had tried to get in with the same crowd Ricky was in; but he just didn't fit. Even so, I had seen the frightened boy beneath the phony facade and had become friendly with him. Many times I joined him in the shower to suck his cock, which seemed positively huge on that skin-and-bones body.

One night, after the 11:30 PM bed-check, I went to Gangster's dorm to see someone else about a date in the shower. It wasn't unusual to see several guys lounging around the restroom area (which we call, with vulgar simplicity, "the shitter"), but it was most unusual to see them all in towels, waiting for the shower. There were four of them, and it took no great brains to realize that one of two things was happening: either one of my "sisters" was holding "open house," or some poor kid was being gang-banged.

I said something like, "It's no wonder they call me 'Mrs. Roper'; men everywhere, and I've got to go begging for a cock!" I went into the dorm area and sat on the bed of the guy I'd come to see. Noticing that Gangster's bed was empty, I asked about him and was told, simply, "He's in the shower."

I've seen it, or heard of it, a thousand times in the past eleven years, but I still haven't gotten used to it. My stomach sank, and I felt a wave of nausea spread over me. I'd been so flip a moment before, but now I felt a flood of pity for Gangster, knowing there was nothing I could do.

Gangster went straight to the unit officer, gave names, and went into P.C. In my status as law clerk, I saw him there and he told me that five of them had fucked him at knife-point. While I felt deep sympathy for him, I'm an old-time con and couldn't condone the fact that he'd turned snitch. I don't say that the so-called convict code is right, but a man must live by it, or expect to suffer the consequences.

DUANE

Probably the least common rape situation is one-on-one. Wolves run in packs, and the lone wolf is a rarity. But Duane became the victim of a lone wolf.

When Duane moved into the empty bunk next to mine, one Saturday morning as I was sleeping late, he pissed me off with the noise he made. But my anger was controlled when I saw what an attractive young man he was, with lemon-colored hair, soft blue eyes, a timid smile, and a slight build. He was a welcome replacement for the slob who'd just moved out. I got up, made coffee, and helped him settle in.

Duane's closest friend was a body-builder named Casey. While some sixth sense told me that these two were an unlikely team and that all was not well between them, it was months before I was let in on Duane's most closely guarded secret.

Duane became my newest favorite, and I joined him in the shower frequently to suck his cock. He admitted to me that he didn't really like Casey, and that he had moved out of his previous dorm in an attempt to get away from Casey. This made me even more curious about why the two spent so much time together.

Casey had a massive physique and was almost too handsome; but his sour disposition, coupled with his obnoxious ego, made him a total turn-off to me. Curiously enough, it was Casey who let the cat out of the bag. I'm convinced that Casey was jealous of the warm friendship between Duane and me; there could be no other explanation for Casey to boast to me about fucking Duane regularly. When I recounted Casey's bragging comments to Duane, he finally told me what had happened.

When Duane was a quiet, timid newcomer to prison, and had been quite lonely, Casey had befriended him. At first Casey had given Duane no cause for fear; in fact, a man like Casey could be a valuable ally.

This particular prison had soundproof, windowless music rooms in the education building. One day, in one of the music rooms, friendly horseplay between the two of them had gotten out of hand. Duane thought they were still kidding around when Casey overpowered him and de-pantsed him. Lying face down on the carpeted floor, his pants down around his ankles, and his left arm in a hammer-lock, Duane didn't believe that Casey was serious until he felt Casey's hard cock probing along the crack between his buns.

At first, Duane got mad as hell, swore at Casey, and ordered him to stop. He struggled against the brute force, but the pain in his shoulder was unbearable. Then he felt the thick cock being rammed deep into his ass.

Afterwards, Casey told Duane that he was now his "kid," his "property." The bodybuilder could fuck the young blond's ass whenever he chose to—all pretense of friendship had vanished. As time went by, Casey tried to regain the friendship that had once existed, but Duane could never again see him as a friend. I'm convinced that Casey was really gay, even though he might not have known it himself, and that Duane did mean more to him than just a piece of ass.

Duane had to keep up appearances of a friendship with Casey, because Casey threatened to break both his arms if Duane ever tried to get out of the arrangement. If Duane tried to refuse to give up his ass whenever Casey wanted it, Casey would also spread the word about Duane, and the young blond would become prey to all the coyotes in the joint.

Duane never balked. I believe that he came to enjoy having sex with Casey, although he never admitted it. Months later, when I was transferred to another prison, the two of them were still in the middle of their uneasy alliance.

These are only three of a thousand stories. There are more brutal forms of rape: I've even heard of kids who were killed in the course of sexual assault. But, as heart-breaking as rape is, there's still another side of the story—the equally tragic cases of the ones who are forced into sexual subservience by threat, coercion, or manipulation.

II. TURN-OUTS

People tend to equate prison sex with the violence of rape or with the promiscuous activities of the flamboyant, declared homosexual (or "joint sissy") who cell-hops. The turn-out is neither of these; he is a guy who is forced into sexual activity by the use of threats, coercion, or manipulation. Sometimes the nature of the threat comes close to rape; other times a man is manipulated into compromising himself; and still other times a guy can be coerced through extortion.

The turn-out and the rape victim share a few things in common: fear is the primary lever used against them; their bodies are used for the sexual gratification of supposedly straight men; their participation is involuntary; and they are looked down upon, derided, and scorned by the average convict. In prison, strength is revered, while weakness is exploited.

*   *

LYNN

Victims of rapes and turn-outs are usually young and attractive. Lynn was no exception to that rule. At twenty-three, he looked more like eighteen, with the boyish good looks and adolescent body that can be so valuable on the streets, but which are anathema in prison.

I met Lynn shortly after my transfer to this particular prison, which had one- and two-man cells. This was a welcome change from dormitory living; instead of the semi-public dorm shower, a cell offered all the privacy one could want. This particular joint was better than most, since the cell doors were solid, rather than barred, and they had a mere 6" x 6" window centered in the upper half. Although it was against regulations to obstruct the view into a cell, the windows were often covered with cardboard. Also, cells were only locked during "count," and for eight hours at night.

One hot summer afternoon, I passed Lynn's cell and saw him lying on his bunk wearing only his boxer shorts. By that time, he and I were friends, and I had sucked his cock on numerous occasions. After poking my head in and saying hello, I entered his cell, closed the door, put up the window cover, and sat next to him on the bunk. I ran my fingers along his velvety smooth legs and then up into his shorts. Lynn was very quiet, but I thought little of that; we rarely talked when we both had sex on our minds.

He was easily aroused, and by the time my fingers were on his cock it was already stiff with anticipation. Wordlessly, I tugged at the waistband of his shorts. He lifted his hips and allowed me to slide the patterned boxers completely off him. I moved between his long, almost hairless legs, and began to lick his fuzzy nuts, while my hands glided along the sculptured contours of his abdomen and chest. His skin was soft as chamois cloth, and he was very responsive in sex, unlike so many guys who just lie there like rubber dolls. His hands always found my shoulders, and his body rhythms would accelerate the moment my tongue began playing along his thighs, on his balls, and down to his ass. It was always exciting for me to suck Lynn's cock—his youthful body and passionate ardor were sensual changes from the hairy chests and dead fish around that particular prison.

I slid my mouth onto his fleshy dick and felt his legs wrap around my upper body, while his pelvis gyrated with pleasure. His tits were highly erogenous; when I began to fondle them, he writhed ecstatically. His cock fucked my mouth then with a driving urgency.

Then his body convulsed, his legs clamped tightly around my body, and his cock erupted with a delicious load of cum. His hips lifted off the bed, and he forced his cock as far into my throat as it would go. After several ejaculations, he relaxed and lay motionless beneath me.

It was only then that I realized something was wrong. His radio wasn't playing, although he always kept it turned to a rock station. I asked him what was bothering him, but he remained silent. When I prodded him with more questions, he just shrugged them off. I had always been able to talk to him before, even when he was in a sullen mood. Whatever it was, it troubled him too deeply to discuss, but I was too concerned to give up. Finally, I asked, "Are you being pressured by anyone?" When he didn't shake his head, I knew I had hit the mark. It took a long time for me to get the whole story. Through that long, drawn-out conversation, this is essentially what he told me:

A guy named Tracy had come into his cell. After a lot of casual, meaningless talk, Tracy started talking about sex. He then hinted that Lynn could make a lot of money by selling his body to horny guys. Tracy finally asked. "Have you ever been fucked in the ass?"

Lynn knew where the conversation was leading. He tried to put a stop to it. "No," he answered, "and I don't intend to start now. So, why don't you just leave?" But, the next thing he knew, a powerful hand was gripping his throat.

"Don't talk to me that way, punk! When you can whip my ass, you can fuck me. But right now, it's the other way around—and I'm gonna fuck you!" Tracy made it very clear that he intended to fuck Lynn. If Lynn wanted to, he could put up a fight first, but their size and strength differences left little doubt as to the outcome. Lynn's other option was to cooperate and not get hurt.

"What was I supposed to do?" Lynn asked me. "You know how big he is. He could have choked me to death with his left hand. Tracy made me strip naked, and then forced me to take his clothes off of him. I had to unlace his shoes, and everything."

He made Lynn lie down on the bunk, face up. With his finger, he drew imaginary lines on Lynn's bare flesh, telling him how he would carve him up with a sharp knife if Lynn were to snitch on him.

"Tracy," Lynn told me, "is as queer as you are, Bob—no offense. What I mean is, he started feeling me up, the way you do. He even played with my cock, trying to get it hard. But I was too scared to get hard."

Lynn was then ordered to turn over. Tracy mounted him and, according to Lynn, hurt him quite badly. Aside from that, Lynn would not discuss the sex act, itself. He asked me what he could do now.

Essentially, there were only three alternatives: (1) He could become Tracy's "kid" (or "punk," or "little girl," or "sissy," or any one of a dozen other derogatory names), with the understanding that he would soon be made available to the rest of the prison population, at whatever price Tracy wanted to charge; (2) He could ask for Protective Custody, which is a last resort because of the many deprivations P.C.s suffer; (3) He could find, buy, or make a shank and kill Tracy, or get killed trying. Needless to say, none of the alternatives was very attractive, and the decision was not an easy one.

It does no good to discuss this kind of problem with members of the prison staff. To begin with, it's one man's word against another's, so prosecution is out of the question. Then, too, staff would insist on names, and the minute a con informs on another con, he becomes a snitch (the lowest thing in the world, to other cons). Finally, staff really has no sympathy about such things—their attitude is generally that "those are the breaks. You shouldn't have broken the law."

Lynn didn't want to take the chance of picking up a new beef for murder, so he ruled out the third alternative. Protective Custody was also discarded as an option—suffice to say that P.C. is the hell-hole of prison life. So, Lynn lived with his unfortunate circumstances, and I kept in close touch, following the situation.

Lynn was smart enough to strike an arrangement with Tracy. Before Tracy ever broached the subject of putting Lynn up for sale, Lynn made it clear that he would seek P.C. before he'd ever let himself be used as a whore. He would allow Tracy to fuck him, but nobody else. Tracy didn't like it, but Lynn had impressed him with his sincerity. No doubt was left in Tracy's mind that he would lose Lynn to P.C. if he ever gave Lynn reason to believe he would be turned out to the general population.

With me, Lynn was passionately responsive in sex. When Tracy fucked him, he lay as still and motionless as possible. Despite all of the big man's best efforts to show some life when being fucked, Lynn wouldn't give him the satisfaction. Within a few months, the frequency of Tracy's visits tapered off.

Once, Tracy tried to lean on me to stop sucking Lynn's dick. I had initially thought Tracy was an okay guy, but by that time I loathed him. When he tried to pressure me into leaving Lynn alone, I spoke to the right people. Tracy, a lone wolf, was told in no uncertain terms that I was a gang member's "ole lady," and that leaning on me was the same as leaning on the gang. Tracy could have been put in the hospital with multiple fractures if I had complained about him once more—if I had lied about Tracy, and been discovered, I would have been the one ending up in the hospital.

In time, Tracy got tired of Lynn. To my knowledge, Lynn was never bothered again. He wasn't the type to draw attention to himself, nor did he ever step on anyone's toes. He handled Tracy in the best possible way, suffered through an ugly situation, and came through unharmed.

ANDY

Andy was as different from Lynn as I am from Tracy. Andy was a short, stocky, handsome blond with a positively beautiful body and face. He was a tough, smart-assed kid. Soon after his arrival in prison, he became a "prospect" (analogous to a fraternity pledge) for the same gang that my old man belonged to. As one of my old man's prospective brothers, he was to become one of my regular tricks. Although his attitudes were unpleasant, and he was unlikable, his body was glorious, and it was a pleasure to suck his cock.

He must have been equally abrasive to the members of the gang, for he never became a brother. When the gang made their decision, they didn't tell Andy—they decided to turn him out.

As long as I took care of my old man, he didn't care what I did, nor with whom. The day he told me not to have anything more to do with Andy, I knew that Andy was in trouble. The gang had begun the slow process of manipulation to make Andy a turn-out.

Still believing that he was a prospect for the gang, and under the impression that he was in a new phase of his trial period, Andy was made into a virtual slave: he swept and mopped floors, made beds, washed clothes, and acted as a waiter and gofer. By subtle, and not-so-subtle, means, he was led to believe that the final test for brotherhood would involve mutual sex with his future gang brothers. Andy was incredulous, at first, but *everyone* told him the same thing. Even so, I suspect he still didn't believe it even at the very last moment, the night of his initiation into the gang.

I didn't have any choice but to participate in Andy's undoing. After the 9 PM count, fifteen guys crowded into the shower room, wearing only their towels. Everyone except the leader was blind-folded, and the lights were turned out. Andy was told that he would have to suck a cock. He objected, but was told that the leader himself would suck Andy's cock first. The leader stood in front of Andy, telling him that he was sworn to secrecy regarding initiation rites. Andy was told to drop his towel. The leader took that opportunity to step back, and I glided to my knees and sucked Andy's cock (very inexpertly, I must add). I sucked him until he was hard, and then tapped the leader's leg. I moved away silently, as the leader told Andy that it wasn't necessary to make a man cum, just to get him hard.

Everyone watched as Andy, naked and hard, got to his knees and sucked the leader's cock into his mouth. When the leader was hard, he signalled to me and I turned on the lights. The other men had removed their blindfolds—they had all caught Andy with a cock in his mouth. Andy tried to argue with them, but when he saw me he realized that I was the one who had sucked him.

He started to stand up, but the leader slapped his face and told him to finish the job. The brothers were menacing him, calling him "punk," "faggot," and "cocksucker." To the delights and taunts of the gang members, Andy resumed the blow-job. I left, just as the first guy had inserted his cock into Andy's ass. I knew that Andy would get no rest until all of them had fucked him.

About a week later, Andy was shot off the fence while trying to escape. A 30.06 bullet in his back hit a vital organ and killed him. It was a poorly planned escape, and I'm certain, deep inside, that his objective wasn't to escape from prison but to escape from his tormentors.

RUDY

I hadn't paid much attention to Rudy. He was rather nondescript. I had seen him naked once, in the shower, and he had one of those boyish, hairless bodies, attractively put together; but, frankly, he didn't interest me. It took me by surprise, then, when he came to me to ask for advice, and began by telling me he was gay.

He had chosen to stay in the closet during his four year prison term, because he was repulsed by the "open market" attitude toward sex. To him, sex was a private thing, and he had no desire to get down with a guy unless he felt some sort of emotional involvement.

He had started hanging around with one of the joint's numerous bodybuilders, a handsome guy named Mel. The two of them became close friends. After several months, Rudy finally told Mel about his true feelings for the bodybuilder. Mel wasn't gay, but enjoyed Rudy's attention and affection. For a long time, Rudy enjoyed the kind of intimate relationship he had wanted, even though sex with Mel was strictly a one-way street. In time, Mel was transferred to another prison, down-state. Rudy discovered, to his dismay, that Mel had not been close-mouthed about their relationship.

Some of Mel's friends, who had kept their distance while Rudy was under Mel's protection, decided to move in once Mel was gone. They were cautious, at first, merely patting Rudy on the butt and making lewd comments and suggestions. Rudy now wanted to return to the closet, but these guys wouldn't let him.

The pressure was steadily building. "I can't even take a shower by myself," Rudy told me. "If any of them see me head toward the shower, they follow me in. They don't keep their hands to themselves the whole time I'm under the water. Once, they took my clothes and my towel. I had to run back to my cell naked. And I have to keep my cell door closed to have any privacy."

His radio was taken when he was in the shower; a bathrobe disappeared one day when he was at lunch; his bedspread was gone; cigarettes and coffee had a way of vanishing. Then a guy named Spider told him that those things would probably show up if he put out.

The reason Rudy had come to me then was that a guy by the name of Floyd had just told him that morning, very bluntly, that he either put out or the whole prison would know about his being gay. "If I take care of him and Spider and three other guys, he says everything will be cool."

Because of his sensitivities, and the constant pressure, this was very difficult for him to handle. My advice to Rudy was to come out of the closet and enjoy the wide variety of sexual experiences he could have while in prison. His only alternative was P.C.

Rudy compromised and made himself available to the five guys who were pressuring him. He hoped he could limit what was required of him. But, a month later, he was back to talk to me. The circle of five had slowly expanded to more than ten, and nobody paid any attention to Rudy's objections.

Eventually, Rudy went into Protective Custody. With only a few more years to go, and a chance of parole before then, he got out of a distasteful situation (but he never did get his radio and other items returned).

Although Rudy was gay, he was still a turn-out because he preferred to remain in the closet. Definitions aren't always clear. Both Lynn and Andy would certainly have been raped if either had put up a fight. Duane (discussed in part 1), although raped, became a turn-out by continually giving in to his bodybuilder friend's demands. Rudy was turned out, but if he had *come out* he would have been classified as a joint sissy.

III. JOINT SISSIES

"Joint sissy" is the name given to an openly gay man in prison; it is up to such a man to adapt to his surroundings and to make the most out of an otherwise miserable predicament in his life.

Tall, short, average, blond, redhead, dark, muscular, skinny, fat, slender, hairy, smooth, blue eyes, green eyes, brown eyes—you name it, you'll find it in prison. I have seen, known, and had sex with some of the most superbly beautiful men in the world. That is not intended as a boast; it's a simple statement of fact. Most prison sex is one-sided, so he-men readily fuck a "sissy" or get their cocks sucked. Essentially it is up to the homosexual inmate himself to adapt to his surroundings and make the most out of an otherwise miserable predicament.

*   *

"FISH"

My first time in prison, I preferred to stay in the closet. I had one brief fling with a guy named J.M., who was also gay and in the closet. But, as of my second prison term, I threw open the closet doors, and time passed much more swiftly.

A newcomer to prison is called a "fish," whether it's his first time in or he's returning after having been in and out. The reception center of the joint is called the "fish tank." At the joint I entered in 1978, fish were locked in their cells, except for meals, showers, and an occasional release for the testing, counseling, medical, dental, and psychological interviews that were part of the induction into the prison system.

At the end of my first day there, after the fingerprints, mugshots, and questionnaires, I was locked into my two man cell along with a twenty-one-year-old named Stan, who was a powerfully built six-footer, with a masculine face, brown hair, and green eyes. Once I learned he'd been in prison before—an "old fish" who wouldn't have the hang-ups of a newcomer—I came out of my temporary closet.

That first night with Stan set the pace for the following four weeks. After showers, we talked until lights-out, getting to know each other. After the 11:30 count, there would be three hours before anyone looked into our cell again. By now, not only did Stan know I was gay, but I had learned that he had fooled around with joint sissies in his last joint.

Even though the cell was dark, the prison yard was brightly lit by floodlights that gave Stan's body the appearance of a reclining marble statue, lying nude on the lower bunk. I sat beside him, running my hands over his lightly hairy body. His wide chest tapered to a narrow waist, smooth as satin to my touch. When my hands reached his cock, it was rigidly erect, eagerly awaiting the attention we had talked about earlier. For a long time, I teased him: stroking his large cock, playing with his velvety nuts, sliding my hands along his thighs, and then back to his firm stomach.

I leaned over him and began to nibble on his neck, using my lips and tongue in a light, feathery way, down to his large nipples, working on them and getting them hard. I moved down the long expanse of his youthful, manly body. Several times he trembled and shivered at the delightful feel of my nibbling lips. I bypassed his throbbing cock, lingered for a while in the area below the scrotum, and teased the bud of his ass.

By the time I finally worked my way up his pulsating cock, he was squirming and writhing beneath me. I had twisted my body around, so that my back was toward his head and my lips were all the way down on his eight inches. He was so caught up in the erotic pleasures of the moment that his right hand wrapped around my waist and his left hand played with my buns. His fingers searched for, and then found, my ass.

Several times I pulled my lips from his thrusting cock when I sensed he was close to orgasm. It frustrated and delighted him at the same time. He let down certain of his inhibitions and soon had my cock firmly grasped in his right hand, while the fingers of his left were probing my ass. His fingers on my cock were rapidly urging me toward climax. I returned to his swollen dick, afraid he would stop jacking me off (most "straight" guys in prison worry about their images and won't reciprocate). To my surprise, not only didn't he stop, he seemed to enjoy jerking me off.

I reached orgasm before he did, and felt my cum on his sticky fingers. His climax was only moments later. When he shot his load, his moans were so loud that I was sure he would bring a guard.

Luckily, Stan was very sexual and we practiced the same routine fourteen nights in a row, with minor variations.

"ON THE YARD"

"The yard" doesn't necessarily refer to the prison yard, itself; it is an expression which refers to any nonlockup status. When a fish is released from the fish tank, he is said to "hit the yard"; someone in protective custody is no longer "on the yard"; while a man on death row might never hit the yard. In some prisons, they simply say a man is on the "mainline."

When Stan and I hit the yard, we were assigned to different housing units. I saw very little of him after that. I was too busy with "fresh meat." In my ten man dorm, six of the other nine guys were fairly young. Of those six, Ross was positively gorgeous; Wolf was ugly as sin, but with a beautiful body; Ed was nineteen, skinny, but sexy as hell; Tom was quiet, introspective, and classically handsome; Gary and Lee were rather average in most respects, but they were rowdy and fun-loving. The other three cons in our dorm were older and looked as though they wished they hadn't been put in a dorm with so many youngsters.

I confess to entertaining all six of my youthful dormmates, individually, in the large dorm shower. But the most memorable night of all was the time I did all six of them, in their beds, one after the other. Gary and Lee had scored some grass, Wolf had brewed ten gallons of "pruno" (home-brew), and everyone was feeling horny and in a festive mood.

It started as a joke. Ross, my favorite of the six, started it by suggesting that I do all of them in the shower. (I had never done more than three in one night.) But it was Tom, the quiet one, who suggested that I bed-hop, right down the line. What the hell! We were stoned and feeling good, and it was between Thanksgiving and Christmas. The three older cons grumbled a little, but Gary and Lee quickly shut them up.

Wolf was first. His beautiful, muscular body more than compensated for his unattractive face. His rippling muscles responded to the touch of my hands. At first, the other guys watched me sucking him, and they teased Wolf. But each of those guys wanted his turn, and the longer it took me with Wolf, the longer it would be before I got to each of them.

Ed was next. Tall and skinny, he was the sexiest of the lot because he knew how to use his cock just right. He didn't just lay there, like Wolf and Lee, but neither did he try to fuck my face. His hairless body was as smooth as a baby's butt. Ed was also an intelligent and likeable fellow with whom I spent most of my free time.

Then came Ross, my favorite because he was the most over-all perfect: beautiful features, a fun guy to be around, and a sexy body that wasn't overly muscled, but not slender, either. In the privacy of the shower, he was always experimenting with new positions. After several months, he was reciprocating in sex, and the two of us ended up having some wild sixty-nines.

Tom was as inhibited at sex as he was quiet. But, because he was so incredibly good looking, I became most excited while sucking him —it was like going down on Donny Osmond, Matt Dillon, and Christopher Atkins, all at the same time.

Lee was nothing special, except for being the only blond in the group. Gary was a real face-fucker; it was hard to catch my breath while doing him. The only way to handle his bucking bronco approach to sex was to position my head and hold it firmly in place while he pounded away.

Have you ever heard the expression *cum drunk?* I found out, that night, what it meant: drunk on pruno, stoned on grass, and hyperventilated by so much oral sex activity, I was really cum drunk. Needless to say, I never repeated that performance.

In a dorm, guys come and go. Within six months of my arrival, I was the only one left in that dorm of the ten who had been there that infamous night. Everyday prison life has its ups and downs and is a subject worthy of an aritcle altogether separate from this one. There were times when I had more tricks than I could have believed possible, and other times I went hungry for cock. Sometimes, a guy would surprise me in the shower by going down on me or by asking me to fuck him. Reciprocation is rare, but it does happen. Generally, a joint sissy must be content to suck cocks, or to be fucked, and later jack-off, quite alone.

"FLIP-FLOP"

Someone who reciprocates with you is said to "flip-flop." A common expression among guys who do not fool around with sissies is: "If you'll flip, you'll flop." This implies: If you'll fuck a sissy, you'll let a sissy fuck you. There is no basis for that statement, of course. Most guys in prison will not flip-flop, and their only reason for sex with another man is to get their nuts off.

Cliff was one of those few who flip-flopped. I see no sense in a debate as to whether he was gay, or bisexual, or whatever. He was essentially "straight," and only the few who fucked him ever knew that he flip-flopped. When I met him, he was twenty-four, and had been in and out of prisons since the age of seventeen. (I suspect, but have no proof, that he was turned out at that tender age.)

The first time I gave him head, in a dorm shower, he asked me to let him fuck me. For various reasons I refused. Twice after that, while enjoying his cock in my mouth, the water cascading down our naked bodies, he asked again about fucking me. I still said no.

The fourth time we were in the shower together, we soaped each other's bodies before getting down to sex—this was usual for us. What was unusual for us was that he soaped up my cock, instead of avoiding it as he usually did. Without a word between us, he turned his back to me, bent over, braced himself with his left hand, and used his right hand to guide my cock into his ass.

Cliff had the finest buns in the joint. When I'd sucked his cock, I had gripped those firm, muscular mounds and had enjoyed their plump fullness. At last, I was enjoying them from the other side, my arms wrapped around his narrow waist, one hand stroking his cock, the other pressed against his flat stomach.

After that, it was his turn. I couldn't very well refuse. Cliff proved to be a veritable acrobat. Over the months, he must have fucked me in every conceivable position, within the confines of the shower.

In one prison, consisting entirely of single cells, I paid a midnight visit to a guy named Fred. He was naked and I was in my boxer shorts when I went down on his cock. I felt his hand travel up my thigh and into the fly opening of my shorts. He stroked my cock for a while, and then made tugging motions—as if he wanted me to come closer. I inched closer to his upper torso. Soon, he twisted around, and then his warm mouth encircled my cock. The position was uncomfortable, but instead of assuming a conventional sixty-nine, Fred remained flat on his back. I crawled on top of him, the backs of my knees interlocked with his armpits, my head nestled snugly in his crotch, and my cock sucked into his mouth.

Fred was a married man with three kids, and I was amazed that he flip-flopped. But it was not the first time it had happened. More surprises keep coming my way all the time.

An out-front joint sissy can do relatively easy time in prison. For a closet queen, prison can be a constant frustration. The turn-out makes the best of a nightmarish situation, and the rape victim, like victims of rape everywhere, must live with the trauma for the rest of his life.

IV. PRISON GUARDS

Among convicts, there is an unwritten rule against fraternizing with prison guards. Anything more than the most casual of conversations can be misinterpreted and could lead to trouble. Snitches ("rats") are an ever-present danger to those cons who don't behave within the framework of prison regulations; men who are overly friendly with "screws" are quite likely to find themselves wearing a "snitch jacket" (labelled a rat). So, as a gay convict, I made it a point to avoid developing any interest in brown uniforms—the color of the uniforms worn by the guards.

But, I'm only human, and not all guards are the stereotypical Southern sheriff type of redneck. In fact, a lot of screws are young guys who found it easy to qualify for the corrections department when the competition was too stiff for other jobs. My first sexual encounter with a prison guard involved just such a guy.

*   *

PAUL

I first saw Paul when, as a nineteen-year-old trainee, his In-Service-Training (IST) group was touring a Southern California prison. At that time, I was the Program Administrator's clerk. The P. A.'s office was in a trailer, some two-hundred yards from the main Administration Building. Since the P. A. was a prison big shot, the trailer was modern, spacious, carpeted, air conditioned, and even had a complete bathroom set-up and a kitchenette. As the P. A.'s clerk, I was some sort of a big shot myself; in con jargon, I had a lot of "juice." I.S.T. groups always stopped in our office for a speech by the P. A.

Sitting at my desk listening to my boss's routine spiel, I was totally captivated by the youngest member of that particular group. Paul's Levis hugged his body so tightly that nothing was left to the imagination. He wore a blue T-shirt which showed his magnificently defined chest and accented his soft blue eyes. He was the sexiest and most desirable trainee I had ever seen. He had a handsome, boyish face—still a teenager, but definitely all man! Since he was not yet in uniform, I found it hard to develop a "hands off" policy. Right then and there, I resolved to seduce him one day—prison guard or not! Several months passed before my chance came.

One of the fringe benefits of my job was access to the trailer on weekends. I had my own key, but seldom locked the door while I was there (except for an occasional trick, which I kept to a minimum. I didn't want to chance spoiling my beautiful set-up.) Once in a while, one of the "Yard Patrol" screws would drop in for coffee in the winter, or for the air conditioning in the summer. The day Paul walked in, I damn near came in my pants! I hadn't seen him since his I.S.T. days.

As a well-known "joint sissy," I had all the men and boys I wanted—in prison blues. A brown uniform had become a conditioned turn-off. But the sight of Paul, sweating profusely in his brown uniform, changed all that.

"I'm on my lunch break," he informed me, "and I've heard this is the coolest spot in the prison." He slumped into the chair at the end of my desk. Large stains at the armpits were threatening to ruin his uniform shirt.

I talked him into letting me rinse the stains out, by assuring him that the shirt would dry in time for him to go back to work, that the office door was locked, that he would feel more refreshed for the balance of his shift, and that I had done this several times for other guards (a blatant lie!). To my delight, he wore no undershirt. His hairless, athletic chest glistened with perspiration. His nipples stood erect where the coarse material of the shirt had rubbed against them.

After washing his shirt and hanging it in front of the air conditioning unit, I brought a damp cloth. "Let me cool you off," I said, casually. He looked at me rather hesitantly. "I do this all the time," I lied. "Just one of my many duties as the P.A.'s clerk." I knelt between his spread legs and ran the cool cloth over his gorgeous torso. "Relax," I instructed. "This is your lunch break. Take off your utility belt." Before he could object, I had unlocked it and placed it on my desk. It was only a superficial belt, to hold handcuffs and a truncheon, but the act of taking off this second piece of clothing had a psychological effect—he had placed himself in my hands. After that, it was easy. A couple of times he started to object to one or another of my actions, but only half-heartedly.

I washed his muscular torso, then unbuckled and unzipped his trousers, while assuring him I was merely "cooling him off." Actually, I was trying to get him hotter than hell. I succeeded, for by the time the cloth reached his cock, Paul had a throbbing hard-on. I glided my hands up his chest then back down along his sides. When they came to rest at his hips, just inside the waistband of his trousers, I applied an upward pressure. "Lift up," I whispered. Silently, and with his eyes closed, he obeyed. I quickly slid his trousers to his knees.

Paul's cock was not as large as I had fantasized, remembering the tight Levis, but it was beautifully thick and definitely above average. I can still vividly recall the fleshy feeling of the underside of his cock as I explored it with my tongue.

When I wrapped my mouth around the crown, I heard him let out a long, loud sigh. The sound was a wild turn-on. Taking his whole cock in my mouth, I let my hands enjoy the sensuous feel of his silky smooth skin. The shaft of his cock was rock hard, but the flesh around it was soft and pliable. As I was enjoying this wildly erotic sensation, the knowledge that he was a guard, a screw, kept playing in my mind. A cocksucker is considered a bottom man, but there was no doubt in my mind that I was in charge. Paul, the symbol of uniformed authority, was under my control. There he was: forbidden fruit, the brown uniform making him one of the enemy. To most cons, a screw is a screw; to me he was a beautiful young man with a gorgeous body and a delectable cock.

Paul was a very vocal young man when he reached a climax. Nearing the moment of orgasm, his soft moans of pleasure became louder and more insistent. When he erupted into my mouth, thrusting his cock as deep as it would go, his groans of ecstasy were so loud I was afraid they could be heard beyond the walls of the office trailer. For a long time, I savored the delightful taste of his cock while my hands glided feather-like across his body.

I pressed his shirt with the iron in the kitchenette and then I watched him dress. He remained silent until he left. That first Saturday had been slightly awkward, but we soon became quite friendly and Saturday afternoons worked into a ritual between us. Once he got to know me and trust me, he began to bring in marijuana for me. Eventually, though, he quit his job. He really wasn't cut out to be a screw; he was too nice a guy, too easy-going, too laid back. In my own mind, I never really thought of Paul as a Correctional Officer. He was very handsome in uniform, and the only times I saw him out of it were when he stripped in my office, but to me, he was just a gorgeous stud who played at being a guard until he got tired of the game.

ED

The ice was broken: I had screwed around with a screw! The first time I saw Officer Ed, I knew I would do it again. At thirty-two, he was as macho as a guy could get. Ed had blond hair and steel grey eyes. Like Paul, he had started young in Corrections; when I met him, he had nine years in service. When the staff sponsor of the bridge club retired, I, as club chairman, asked Ed to step in. He had played in a couple of our tournaments, so he accepted.

As chairman, I had to do everything: direct the tournaments, put out a weekly newsletter, act as secretary and treasurer, teach novices, and be janitor. Once everyone had gone, on Sunday nights, I had a half hour to clean up our club room; Ed always stayed till I was finished.

Unlike Paul, Ed was "all cop," never allowing infringements of prison rules and regulations. Since Sundays were one of his days off, he was never in uniform at our club games. This fact helped to ease my no-longer-rigidly-enforced self-imposed ban on brown uniforms. In his street clothes, even Ed felt less like a prison guard. We became quite friendly, and, since he was technically off-duty on Sunday nights, he gradually loosened up to my constant attempts to grope him and feel his body.

One night in mid-winter, he had had a few drinks before coming to the club meeting. He was having marital difficulties, and was unusually quiet. That particular Sunday night, Ed was vulnerable. When the room was deserted, I followed him into the restroom and came up behind him just as he finished pissing. I wrapped my arms around him and said, "What you need is something to take your mind off of Joyce."

When he didn't answer or shrug me loose, I sensed the time was ripe. I let my hands fall to his belt. Meeting no resistance, I pulled his pants and shorts down to his ankles. Awkwardly, he turned around. I cupped my hands around his large, beefy buns and vacuumed his dick into my mouth. He let his hands rest on my head. As I worked his cock up to a throbbing erection, his hands became more passionately involved. Soon, he was working my head back and forth along his cock in a rapid frenzy. When he reached climax, his knees buckled and his body jack-knifed in a convulsion of unrestrained orgasmic pleasure. Gobs of delicious cum shot into my throat. I thought he would never stop.

When at last he had shot his load, he sank to his knees, facing me. "If we were caught," he said, panting heavily, "I'd get fired and you'd go to the hole." Then he smiled—a melancholy widening of his lips—and said, "But it was worth it. I wish I'd given in sooner." All I could say was, "Yes."

A few weeks later, he came to the club in uniform; he was working for someone who had called in sick. That night, when everyone was gone, he asked if he could fuck me. I readily agreed, dropped my prison blues, and bent over the table where one of my students had, just a short time before, bid and made a grand slam.

Acting out some sort of fantasy (I'll never know what it was all about), Ed snapped his utility belt around my naked waist. Several times, he held onto it as though he were a cowboy gripping the reins of a bucking bronc. Mostly, he was gentle, but as he pounded away, grand slamming toward a climax, he rode me as if I were a wild mustang. When he exploded into the far reaches of my ass, he again jack-knifed, this time crumbling on top of me.

GIACOMO (a.k.a. "JOCK")

My liaisons with Paul and Ed were never noticed by the general inmate population. Even so, before I gave consideration to having sex with a prison guard, he had to be wildly appealing. Paul was young, handsome, athletic, with a centerfold's body; Ed was mature, macho, ruggedly handsome—the strong silent type; Giacomo, called Jock, was more than just special, he was indescribably beautiful.

Jock was 100% Italian, of average height, with a slender, boyish body, black wavy hair, the most sensitive, large brown eyes I've ever seen, and a dark, pretty handsomeness that I fantasize about but rarely see in the flesh. I was in a maximum security prison that had just undergone a violent, ugly riot. Once the riot had been quelled, prison staff hired twenty new guards. Jock was one of the "fish screws" (rookies).

When I first saw Jock, I was so overwhelmed by his delicate, almost fragile beauty that I couldn't keep myself from staring at him. Fish screws learn early never to let a convict stare them down. My stares were not hostile, but Jock didn't know that. He glared back at me with what I feared must be hatred. I was off to a bad start.

Slowly, the strict, austere conditions of the locked-down prison were relaxed. I was eventually let out to go back to work as the Property Sergeant's clerk. The property room was in an old section of the prison. There were many nooks and crannies amid rows of shelving and boxes and crates piled into out-of-the-way places. My first few weeks back on the job were spent busily typing, sorting, and filing forms. Before the riot, it had been just the sarge and me; with the tremendous backlog, we needed help. You can't begin to imagine the thrill I experienced when Jock was assigned as the sergeant's assistant.

His anticipated hostility either melted away when it was apparent that we would be working together, or it never actually existed. It was easy to like him; he had an effervescent personality and enjoyed laughing and smiling. As pretty as he was, he took a lot of ribbing from the cons.

I won't bore you with the details leading up to the seduction of Jock. I had to lay a lot of groundwork. A prison guard is not very anxious to lose his job just to get his rocks off. But when the sarge called in sick one day, I knew I had to act. We had caught up with the backlog and things were quiet. Unseen by Jock, I followed him to a stack of boxes in the back room. Caught by surprise, he said, rather flippantly, "Sneaking up behind me, huh? What are you gonna do, molest me?"

"You know that I want to," I answered. His smile faded and an almost dreamy look flooded into his huge, liquid brown eyes. "I know," he answered softly. I put my hands on his narrow, trim hips, and quietly asked, "Do you want me to?" His answer was a silent laugh.

In no time at all, his pants were down to his ankles, I was on my knees, and his beautiful, uncut cock nestled warmly in my mouth. My hands glided across his satin smooth, tiny, firm buns. My right index finger found and began to probe the hairless opening of his ass; when it slid in, he plunged his cock deeper into my mouth. His cock was not large. Like the rest of him, it was small but perfect.

My left hand worked its way under his brown shirt up to his chest and began to toy with his hard nipples. My right hand continued to play with his ass. After a few moments, I heard him whisper, "Do you want to fuck me?"

Sexual reciprocation is infrequent for a "joint sissy"—men in prison are too concerned with their masculine images. When it's offered, however, I never wait to have my arm twisted. In answer to his question, I stood up and dropped my pants. Jock dropped to his knees and took my already hard cock in his mouth. My head began to swim in a dizzy sea of disbelief. I looked down and saw a prison guard sucking my cock! The reader, unless he's been a convict, cannot begin to imagine the powerful electric thrill of having my jailer become the instrument of my sexual release.

Even though I liked Jock very much as a unique, real human being, there was a perverse joy in having a screw suck me off. The crazy notion occurred to me again when he stood up and bent over. He propped himself against a crate and guided my cock into his delicious warm interior.

I wrapped my arms around him and began to penetrate and retract in slow, rhythmic motions. I played with those rock hard nipples, correctly assuming that they were highly sensitive, and then I let my right hand drop to his crotch. Once again, the perverse notion of fucking "the enemy" crossed my mind. *Fuck you, pig! Take it in the ass, screw!* and other epithets flitted into and out of my thoughts. Such thoughts, however, did not remain for long. Jock's warm, silky body was too much like that of a teenager to think of him as a hardened, bastard-type prison guard.

When I finished, Jock fucked me. It didn't take long, and I was ready to go back for seconds. We decided to wait till the afternoon, but that turned out to be a mistake. A bus of new arrivals came in just before lunch, keeping us too busy to return to the back room. A few weeks later, Jock was rotated to the graveyard shift. I never saw him anymore.

Uniforms, per se, don't turn me on. Men turn me on. As a convict, men in brown uniforms used to be taboo, forbidden territory. It's easy to overlook the man and see only the uniform of the adversary. I still restrict my contacts with prison guards to "strictly business." Frankly, I still see most of them as assholes and sadistic morons. My attitude is typical of most cons. But every now and then, there's a man hiding behind the uniform—or a beautiful boy, almost a man. Then, look out, because all is fair in lust and war.

*   *

As long as men put their fellow men in cages, sex in prison will exist. Men will seek other men for sexual release. Some will go to those who are willing and more than anxious; some will try to force or coerce others; and some will rape, especially if judges continue to sentence boys to men's prisons.

I have no moral to preach. I simply set out to chronicle the stories I knew—to tell it like it is. Believe me, even for an out-front gay man, sex really is better outside than it is in here.

PRISON SPORTS

WHEN MEN ARE CAGED away with nothing but other men, sexual sparks are bound to fly, and one way or another men are going to get down with other men, whether it be by mutual consent or by force. In the living units, the mere proximity of other bodies, warm flesh, will trigger hidden desires, urges that most men would deny under more "normal" circumstances. The sight of a boyish body, fresh from the shower, will excite even the most macho of men, if he has been deprived of women long enough.

Aside from the living units, where naked and semi-naked bodies are a common sight, the gymnasium is probably the other most visual and sexually stimulating location inside of a prison. In some prisons, such as the one I'm in right now as I write this, there is a modern, well-equipped gym and it is frequented by all the macho studs on the "yard" (*yard* is a general, all-encompassing term which means the entire prison as a whole). Except for sports, there is very little other organized activity, and sooner or later most men will find themselves at the gym. Even the gays.

We gay men have earned a degree of acceptance at this joint that is not often found in most prisons. Most of the time, we are seen only as faggots, queers, homos, or weirdos, to be used only for that rare sexual outlet when the guys get tired of beating off. Here, the men have gone along with calling us "moes" (which is a word we ourselves coined: *mo* is short for *homo* and is not used as a derogatory term.) We moes have formed our own teams to compete with the macho types, whether it be in baseball, volleyball, basketball, or even football.

Last summer, our gay baseball team took first place. By being athletically inclined and being able to compete against "the fellas," we have earned a high degree of respect. Right now, it's the volleyball team that is taking away all the honors. Two weeks ago, at our first practice game, the "Wrecking Crew" walked all over us. Their team consisted of the most athletic, muscular, and macho guys on the yard. We moes decided that we had a lot of getting into shape ahead of us. In the re-match we waxed them.

After the practice game, though, the gym showers got more steamed up than usual. There are eight shower heads; so we took turns in the shower. By the time that John, Randy, and I stepped into the showers, most of the other guys had finished and were getting dressed. There were only three members of the "Wrecking Crew" who had not yet showered. All three were in their early twenties, with muscular bodies (they were also weight-lifters and all-around jocks), and all three had been known to occasionally "fuck around" with the moes. Danny was blond, but not too terribly good-looking (gorgeous body but nondescript face). Phil was the most handsome of the three and had long brown hair and just a small patch of curly hair in the center of his chest. Carl was the tallest and had thick, wavy black hair with eyes like blue ice.

There was, of course, lots of sexual teasing, but I really hadn't expected anything to happen right there in the gym shower. Danny, who had twice his share of cock size, started by teasing John about the size of John's cock, which was easily as big as Danny's. Phil taunted Danny: "Peter-gazer! Tell ya what, Dan, mine ain't as big as John's, but I'll let you suck on it, if you want to."

The taunts went back and forth. We moes joined in. Randy said something like: "Let an expert show you *how!*" Then Carl said to Phil, "You ain't got a hair on your ass if you don't let Randy suck it right here and now!"

By this time, the six of us had tacitly formed into partners: John and Danny, Randy and Phil, and me and Carl. In point of fact, we had already previously gotten down together in that same pairing. Out of respect for Randy, I would *not* get down with Phil; out of respect for me, John would *not* get down with Carl; and so on. The actual sex acts began when Randy let his hand glide over Phil's ass and said to Carl: "He's got more hair on his ass than you do on yours!" He then sank to his knees and sucked Phil's already hardening cock into his mouth. For a minute, not a word was said; each of us was taken by mild surprise. Then Randy stood up and said to

Carl: "You've got a hairless cunt if you don't let Bobby suck your dick!"

Rising to the occasion, I too sank to my knees. Meeting no resistance, I took Carl's beautifully shaped dick into my mouth. The water streamed down over both of us, and I let my hands glide up along his smooth torso. I heard John cry out: "Oooh, get on it, girl!"

Then Randy said "What's the matter with you, John? Are you on the rag? Hit it, girl!"

(We moes use a lot of those female terms towards each other; so do the guys. We have learned that no matter how macho the mo is, he is better off—in prison, at any rate—if he assumes a feminine role. It is easier for the "straights" to accept homosexuality if they are allowed to continue to play their man-roles.)

Before long, the only thing to be heard was running water; each of us was lost in the ecstasy of the moment. Carl had one of those bodies that magazine editors pray will turn up in portfolios submitted by freelance photographers: nicely muscular, with contours that are flattered by lighting; a well-shaped, nice-to-look-at, mouth-watering cock that wasn't too big and not too small; and eyes that could stare out from a cover with a look of seduction guaranteed to melt and to mesmerize the magazine stand browser. I let my hands cup his full, firm, fleshy buns while my mouth worked insatiably on his now rigid cock.

Carl's stiff piece of meat had swollen to large proportions, and I watched it glide in and out of my mouth, seeing it through a cascade of water, like some huge phallic monster poking its head out from behind a waterfall. My hands glided over his body, made even smoother by the warm water and the soap which had not yet dissolved and rinsed off. The sensuous feel of his silky-smooth athletic body, with muscles tensed in delight, flexing and responding to my touch, sent a shiver of pleasure racing to the head of my cock. As I reached to take hold of my own dick, he thrust his cock deep into my mouth. For a few minutes, he fucked my face in pounding jabs.

When he slowed down, I glanced around to see how Randy and John were doing. Randy was bent over with his back to Phil; Phil appeared to have his whole fist up Randy's ass. When I later asked Randy about it, he told me it was true: Randy loves to be fist-fucked. Phil had worked his hand into Randy's ass and had then worked his cock into it. Both at the same time.

Danny had taken John to the floor of the shower and was ramming away in family style.

Carl reached around behind him and turned down the cold water. Soon, the hot water flooding down on us was almost scalding hot. I had to admit that it was magnificent. The heat was intense. Not much later, Carl reached a shattering climax.

We finished before the other four guys; so we completed our showers and walked into the dressing area to dry off.

It had been my first experience with sex in the gym, but it definitely was not the last. A few months later, there was a new inmate clerk. He was from Dallas, and his thick Texas accent was the cause of his real name being quickly forgotten; he was known as "Tex" to one and all. Tex was six-foot tall and built like a pro football player—huge, muscular chest; broad, powerful shoulders; thick biceps and thighs; a hulk of a man. At twenty-three, he still had boyish good-looks, with flashing hazel eyes and straight white teeth. He had done time in Huntsville; so joint sissies were not a shock to him.

I first met him through John. I had just gotten out of the "hole" after fifty-two days of lock-up for getting caught giving a young stud some head. Randy had gone home on parole during my period of incarceration in my jail within a jail; so John was quite naturally the friend to whose cell I went first, upon my release from the hole. I walked into John's cell and spied this gorgeous hunk of a stud sitting next to John's bed. John is an attractive, handsome man and seems to have no difficulty picking up the most attractive and handsome men on the yard. Seeing the new man in his cell, I said: "You have all the luck, John. Gorgeous men all over the place."

Somehow, I made a good impression on Tex, for that same day John came to me and told me that Tex was interested in me. That night I went to the gym after the evening meal and struck up a friendship with the guy from Dallas. Before the night was over, we had agreed to make it official that he was my "old-man" and I was his "old-lady." The next day the gym was going to be closed because the coach had to go out of town; but Tex had his own key and was allowed to go to his office in the gym at almost any time of the day, even without the coach being there. We made a date for the next afternoon.

When I arrived, Tex was wearing nothing but gym shorts and a jock strap. He had been in the middle of his work-out, and his sexy body glistened with perspiration. We went straight to the weight room. He confessed that he had a fantasy he wanted to experience while he worked-out his muscular body. He described it to me, then we set about doing it.

I stripped and put on a jock strap; Tex removed his gym shorts. He put 275-lbs on a bar and lay down on the bench press. I assumed a position on my hands and knees between his legs. After very little coaxing, through his jock strap, Tex's cock was alert and eager. I then pulled the elastic pouch material aside and caught my first glimpse of his beautiful cock; his balls were already beginning to creep up tighter toward his groin.

We then began to choreograph our actions in accordance with his fantasy. He heaved the weight bar off its rest and brought it down to his chest. As he pressed the heavy weight upward, I went down on his rigid shaft; then as he brought the weights down to his chest again, I came up. When he pushed up, his cock seemed to strain along with his chest and arms; then when he relaxed, I let my mouth ride to the tip of his dick. Like a teeter-totter, we worked back and forth—I went down when he pushed up; when he brought the weights down, I came up. He did ten reps, then he put the weight away.

We moved over to the dumbells and did much the same thing, but in a standing position this time, while he did curls with one weight in each hand. We progressed through the balance of his work-out routine in this fashion: each time he pumped a muscle, I pumped the muscle between his legs.

Next we went to the rope pulleys. I faced the wall and braced myself; he grabbed a pulley in each hand, then nudged his cock against my ass. I glided him in, then he began to slowly pump my ass in rhythm with pulling down on the rope grabs. I ground my ass into his cock each time he grunted with exertion. His sweaty body slapped against me, and the heady aroma of masculine perspiration filled my nostrils.

For his next routine, we went to the Universal. I sat with my back to the unit, facing him. This time, I was the recipient of the sexual pleasure. He lowered his ass onto my cock, then gripped a wide bar, attached to weights by metal cables. Each time he pulled down on the bar, he sat down on my cock. After awhile he tired of pulling the bar and let it go. To my surprise, he kissed me firmly on the mouth while my cock nestled warmly in his ass.

The work-out was over; now we were getting down to business. Up 'til now we had worn our jock straps, cocks jutting out the side. We took them off, and Tex lay down on the wrestling mat. I crawled between his legs and sucked his cock into my mouth greedily. He wrapped his legs around my shoulders, and I slipped a couple of fingers into his warm ass. Soon his legs were high in the air, and I pulled my mouth away from his swollen rod. I pushed against the backs of his thighs, then quickly slid my cock into his ass. There had been so much sex play leading up to that moment, it didn't take me long to shoot my wad.

Exhausted, I rolled over, spread eagle, and lay beside him. He hadn't yet cum; so we decided to finish in the shower—the same one which had seen lots of sex play between convicts. Under the running water, he must have fucked me in every position conceivable.

Tex was one of the very few jocks I've had in prison who liked to reciprocate sexually. Labels are a convenience that can often be misleading; but Tex was labeled as my jock, or my old-man, thereafter. And most jocks are thought of as straight. For his macho image, no one knows that he reciprocates with me.

He takes a lot of kidding at this particular prison. But he can handle it. In Texas being a jock with a sissy is a status symbol. Here the so-called "men" play their little games: almost every guy on the yard fucks around (if a sissy will have him, that is), but no one admits it openly. Only a few *real* men, like Tex and John's current old-man, openly flaunt it. They are rapidly changing the attitudes of the other guys. No one will fuck with a hunk like Tex, and he knows it.

The day after our heavy work-out, he and I went to the gym, which was open because the coach was back. We exchanged knowing glances every time we saw someone using the same equipment we had used the day before.

Tex is on a softball team called "The Bad Guys"; I'm on a team called "Pandora's Box," made up of gays. So far, our two teams have not played against each other; but after each of his games, I manage to slip into the shower with him. As I write this article, I've known Tex for only six days; we are already making plans to visit the gym the next time the coach takes off. He tells me that there are lots of other sports we should do together.

Whenever I ask him, "What kind of sports?" he simply answers, "Prison sports," and smiles broadly . . .

SLIPPERY SEX

T HE SHOWER STALL was huge. There were only two spray heads, but twenty-five men could have stood comfortably in the enclosure. A mildewy, tattered blanket served as a shower curtain, draped across the narrow end of the enclosure. This shower served a ten-man prison dorm, so no more than one man ever showered at a time, unless, of course, the men were doing more than just taking showers.

There is an unwritten rule in prison that a man is given privacy in the shower. Nobody opens the curtain when the water is running—not even the screws. A screw (guard) could be laughed out of the joint as a "peter gazer" if he were to draw aside the shower curtain.

I was wearing only my boxer shorts when I entered the shitter (our colorful name for the latrine), which was empty. I ducked quickly behind the shower curtain, took off my shorts, and hung them over the unused spray head.

Marty was already waiting there for me. At 6′3″ he towered over me by six inches. His body was a mass of gorgeous muscles, developed through years of devotion to the iron pile. His body was nearly hairless, except for tufts of light brown hair at his armpits, a light fuzz on his legs, and a patch of wiry hair forming a triangle above his cock—like an arrow pointing to a landmark. His cock wasn't really small—a little short of seven inches. But in contrast to his large body and inflated muscles, it appeared to be disproportionate in size.

Marty was a closet queen. I was the only one in the joint who knew he was gay. In front of the other cons, he had to protect his macho image; behind the shower curtain, we enjoyed each other's bodies with reckless abandon.

Often in the past we had soaped each other's bodies. This particular night, after sudsing up a rich lather on my body, Marty pulled me out of the spray. I caught on quick and covered his entire body with a thick lather. We then pressed our bodies close together. Marty's body had always felt smooth, especially under water; the soap suds added a new dimension to his slippery smoothness. My hands slid down his silky back and onto his incredibly slick buns. We pressed our hard cocks against each other's as our bodies squeaked with a flapping noise. The feel of his body was deliciously sensual, the lather heightening the pleasurable feel of his satin smoooth skin. Our bodies, slipping and sliding against each other, felt even more naked than ever.

Our backs, exposed to the air, began to dry before our groins did. Our cocks continued to struggle against each other, like two mud wrestlers trying to get a firm grip. The sensations were fantastic, like nothing I had ever experienced. Until then I had thought that sex under running water was the height of sensual delight. If lubricant added a certain degree of pleasure while fucking, then soapy lather all over the body increased the joy a hundred-fold.

We discovered some drawbacks: under the water the soap rinsed off, and out of the water the soap began to dry. We stepped back under the spray. After rinsing, I stood with my back to the nozzle, blocking Marty's body from the water. I again soaped his smooth body into a slippery lather, and then had him turn around and bend over. I lathered my cock with the soap, then I worked it between his fleshy buns and into his hot ass. I wrapped my arms around him and slid my hands down the slippery front of his body—down his creamy thighs, across his massive chest, over his rippled stomach, and down to his hard-on. The slippery front of my body created a slapping noise against his wet buns. I fucked him with a frenzy, generated by the heady intoxication of this new delight—the feel of his slippery flesh.

After I climaxed, Marty soaped up my body and did the same to me. I was shielded from the water by his body when he turned me around and slid his cock into my ass, wrapped his powerful arms around me, and ran his hands all over my slippery body. The feel of his hands, slipping and sliding along my chest, stomach, thighs, and then grappling with my soapy cock got me hot all over again. My cock was rock-hard again as Marty pounded away at my ass, his thick cock driving with a fierce, single-minded purpose.

Marty didn't know his own strength. When he erupted inside of me, he drove his cock with such fury, he nearly knocked me over. It had obviously been as sensuous for him as it had been for me.

From then on we always worked up a full lather of suds before fucking. If we decided on oral sex, we would soap up all over, except our cocks. (Soap feels marvelous; it tastes terrible.)

Several months later I was transferred to a prison that didn't have dorms; men were housed in single and double cells. Randy was one of my favorite tricks there: a slender youth of twenty with black curly hair all over his body.

I talked Randy into letting me smear body lotion all over him before sucking his cock. I started by giving him a rub-down in the privacy of his cell. Randy had never had any qualms about getting totally naked when I gave him a blowjob. He was very relaxed. Even though most of the young straight guys I blew were averse to letting anyone touch their buns for any reason, Randy lay on his bunk, face down, his beautiful buns exposed, as I applied a generous amount of lotion to his body. I worked it in gently, allowing my hands to glide along the slippery contours of his back, occasionally making smacking noises—usually when I was rubbing his fleshy buns. I had used so much lotion that it took a long time to rub it all in. His back wasn't completely dry when I had him turn over.

A mat of furry hair on a man's chest can be nice to feel; but when I drowned that mat of fur with lotion, it became even nicer. His abdomen and the upper part of his thigh were still almost hairless—there was only the slightest hint of what promised to be wall-to-wall carpeting by the time he was twenty-five. I smeared the lotion all over the front of his body, from neck to ankles, avoiding only his cock.

Stripped to my shorts, I added a fresh dab of lotion to his chest, stomach, and thighs, and then I crawled between his legs. His cock was rigidly erect. As my mouth descended onto his rather large tool, my hands glided from his slippery thighs up the sides of his body to his nipples, tiny but rock-hard.

I felt him tremble beneath my touch—an involuntary shudder of erotic sensation. I was sure that the slippery sex was as exciting for him as it was for me. Although Randy had never been the "dead fish" type of trick, he wasn't usually overly demonstrative. That day, however, he became passionate; he squirmed and writhed beneath my touch, his legs wrapped around me, slipping and sliding along my sides and back as his pelvis rocked up and down to the urgings of my greedy mouth.

I cupped my hands around his buns, lifting from and returning to the bunk. My hands were still slippery from the excessive amount of lotion I had used. My right index finger found his ass. It plopped into the tight orifice, just as he was reaching his climax—perhaps my finger at his asshole was what pushed him over the edge.

After that, I used my "lotion technique" with anyone who was willing to get slippery for a sexual encounter. Everyone who tried it with me admitted that it was superbly wild.

But the ultimate in slippery sex came after I had been paroled. Curt and I became lovers for a short while, (though it didn't last long since both of us had roving eyes). Curt's body was almost totally hairless, and he liked other men to be hairless, too. For him, I bought a supply of *Neet,* and stripped away all my body hair, except for the small patch above my cock. It was like being more naked than nakedness itself! And, it really increased my pleasure in slippery sex.

Curt had a waterbed. I bought some black polyurethane—called "visqueen"—which we placed on the bed after removing the covers and sheets. I know that Curt and I weren't unique in using Crisco as a lubricant for fucking. But, while most gay guys will just smear it on their cocks and asses, Curt and I rubbed the Crisco all over each other's bodies. Just applying that lard to one another's flesh was tremendously exciting. It was more fun than playing with mud pies as a kid.

Unlike soap or lotion, Crisco doesn't evaporate or dry out. And it doesn't taste bad either—not good, but not bad. Curt and I were ready for a marathon sex bout. While the plastic of the visqueen would have been sticky against our naked bodies, our Crisco-covered bodies slid wonderfully on that surface. Meanwhile, the plastic helped to keep the mess from permanently ruining the bed.

Forseeing the problem of the sticky bodies against the bed, I started by pouring half a bottle of salad oil onto the visqueen and having Curt lie in that. (Since this was a waterbed with a wooden frame higher than the mattress, there was no spillage.) Then I heaped gobs of Crisco onto Curt's back, caressingly spreading it out along the length of his lovely body, even squishing it between his toes. Although the front of his body was already covered with oil, I had him turn over, and I smeared the Crisco everywhere. Curt's already smooth body was now slippery.

Then Curt did the same to me. We were so hot and horny that the Crisco started to melt against our bodies and the visqueen. Curt started laughing at this, and then the two of us were as giddy and playful as schoolboys. We wrestled, laughed, slipped, slid, and carried on like maniacs. The rocking motion of the bed combined with our own slick, smooth feeling to increase our sexual appetites.

There were problems for us. When Curt tried to mount me from the front, my legs in the air, it was almost impossible for his knees to get any purchase against the visqueen. He collapsed on top of me in a fit of laughter, then slid down my body until we were united in a deliriously sensual *sixty-nine*.

The taste of Crisco was soon gone, and the taste of his male body was all I was aware of. Soon the laughter was gone and we were earnestly involved in the erotic pleasures we were sharing. My cock was nestled in Curt's mouth; Curt's cock, swollen and throbbing, was deep in my throat. His hands sent tingling sensations through my greasy body as they slid over me. The slick feel of his body was overwhelming to me.

Now I am back in prison. I miss the Crisco and the visqueen, but between soapy showers and my bottle of hand lotion, I still enjoy slippery sex with any handsome guy who's game enough to go for it.

PRISON SLAVES

W HILE DOING TIME at Nevada State Prison in Carson City, I saw things I had previously considered to be products of fiction-writers' imaginations. A young guy, whom I'll call Quinn, found himself pressured into becoming the slave of a convicted murderer. Quinn could have gotten out of the situation by going into Protective Custody, but such a move is like jumping from the frying pan into the fire. P.C. is a terrible place to do one's time. All the food is prepared and served by inmates and is frequently tampered with (snot in the oatmeal, sperm in the fried eggs, urine in the soup, and so on). P.C.'s are not allowed to use the exercise yard with general-population inmates; thus they are given extremely limited access, and recreation is severly restricted. Whenever a P.C. inmate goes anywhere (to the doctor's, on a visit, to see his counselor, or anywhere else in the prison) he is taken there under escort because the man's physical safety is threatened simply because he's in P.C. Prisoners enjoy very few privileges, but P.C. inmates enjoy even fewer. Living conditions are subnormal. Unless a man has actually done time in prison, it's difficult for him to understand why and how P.C. can be a last resort and something to be shunned like the plague.

Quinn was nineteen: not too terribly attractive, but he had a youthful, pretty body—slight build, little, round buns, flat tummy, slender legs, and very little body hair. He was doing time at Max because he had pulled an armed robbery and had been sentenced to fifteen years for the robbery and another fifteen for the use of a gun in the commission of a felony. The thirty years of his sentence disqualified him from consideration for the Medium Security prison.

Someone like Quinn is almost predestined to have problems in a prison like Max.

Quinn's problem took the form of a brute of a man whom I'll call Dominic (Dom, for short). Dom was doing six life sentences. I once heard Dom joke about it: "God gave me only one life," he had said; "the judge gave me six of 'em!" Dom will never see the outside world again; he has nothing to lose. If the price is right, he'll even kill a man because the courts can do no more to him.

We lived on the first floor of the ancient building. The cells were spaced closely together in a long row, with a corridor running the length of the tier. Sets of twenty cells were caged off by steel bars and were designated: A-Tier, B-Tier, C-Tier, etc.

At that time my old-man was a guy named Brad who happened to be a freind of Dominic's. In no sense of the word was I any kind of slave to Brad, but I enjoyed doing little things for him like making his bed. I once helped Brad do his laundry, but when he later asked me to do it for him by myself, I quickly let him know that I wasn't about to become a servant. Nonetheless, Brad's stature on the yard was enhanced by the fact that he had an "old-lady" who "did things for him."

Dom was jealous of Brad in many ways: Brad was strikingly handsome, well-built, athletic, and had lots of "things" (TV, radio, carpets on his cell floor, a bedspread, macrame hangings, and the other relatively few niceties one was allowed to have in his cell in that prison). Dom was balding, going to fat, lethargic, and had no "things" to show off to the other cons. Thus, when Quinn moved onto the tier, Dom saw his chance to run over a weak kid and gain a little stature for himself among the tougher cons.

Dom wasted no time. As the tier porter, he was out of his cell all day; the rest of us enjoyed only six hours in the late afternoon and evening. One day, Dom stopped in front of Quinn's cell, which was only two cells away from mine. The tier was quiet, and I was able to hear Dom's side of the conversation. After some small talk, he got to the point: "This is the way it is, kid—you're gonna be my punk! If you think you're bad enough to whip me, try it. 'Cause if you don't whip my ass, I'm gonna fuck you! When you come out of your cell at three o'clock unlock, we're either gonna fuck or we're gonna fight."

There was no doubt in anyone's mind who the winner of such a contest would be, but just to be on the safe side, Dom talked to a couple of his buddies. When the cell doors came open at three, there were four guys flocking to Quinn's cell. I didn't see what happened, but later that evening everyone on the tier knew about it. Quinn had submitted without a fight; he had obeyed each of Dom's orders to strip, lie down, grin and bear it.

Drunk with the feeling of power, Dom began to be more assertive. Within a few days, Quinn was totally subservient to Dom. Not only was he an unpaid domestic servant, making beds, doing laundry, cleaning the cell, and so on, he was also a sex slave. Nor were his sexual services restricted to his master—Quinn was required to be available to Dom's friends.

Often, while I was sitting in Brad's cell, listening to his stereo or watching his TV after a delightful bout of hot, passionate sex, Dom or one of his friends would come in and tell us in luridly descriptive terms about the new "uses" they had come up with for Quinn.

Quinn's unfortunate circumstances were pathetic, and I felt extremely sorry for the young man; but there was nothing I could do to help. As a result, I made it a point not to become familiar with him. I am too soft-hearted, and familiarity would have only increased my own feelings of impotence. Quinn would have to work it out for himself.

Of the many things described to Brad and me, a few stick out in my mind. On one occasion, Quinn had been sandwiched between Dom and a guy named Lee. Dom was fucking Quinn while Lee was getting his dick sucked. On another occasion, Quinn had been required to give seven or eight different guys blow-jobs, one after the other without let-up. One day, Dom even made Quinn give him some face through the cell bars.

Quinn never seemed to have any free time to himself. The six hours of unlock were completely preoccupied by the demands that Dom and his friends placed on the increasingly unhappy youngster.

Master-Slave situations in prison are not like the fantasy trips one reads about in gay magazines between two willing adults. It is not fun-and-games. Convicts play for keeps!

The straw that broke the camel's back was Dom's decision to have a tatoo put on Quinn's lower abdomen: "*I belong to Dom.*" Quinn spoke briefly to a guard in the chow hall one day; that same afternoon Quinn was in P.C.

Dom laughed about it later, after he finally blew off a lot of steam. It had been a new experience for Dom. It was not to be his last. About a month later, another pretty-boy moved onto B-Tier. That was several years ago. In the intervening years, Dom has had at least eight slaves that I know of, perhaps more.

There is yet one other side to prison slavery, and in this circumstance the roles are reversed. The joint I'm in while I'm writing this article is a fairly loose prison. We gays enjoy a lot of attention and are treated well. There are very few of us in ratio to the general population (ten or twelve of us to five or six hundred men). Needless to say, they curry our favors.

Each of us has his own stable of studs to do his bidding. It is no exaggeration to say that these guys literally drop what they are doing to fulfill our whims. "Do this for me"-"Do that for me"—"Go somewhere for me"—"Bring me this or that"—and so on. Obviously, this is not quite the same as the above example of prison slavery. However, it *is* a situation that one rarely encounters in the free world.

The aspect that makes it delightful is the willingness of the slave. Forced subjugation is intolerable. What Dominic did to Quinn and others like him leaves a bad taste in my mouth.

Tex, my current old-man, willingly obeys my commands to strip, to lie down, to turn over, and to lose himself in an hour of sexual carousing. Now, that's my kind of prison slave!

BUTCH VIRGINS

Of THE MANY SEXUAL EXPERIENCES to be found behind bars, none is perhaps as exciting as being the first joint-sissy to get a hold of a guy who has never been to bed with another man. Butch Virgins—I mean, truly "straight" guys who have never had any kind of sex with another guy—are often the most adventurous challenges and offer a special satisfaction.

"I don't fuck around" is a common expression among the Butch Virgins, implying that they are unattainable. The first time I put the make on Noel B., he put me off with those very words. Doing a lightweight four-year sentence, Noel was one of the incredible Greek-God types: tall, broad, powerfully muscular, startingly handsome. He had perenially erect nipples (like a Tom of Finland drawing) set on beefy, silky-smooth pecs. When I finally got him alone, he told me that he wasn't doing enough time to start "any funny stuff." He was very pleasant, but very adamant; he had never fucked another man, nor had he ever had a blow job (not even from a girl), and he had no intention of starting now.

Two years later, with a mere thirty-eight days before his release, Noel (with whom I was only casually friendly), dropped into my cell one evening after chow. This in itself was highly unusual. Even more unusual was the very personal nature of our conversation. A month earlier he had received a "Dear John" letter. Now, with less than six weeks to go, he said, "Fuck it! What am I saving myself for? Some cunt?"

Many times I had seen him on the yard, stripped to the waist, and had drooled over the thought of taking that magnificent body to bed. I had eventually given up hope; but here he was in my cell, hinting very strongly that he was "ready." He didn't come right out and say it; instead, he asked, "I've heard you give a good massage. Would you like to give *me* one?"

I covered my cell door and instructed him to strip. He followed orders, except for his white boxer shorts. "Those, too," I insisted. The massage, of course, was merely a convenient form of foreplay. By the time I had him turn over onto his back, he had a throbbing hard-on. After years of fantasizing that moment, I finally got to feel those muscular arms, that massive chest (with those pencil-eraser nipples), those powerful legs, that flat, fleshy stomach, and that gorgeous cock!

Noel was nervous and apprehensive. He started at every sound coming from the corridor. When he had turned over, exposing his raging erection, he reached down to cover it with his hand. I immediately began to massage the bicep of the offending arm, moving it away from his groin. At that point, he closed his eyes. I don't believe he opened them again till after I had brought him to an orgasm.

Like most Butch Virgins, he wasn't very responsive. They seem to think that if they become too involved, it will somehow lessen their manhood. Some of them do get "carried away" in their love making; but most lay there like dead fish. Although Noel fell into the dead fish category for most of our session together, he began to loosen up as his body neared orgasm.

After having let my hands explore every inch of his beautiful body, I climbed onto the bunk, between his legs, and allowed my mouth to do the rest. I couldn't keep my hands off those glorious nipples, as my tongue licked its way up his shaft. By the time I vacuumed his cock into my mouth, he had been in a state of expectant erection for nearly fifteen minutes. I heard an almost inaudible sigh of pleasure as I took his prick and lightly pinched his nipples.

His cock was average size, beautifully shaped, sensual, and silky. It wasn't long before I realized he would climax with very little more urging; so I took my mouth away from his throbbing tool and licked my way up his abdomen to his chest, carefully avoiding any contact with his dick. His nipples were rock-hard mountains set into spongy tits, surrounded by acres of hairless, muscular flesh. I was getting so excited myself that I knew I had to bring him to orgasm quickly or I would find myself creaming in my jeans.

I quickly licked my way back to his dick, took it into my mouth, and urged him toward a passionate climax. At this point, he tentatively placed his hands on my shoulders and carefully moved his pelvis up and down. In no time at all, his body convulsed in spasms, and his cock exploded with a uniquely delicious tasting cum, thick and creamy, suggesting that it had been a long while since his last orgasm.

Afterward he asked me: "How does the size of my cock compare to other guys?" Curiously, this is not an uncommon question. Noel's cock was an average 6″ to 6½″, but Noel was convinced that his cock was small. On his massive, broad physique, I must admit, it looked small; but in my mouth it was the perfect size. I told him so. Apparently, the girl who had recently jilted him had had the effrontery to tell him that his cock was small. I assured him it was not, and I probably had had a thousand more cocks than she could ever hope for. He went away content and returned several times before getting out of prison.

For all his magnificent good looks, Noel was a quiet and shy person. Jeff W. was quite the opposite: blustery, egotistical, full of bravado and swagger—but quite likeable, nonetheless, with an infectious smile and a witty personality. Jeff had never said, "I don't fuck around." In fact, he flirted with all the sissies in the joint. I naturally assumed that he frequently "fucked around." I continually invited him to my cell, but he always found some excuse not to come. He was only twenty, but he seemed so worldly. When I first saw him, he had a gorgeous physique; but by the time he finally paid me a visit, inactivity had taken its toll. He had begun to develop a bit of a pot-belly, but it had not gone so far as to become unattractive. His body was smooth and sensuous.

"Hi, Babe!" he announced with a flourish, coming into my cell. "I've come to *fuck!*" With what seemed like one continuous motion, he closed the cell door, covered it, and began stripping off his blue jeans. Wearing no underwear, he was soon naked. He lay down on my bunk and said: "I don't really want to fuck; I want some *screamin' skull,* beautiful."

I went straight to work. I assumed my favorite position (crouched between a man's legs) and worked his flaccid cock into a pulsating hard-on. Once his dick was hard, I began to lick his nuts. He wrapped his long, smooth legs around me and squirmed. Uttering low, soft moans, he massaged my shoulders like an experienced lover. With his legs up, his ass was accessible; so my tongue worked its way toward that tight, knotted orifice, while my hands played with his cock and balls. "Oh, Baby!" he sighed.

After a while, I returned my attention to his cock. His hands feverishly felt my neck and shoulders, while his pelvis pumped up and down with frenetic urgency. I ran my hands up his body to his chest, enjoying the baby softness of his delicate skin. "Oh, yeah, Babe! Yeah!" he exclaimed, thrusting and retracting his cock, as he fucked my face.

At the moment of orgasm, his body jack-knifed, his hands reached down my back almost to my buttocks, his legs clamped around me like a vise. He muttered "Oh, Baby" over and over again, as gobs of delicious sperm shot into my mouth.

When it was over, I asked him: "Well! How did that compare to the other sissies in this joint?"

"All I know is," he answered, with a contented smile on his lips, "it was damned good."

When I pressed him for a comparison, he finally admitted that it had been his first blow-job. He shrugged off his months of bravado by saying that he had been thinking about it for a long time but just "never got around to it."

He had been such a responsive, active lover that I found it hard to believe it was his first experience. So I discreetly checked with every sissy in the joint. It was true: Jeff had never gone to bed with any of them. His passionate love-making had simply been a part of his blustery personality.

Another standard trait of the Butch Virgin is his tendency to play hard-to-get. Most Butch Virgins in prison remain aloof from the joint-sissies, fearing that any association will reflect on their masculinity. This is especially true of the young, straight guy who could conceivably become the object of sexual advances from other straight cons.

Gerry C. fell into this category. Gerry was 21 when he came to prison (fifteen years for robbery), but looked like a 15-year old. I'd never seen more beautiful eyes in my life! I will never know how he avoided being "turned-out," but somehow he managed. One thing is certain: for four years he never spoke more than two words to any of the sissies. By the time he was 25 (looking more like 18), he was buffed-up to god-like proportions and feared no man on the yard. Also, by that time, he realized that "fucking around" was common practice. For four years he had been unattainable—wasted years in my opinion. When he finally decided to "do it," it was my good fortune that one of Gerry's closest friends was a regular trick of mine.

Gerry would not come to my cell alone. Before he finally took the plunge, he visited me several times in the company of T. M. One day they arrived together; then T.M. excused himself. When Gerry remained behind—alone—I knew the time had come.

He refused to strip naked. In fact, he wanted only to take his cock out of his pants, fully clothed. We struck a compromise: he pulled his pants down to his knees, but was otherwise still fully clothed. He leaned against the wall, and I dropped to my knees.

Knowing that this was the first time a man had sucked Gerry's cock was an intense thrill for me. When I cupped his buns in my hands, he moved quickly to push my hands away. Not wanting to argue, I restricted my hand movements to his thighs and lower abdomen. He remained motionless after that, and it took a long time to coax him towards orgasm. I asked myself if it had been worth the wait. The excitement of getting a Butch Virgin was rapidly wearing off. The beautiful young man in front of me might as well have been a foam-rubber sex doll. After a while, I began to believe he would never cum.

I pulled away. I was going to ask if he wanted to try again later. Before I could speak, he said: "Don't stop now. I'm ready to shoot!"

Within seconds of returning my mouth to his cock, I felt his hot sperm shooting into me. But even at the moment of eruption, there was very little movement in Gerry's body; his contractions were slight—not at all explosive.

To my amazement, he showered me with praise. He loved it, he insisted; it was great. And so on. Since then, I've had Gerry numerous times. He even gets totally naked these days and has livened up considerably. We've become friends, and he has confided in me that not only was I the first *man* he had ever had sex with, I was the first *person*. Gerry had been a virgin in every sense of the word.

TANK BOSS

I WAS UP ON A FORGERY CHARGE. I had been issued a blue jump-suit, a pair of shower thongs, and a towel. Everything else was taken away, including underwear and socks. I was taken upstairs to A-Tank, given a one-inch thick mattress, two sheets, and two blankets. The steel-barred door to A-Tank was opened; I was told to find a bunk. Then the door clanged shut loudly behind me. I was in a narrow corridor, to my left was a row of seven four-man cells, to my right was a large day-room with several plexiglass windows, four-feet square.

I lugged my bedding down the corridor until I found a cell with an empty bunk. It was 10 AM and nearly all the inmates were still sleeping, but I had seen three young men in the day room. Each of them had rolled down the upper part of the jumpsuit to below the waist and had tied the sleeves in a loose knot in front. I later discovered that this was the universal practice because of the heat. It also exposed well-muslced young chests and abdomens.

The cells were totally enclosed, except for a steel door which was opened or closed electrically by the guards. The bunks were mounted on the walls—nothing but 6' x 3' steel slabs bolted to concrete. There was one upper and one lower on each side of the cell. Centrally located at the rear of the cell was a single-unit toilet and wash basin. The empty bunk in Cell 5 was an upper. I spread the mattress and made up my bunk, trying not to disturb the guy below me.

Across from me, an old man lay reading a book. After a few moments, looking over at me, he introduced himself. "They call me Pops," he said. "Those two are twins. John's the one below you and

Jim's the one below me. Nice enough boys, quiet, and easy going. They got caught burglarizing a stereo store. I'm doing six months for drunk driving—second bust for the same charge.

I looked down at John. Asleep, he looked fourteen. He had a pretty, almost feminine face, framed by long, silky, wavy, blond hair. I couldn't see Jim's face. He was on his side, facing the wall. But because of the heat, I could see an awful lot of his tender young body. His blanket barely covered his legs, and revealed a small, firm, delicately shaped pair of buns and a slender, fair-complexioned back. Seeing as much of these twins as I did, I knew I wouldn't be able to share the same cell with two beautiful young men and stay in the closet.

I introduced myself to Pops. He had also stripped to the waist, and I did the same. Then I jumped down and used the toilet. Flushing it, I turned and saw another young man framed in the doorway. He appeared to be about my age, twenty-five. He had a handsome face, but his body was a little too flabby. He was shorter than my 6'2" by a good six inches. His skin was white and pasty.

Behind him, in the corridor, was an even younger man, firmly muscled, and possessing that strong chest and arm tone that usually turns me on. He was as deeply tanned as I, and his chest was beginning to sprout curly black hair.

"I'm Paul," said the one standing in the doorway. He tried to make his voice sound menacing. From experience, I knew what was coming. "I'm the tank boss. Me and Jack run this tank." He pointed over his left shoulder to the bronzed man behind him. He than went into his spiel—one I knew by heart: who sits where at chow, who does what for clean-up, who runs the poker game, etc. etc.

The sampling of beautiful young bodies I'd seen had made up my mind: this was definitely *not* a closet situation.

The twins had awakened (Jim quickly covering his exposed *derrière*), and were listening to me tell Paul I had done lots of time and that he wouldn't have to worry about me creating any problems. By my behavior, I made it clear that I wasn't afraid of him, nor of his muscle-man.

" . . . And I want it understood from the gate," I continued, "that I've done more time than any six of you put together. I'm also gay, and I'm proud of the fact." A quick look of astonishment crossed their faces. "I won't get in your way, and I expect you to not get in mine. You run the tank however you want, you don't bother me, and I won't bother you. And you can pass the word: if anyone thinks that all gays are weak sissies, he can do whatever he thinks is right."

I could tell that Paul was not happy with the situation. Tank bosses always work on the principle that a show of strength is all that is necessary to instill fear, and fear subjugates. By refusing to kowtow to him, he had lost some of his stature, and by refusing to be on the defensive about my homosexuality, I had put him on the defensive.

He extricated himself as well as he could. "Okay. Just as long as we understand each other. Don't create no problems." He turned and walked back down the corridor to his own cell, which I knew would be Cell 1. Jack lingered, looking at me. I couldn't help but notice that Jack wore his jumpsuit dangerously low on his hips. The thick patch of pubic hairs extended the invitation that I could only hope I had read in his eyes. The jumpsuit was slung so low that if it had hung a half-inch lower, it would have revealed the base of his cock. Jack's jumpsuit had been rolled down inwardly, sleeves tucked-in and adding to the bulk which kept the uniform hanging on his hips very precariously.

After making it obvious that I had studied his body, I let my eyes return to his gaze. The quick movement of his eyes betrayed that he had also been looking at my bigger, more muscular body. He turned and followed after Paul.

I glanced first at Jim then at John. They broke into smiles simultaneously. John was the first to get out of bed, as naked as I had seen Jim, but now I caught the first fleeting glimpse of a cock which I was determined to get to know quite well. Both twins got into jumpsuits which, like everyone else's, rode very low on their slender young hips. I realized that the practice of wearing them so revealingly was not intentional; the jumpsuits had been made in such a way that wearing the upper part rolled down, tightness could be achieved only at the widest part of the pelvis. The narrower the waist or hips, the lower the uniform slipped.

Lunch, like all meals, was served in the dayroom. There were tables and benches (bolted to the floor), a TV at one end of the room (mounted in a steel frame and bolted to the wall), and a shower stall at the opposite end of the room. Our cells were unlocked at six in the morning. Until eleven at night, we could roam the tank, from cells to dayroom, and back. There were no scheduled activities; we could sleep whenever we wanted, for as long as we wanted. The remote control TV was operated by jail officials, and books, magazines, and newspapers lay scattered on the long tables. There was one chess set, a Monopoly game, dominoes, and playing cards.

At lunch, I learned that I had fallen into a veritable paradise of beautiful young bodies: at least twenty of the twenty-six inhabitants of A-Tank were under twenty-five; of those twenty, fourteen had slender or muscular bodies. Aside from the twins and Jack, I saw three others that I singled out for early conquest. After lunch, I was pleased to see that two of those three were playing chess. I would get to know them by challenging them at chess.

Word had traveled fast that I was gay. Good; I wanted it that way. I could tell from whispered conversations and from covert glances that I had shattered many preconceived notions about homosexuals. I even overheard this exchange:

"He don't look like a queer to me!"

"Ya can't tell just by lookin'!"

The first speaker was a young man, probably twenty, whose low-slung jumpsuit revealed a white lower abdomen against a deeply tanned upper torso. He handled his cock with his left hand under his jumpsuit as he talked.

Later, after dinner, I took a shower. The shower stall was large enough for four people, but there were only two shower heads. And I had noticed that only one man ever showered at a time, as if by some unwritten rule. After my shower, I challenged one of my three target objectives to a game of chess. His name was Monty. Since I didn't yet know the jail's routine, I waited. There would be plenty of time to figure out the best time and place, but I could tell from his friendly manner that the answer would be yes.

I quickly learned that the only privacy one could find was in the cell, between 11 PM and 6 AM. Even so, that privacy was shared by three cellmates. In cell 5, though, I found all the privacy I needed. Pops was in the habit of going to bed early; according to John, the old man slept soundly throughout the night.

With Pops fast asleep, the twins and I got to know each other. Jim was the oldest, by about five minutes. They were identical, except for the locations of their birthmarks. They had soft blue eyes, and although they were slender and small-framed, their bodies had a tight muscularity which could easily develop into god-like proportions if they were to work at it. Their fragile, delicate, boyish features were a tremendous turn-on.

After an hour of informative personal small-talk, I guided the conversation toward sex. They asked the usual questions about being gay, and eventually I bluntly told them that I enjoyed sucking cocks, I enjoyed the feel of a finely proportioned body. Then I made it clear that I really wanted to suck their cocks. It took another hour for them to talk themselves into it. They admitted that early in puberty they used to get down together a lot, but for many years hadn't done anything like that. They both made it a strong point that they liked girls. Under the present circumstances, however, they were willing to let me do my thing.

For a minute they played at "you go first, no *you* go first." I settled it for them. "Since I've already seen John's cock," I said, smiling at him, "I now want to see Jim's—just to be sure you guys are really *identical*." We were sitting on John's bunk; so I told Jim to stand in front of me, facing me. With one hand, I loosened the knot in John's jumpsuit while he was still sitting on the bed. With the other hand, I did the same to Jim's jumpsuit. It fell to his ankles; John's didn't appear to move much, except in the rear. I told Jim to step out of them. I told John to stand up and step out of his. It was wild! It was like looking at one guy from both sides at the same time. I felt my dick stiffening.

I cupped my hands on Jim's soft but firm buns and nudged him closer to the bed. I licked his navel, then ran my tongue down the soft fuzz of his abdomen. Soon my mouth encircled his still-flaccid cock, but by sucking and by licking the head, it was soon hardening. I pulled my mouth away and stood up, pressing our bodies tightly together. Then I released him and motioned him to lie on John's bunk. Next, I sunk to my knees in front of John. It was like an instant replay, and my cock became hard as steel. As soon as he was hard, I stood up. I said to him softly, "stand near the head of the bed and watch."

I went to the foot of the bed, let my jumpsuit fall, stepped out of it, and climbed onto the bunk between Jim's slender, finely downed legs. I crouched into position and ran my hands up the insides of his thighs. His legs felt hairless and smooth as silk. My hands reached the fuzzy scrotum; my fingers began to toy with his balls. As my tongue began a flicking, darting movement between his thighs, my hands left his balls and began to feel the firm, flat, sensual softness of his tight abdomen. I was now purposely avoiding any touch of his rigidly erect penis. At last my tongue found his nut sack. I softly sucked his left ball into my mouth, then the right. My mouth gently massaged his balls; my hands floated feather-like over his chest, shoulders, arms, and neck. My chest lay between his thighs, and I sensed the slow working of his leg muscles. I could see his dick bobbing in front of my eyes. It hadn't been touched since I started, and it was begging for immediate attention. I released first one, then the other, of his balls, and I started licking around the base of his cock. I licked the entire length of it, with the exception of the head. Jim was now more than excited, he was passionate. I felt the erotic thrusting and gyrating of his pelvis; he chest heaved with heavy breathing; his hands had found my shoulders and were gently massaging, urging me onward—or downward.

My tongue finally touched the head of his dick. He thrust upward, his dick crying out to be taken. I let my hands slide down the edges of his body to his hips. Again I licked the head of his dick and again he thrust his pelvis upward. My hands quickly slipped underneath him, cupping and prodding his buns.

At last, I gave him the relief his cock was craving. My mouth wrapped firmly around the head of his swollen, throbbing dick. It lunged deep into my mouth; my lips and nose nestled snugly in his fine public hairs. I savored the delicious aroma of bath soap and perspiration, that delightful, ethereal odor which is so unique to young men. A virile clean smell, mingled with passionate perspiration. I stayed all the way down on his cock for several moments, his hips doing the labor of love, his arms reaching as far down my back as they could go.

I began an up and down movement with my mouth, enjoying every inch of his delightful, youthful organ. I started to pull away, in order to delay orgasm and to prolong this intensely pleasurable moment. I had already tasted the lubricating semen. I knew he was ready to climax, but as I started to take my mouth away, I felt his hands on my head and knew it was too late. His dick thrust deep into my throat, and I brought one hand from his buns to cup around his balls just as his scrotum contracted violently. Jim's cock erupted into my mouth, his pelvis jerking and thrusting his dick as deep as it would go. His whole body shuddered; the muscles in his abdomen contracted, and his upper body jerked forward. His sperm was thick and creamy. His cock continued to jerk ferociously in my mouth; his thighs tightened around my body. His body trembled, then shuddered as I finally got to taste his cum, sweeter than a lot I've tasted. It had been a long time since his last orgasm, I could tell.

For a long time we lay practically motionless, except for an occasional shudder. My mouth was slowly, gently massaging his spent penis. I released his balls and let my hand wander idly along his body. The pungent odor of satisfied passion washed over me, and I wanted to lay there with his cock in my mouth forever. It did not seem to be going soft. If I continued to suck on it, I knew he would soon be ready to go again. But now I wanted the brother.

I pulled my mouth away, then my body, and crawled off the bunk. Jim lay still for a moment, then swung his legs off the side of the bed. "Wow!" he said, "that was *far out!*" He cast an embarrassed look at his brother, but seeing his brother's rigid hard-on, he lost some of his self-consciousness.

John took his brother's position on the bed. I practiced a similar routine, but I'm sure my own love-making was more intense since John was being even more responsive than his twin. Despite the fact that he had been aroused considerably by watching, he took longer than Jim to cum. His sperm was not as sweet nor as thick; I knew he had masturbated recently.

Afterward, we sat around in the nude and talked. Both twins admitted that they had never before watched someone getting a blow-job. Both had been turned-on while watching. Jim said that watching his twin was like seeing himself getting some head.

The more we talked, the more aroused we became. I told them that I'd love to do it again to both of them, but I was so turned-on by their bodies that I wouldn't be responsible if I shot all over one of them.

John looked at Jim, then back at me, and said, "To be honest with you, Jim and I used to lay on top of each other and come all over each other, so it really won't be anything new. It'll be okay. Okay, Jim?"

Jim smiled at me. "Sure! Look what he's doing for us!" Jim, almost playfully, scooted onto the bunk behind John and me. "I'm first," he said, with a mischievous twinkle in his eye.

John remained seated near the head of the bed. I had been sitting in the middle; so I merely twisted my body around and immediately went down on Jim's majestically proud cock. Since my body was half facing John, I reached over and began to search for his cock with my right hand. I found it firmly erect and began to jack him off. While my mouth sucked on the one, my hand played with the other.

But the position was uncomfortable, so I let go of John's dick and took up my favorite position between Jim's legs. It went much like the first time, but now I felt as though Jim were trying to make love back to me. His hands roamed as much of my body as he could reach, and his legs tried to massage my sides and buns. I deliberately tried not to get too excited this time, but Jim was making it difficult.

Sooner than I had expected, Jim had orgasmed. This time his cock went limp within a short period of time. After a minute or so, the twins changed places. My head was feeling light, and my whole body trembled with pleasure. I threw myself at John's dick and did every trick I knew with my mouth and tongue. Suddenly, I pulled away from his cock. I lifted my body, then lowered it along his length, directly on top of him, our cocks in intimate contact. I pumped and thrust my swollen cock against his abdomen. I felt John's hands on my buns and his pelvis working in time with my own. Then I felt a surging inside of me. Unable to control myself, I kissed him passionately on the lips, then all over his face and neck. John was fingering my balls.

When I subsided and came off him, I discovered that he, too, had reached climax. He looked up at me, smiling through glassy eyes. "Jim, bring the toilet paper," he said.

"Oh, no, you don't," I argued. I began licking all around his balls, his dick, the pubic hairs, the flat, muscular abdomen, enjoying the exotic taste of our mingled juices, and the sensual aroma of his sperm-covered belly. Then I went back to his dick. To my surprise I got him off a third time.

Jim had gone to his own bed, was lying on his side stroking his dick, watching us. I crossed over to his bed, gave him a vigorous rub down, then sucked him off.

The following night was much like the first, with a few exceptions. The twins were thoroughly enjoying our sex play. They loosened up even more, and (although they wouldn't take my dick in their mouths), they saw to it that my needs were met by jacking me off while I was doing one or the other.

It had been easy to get down with the twins, given the privacy of our cell (and Pops sleeping soundly through it all, occasionally punctuating our orgies with sharp snores). But getting down with Monty was going to be a different matter.

For five days in a row, the twins and I slept late because of our all-night love bouts. I learned from Monty that he, too, had been sleeping till noon.

On the sixth day, Jim and John and I had stayed awake until

breakfast. After pancakes and oatmeal, the twins went back to bed. I soon found myself alone in the dayroom with Keith, the one who had handled his penis when talking about me to one of the other guys. He now appeared to be browsing through the paper, but he knew I was cruising him. His left hand turned the pages idly, while his right hand suggestively felt his chest muscles then glided down his body and disappeared into the front of his hip-slung jumpsuit. By what he tried to make look like an accident, the loose bow of his sleeves unraveled and the jumpsuit slid off his hips. He made a half-hearted grab for them with both hands, without bending his body. For five or six seconds, he stood there, his naked body exposed to the knees. He casually looked around the dayroom, as if to see whether or not anyone had seen the "accident." Then he looked me square in the eyes. I looked directly into his eyes, then very slowly let my eyes lower—obviously scanning his body and coming to rest at the level of his dick. Then I looked at his face again. He pulled up the jumpsuit, looped the sleeves, turned, and walked out of the dayroom.

For a minute I was puzzled. But only for a minute. He returned, carrying his towel. He walked to the shower. He turned and faced me as he stripped. I didn't know what to think—his gaze appeared more like a challenge than an invitation. He disappeared behind the shower curtain. I shrugged, went to my cell and got my own towel.

The shower was full of steam when I stepped in. Keith had turned on both shower heads. "Do you mind if I shower with you?" I asked.

"I want you to," he responded in a pleasant voice.

I began to lather him up and soon I was soaping his whole body. The striking contrast between his upper torso's deep bronze tan and the lower half's milky whiteness made him look ten times more naked than he was. The soapy lather gave his body a silken smoothness which heightened the sensual gratification of our close contact. He had one of the most perfectly shaped dicks I had ever seen. While soft, it seemed thick and full, not a wrinkle in sight. The circumcised skin fit smoothly around the head—no scar visible. As I soaped it up, and as it got harder, it achieved exquisite proportions. I sunk to my knees in front of his large phallus. Cupping water in my hands, I rinsed the soap from his dick and balls. As the water poured down over us, I took his proud symbol of manhood deep into my mouth.

While I sucked lustfully on his cock, my left hand roamed across his chest and stomach, reaching down to play with his nuts, then in to finger his asshole. My right hand was busy stroking my own cock. I managed to synchronize my masturbation and succeeded in reaching a simultaneous orgasm.

When we emerged from the shower, the Dayroom was still empty.

That night over a game of chess after supper, I told Monty to be ready the next morning after breakfast. He flashed a timid smile revealing a mouth full of beautiful teeth. His deep brown eyes, accented by thick, luxurious lashes, sparkled in anticipation. His skin was fair; his twenty-year-old body bore witness to several years of body-building. His chest was hairless, and he had a rugged, masculine handsomeness.

Our turn in the shower, however, was to be delayed by several days. It happened so quickly, I cannot recall the details clearly. Paul and Jack were calling Monty names, such as: "faggot's faggot," "queer lover," and "punk's punk." The immediate, superficial cause of the fight was actually unimportant; the real reason was that I represented a threat to their supremacy in the tank, and Monty and I had been spending a lot of time together in the evenings. Some kind of show-down was inevitable, and Paul and Jack picked that evening to force the issue.

Before I knew what was happening, Monty was on his feet, slugging it out with Paul. Jack saw that Paul was getting the worst of it, so he joined in the battle. I figured I had best even the odds, so I tapped Jack on the shoulder and delivered a powerful right to his jaw.

The fight was never really even. Paul was no match for Monty, and Jack was no match for me. The two guys who celled with the tank boss and his muscle man decided to stay out of it.

I was unable to watch how Monty was doing, but I managed several well placed hits against Jack. He scored a couple of rib shots. Delivering an upper cut, I drove Jack into a table. His jumpsuit had been working loose during the fight, and it gave way. Before he was able to redeem his modesty, he had exposed a hard-on. He crumpled onto the bench, obviously giving up.

The iron-barred doors to the tank were opened, and three jail guards came storming in. Since no one would snitch on who had started the fight, all four of us were taken to the "hole."

The jail had two 6' x 6' "strip cells," or "holes." There is nothing inside the thickly padded cells except a hole in the floor, near the rear of the cell, for bodily functions. The word "strip" not only means that the cell is bare, it means its occupants are equally bare.

They stripped the four of us in the hallway. Bare-ass naked, we answered none of their questions, except to indicate how we four should be divided between the two strip cells. Paul and Jack were unceremoniously ushered into the first cell; Monty and I were roughly pushed into the second one.

For a long time, we stood silently, letting our eyes grow accustomed to the blackness of the cell. A faint, exceedingly dim light shone through the tiny window in the solid steel door.

Monty said very softly, as though not wanting to disturb the silence in the cell, "Not exactly the comforts of home." He paused slightly, then added, "but I'll bet it's better than in the shower . . ."

Forgetting the soreness in my ribs and chest, I felt for his body. In the ghostly light, I saw his flashing eyes. The silhouette of his beautifully muscular body showed him leaning with his back to one of the side walls. I crossed to him, put my hands on his waist and edged my body up against his. Both of us were still slippery with perspiration. I rubbed my stiffening cock against his. My hands slid behind him and brushed lightly against his buns. I began to lick the sweat from his neck; it was salty, but clean tasting. I bent my knees slightly, nudging our cocks even closer together, as I started licking his massive chest. I could feel the iron hard muscles beneath the velvety smooth skin of his magnificent body.

Hands softly caressing his large, firm buns, I glided down to my knees. I was now looking at his fully erect cock for the first time. At first I thought I was seeing an optical illusion created by the dim lighting in the cell: it was the largest cock I had ever seen.

When I put my mouth over the head of his collossus, I knew it was not an illusion. He pressed his fingers against my head, urging me to go all the way down. I ignored the pressure; I would have to take this one at my own speed—if I could take it at all. I liked Monty, and I wanted to satisfy him. I wanted *all* of him.

I gagged. I quickly took my mouth away. "Let me fuck you," I heard him ask. "You'd tear me up," I protested. I started again, determined to conquer his veritable Mt. Everest. I went down on the shaft a little, then came back up; then went a little further, then up; then deeper yet. Finally I made it. But I couldn't keep doing it. I kept gagging. I damned myself for being so inept.

I kept trying, but at one point I was sure I would vomit. I came up for air. I stood up and nibbled on his tits while my right hand stroked his iron-hard cock, covered with burning soft flesh. His tits were the only tiny things about him—small, rock-hard islands in a massive sea of firm muscles. I discovered that they were almost as erogenous as the Goliath-sized cock between his legs. As I sucked them into my mouth, first the right, then the left, his body responded in shudders of delight. He arched his back, breathing heavily now. I stroked his cock faster and scraped my teeth against his nipples. I stood up straight and darted my tongue into his left ear.

He wrapped his arms around me and kissed me passionately on the lips. I sucked on his tongue until I thought I'd suck it out of his mouth.

He suddenly unclenched and sank to his knees. "I don't know if I can do this," he said in shallow, gasping breaths. "I've never done it, but I *want* to, because I want to please you, too."

"Let me show you," I said, gliding down to my knees and nudging him onto his side. He responded to my gestures, and soon we were lying on our sides. My face was buried in his cotch, my erect cock pointing at his mouth. "Just do what I do. You'll like it."

For some reason, perhaps the angle, it was easier to go all the way down on his cock in this position. He glided my cock into his mouth with his hand. It had been a long time since my dick had nestled in a warm mouth, and the sensation was overwhelming, especially because I liked Monty so much.

While I was now able to handle his whole cock, my free hand found and began to play with his left tit. Immediately, he was more passionate. He abandoned himself to the frenzy of the moment, and sucked my cock inexpertly, but with a desire to please.

More suddenly than I expected, he erupted full-force into my mouth. The violent spasms and tremors of his orgasm were so powerfully thrilling that seconds later I was thrusting my own cock deep into his gagging mouth in an ecstatic burst of passion. I felt in that moment that I loved Monty more than anyone I had ever known.

Then, our passions deliciously spent, we lay with each other's cocks in our mouths. I enjoyed the smooth feel and the sweet-and-sour taste of his limp cock almost as much as his hard one. The smell of his body, sweaty from both the fight and our love-making, was not offensive; it was youthful, and it was masculine.

At length I pulled away and adjusted my body to lie alongside his, face to face. "You were right," I whispered, "it was better than in the shower."

He stroked my muscular arm, gliding his hand up to my neck and face. I was thrilled by this show of tenderness. "You were right, too," he said, as he flashed me another one of those ice-melting smiles, "I *liked* it!"

We were kept in the strip cell for three days. We talked a lot, and we made love a lot. We got to know each other intimately. It was almost a disappointment when they took us back to A-Tank.

We were greeted like conquering heroes. Paul and Jack had been transferred to the County Jail when it was learned that they were the instigators of the fight and generally disliked in A-Tank.

To a man, the men in the tank asked Monty and me to be the new Tank Bosses, and while I don't really condone the concept of a tank boss, the existence of one is almost inevitable, so I agreed that it might as well be Monty and me.

We moved into Cell 1 and evicted the two men who had supported Paul and Jack. In their places, we installed the twins. Our first night back was an unconditional orgy. After supper, I followed Rusty into the shower, in full view of everyone. Rusty had been the third of my original intentions of conquest in the tank. He was taken by surprise but consented, and in no time my mouth was wrapped warmly around his long, thin cock.

When we emerged from the shower, several heads turned; but if anyone's sensitivities had been offended, no one dared to speak. Later, while running a poker game, I watched a guy named Scott go into the shower. Scott's body was nothing remarkable, but his face was extremely handsome. To a lot of good-natured teasing, I grabbed my towel and again disappeared into the shower.

After lock-up, the four of us sat in Cell 1; the twins and Monty were getting to know each other. Later, Monty and I gave the twins blow-jobs. Then, as they watched, Monty and I got into a *sixty-nine.* Later we managed to coax the twins into a four-way *sixty-nine,* after I had told them that I would take Monty's huge cock.

For the next three months, we four were the tank bosses. At night, we indulged our sexual fantasies. We often slept with each other, cuddling up to soft, warm bodies. Although Monty didn't object to anything we did with the twins, I could see his was jealous whenever I joined someone else in the shower, so after a while, I abandoned the practice. Monty was pleased, and he showed me.

Then I was sentenced to State Prison. Monty was given probation. He writes to me all the time, and he'll be waiting for me when I get out. But as much as I love Monty, I still like sex. And there's a hundred gorgeous bodies here. Steve is eighteen, blond, bronze, and muscular. Dave is twenty-four, with black hair and a small framed body. Mark is just plain pretty. And there's Wayne, Tim, and . . .

WHO'S KIDDING WHO?

I T WAS AN OLD PRISON, built in the eighteen-hundreds. It had been added to over the years, as the inmate population increased. When Dale arrived in 1979, the place looked like an architect's nightmare; the old, the not so old, and the relatively new buildings merged into a chaotic maze of sandstone, brick, and concrete cell blocks, dormitories, alcoves, and after thoughts. It was Dale's second time in prison, and right away he noticed the almost alarming shortage of uniformed staff; there simply weren't enough screws to adequately supervise and police inmate activities. Poker games, prohibited by the rule book, flourished in every dorm and cell block, sheets were hung over cell doors, also against the rules, marijuana and drugs, absolutely illegal, were as common as cigarettes and coffee. Security checks were infrequent, and on the rare occasion when a screw patroled the cell block, instead of breaking up the poker game, he would watch it for a while and joke with the participants.

Behind the unauthorized (but ignored) curtains, men shot dope, smoked pot, got blow-jobs, occasionally beat the shit out of someone, and far too often raped some poor defenseless young kid. None of this, of course, ever came to the attention of staff. There is an unwritten "convict code" which dictates silence. The guy who gets beat up must rely on the old "I slipped and fell in the shower" story. If the possibility exists that an illegal act might be detected by a surprise security check, one man is made to "stand point." The hapless kid who gets raped either suffers in silence, seeks Protective Custody, or gets a shank and tries to kill his rapists at a later date.

For Dale, who used the nickname Candy, since gay were expected to use feminine-sounding names, the illegal (but tacitly approved) curtains over cell doors allowed him all the sexual freedom he needed. In his previous "time down" the only privacy to be found at that prison was in the shower; this time the curtains provided privacy in one's own cell. It allowed him to entertain the many eager hunky studs in the comfort of a bed.

Candy was also a budding writer. Behind the curtains, he was able to find the seclusion he needed when working on his short stories.

Within a week of his arrival, he had latched onto an old man, Jim Folger. Like so many guys in prison, Jim went by a nickname: Hawk. He was a weight-lifter, whose body was at that stage of development midway between a natural slimness and the gigantic proportions achieved by the more zealous body-builders. Hawk's muscles were not rock hard, but Candy delighted in the feel of Hawk's nicely developed body. He was in his late twenties, not really handsome but good looking in a rugged way. He was tanned to a golden bronze above the waistline but suffered from prison pallor on the lower half of his body. Hawk's most striking feature was his eyes: soft blue, watery pools set off by long lashes.

Candy and Hawk had a good working mutual arrangement. Candy had managed to sell a couple of his stories; the profits kept the two of them in coffee, cigarettes, and toilet articles. Hawk's limited finances were thus freed to be used for dope and grass deals, on which he always made a profit. He also kept Candy and a few close friends in grass and dope. Between the two of them, they never lacked for the few necessities and pleasures to be had behind prison walls.

It was more than a year after Candy had settled comfortably into the routine of prison life that Skip moved into the cell block. Melvin Arnold Skipmore was twenty-two, but he didn't look a day over fifteen. A fine peach fuzz lined his face, and his attempt to grow a moustache was abortive. He had silky, sandy brown hair, too curly and too long. It framed his too pretty face and turned heads everywhere he went. His slender body was small, almost fragile. His chronological age qualified him as an adult; his youthful physical appearance was that of an early adolescent.

Candy, a chicken hawk at heart, was immediately attracted to him. Unfortunately for Skip, so was every other swinging dick in the joint. Candy realized instantly that Skip was in trouble.

The newcomer occupied the cell next to Candy's, and Candy lost no time in getting to know him. His large brown eyes twinkled when he smiled and lit up his angelic face, making him even more beautiful. While chatting idly, Candy helped him make up his bunk. When Skip removed the prison shirt of blue chambray and slipped into a T-shirt, Candy caught a glimpse of his naked torso. The smallest blue jeans issued by the prison laundry were size twenty-eight. Skip's waist could have been no larger than a twenty-six, for the jeans hung precariously low on his slender hips, revealing a flat, hairless abdomen (which Candy would have liked to lick and nibble on for hours without end.) The kid's chest was small but not skinny, and there was a delightful fullness to the boyish musculature.

Yep, Candy thought. *This boy's in serious trouble.* Sex-deprived cons are drawn to Skip's type like vultures to carrion, like tomcats to pussies in heat. Candy tried to warn the kid what to expect; he even offered Skip the use of his shank. "Believe me, I have no use for it. Hawk takes care of me. But before a few days go by, you're going to need it."

"I won't need it, Candy," Skip demurred. "In the first place, I don't know how to use one. I'd end up getting it taken away from me and probably used against me. In the second place, I really don't think I'll need it."

During their conversation, Candy made sure that Skip knew that he was a queen. Then he let the younger man know that he would enjoy sucking his cock. He assured Skip that he posed no threat to his masculinity, nor would he ever force himself on Skip. "That will happen," Candy insisted, "all too soon by the coyotes on this tier."

Despite Candy's persistent efforts, Skip wouldn't give in. The curious thing was the wording of his refusals. "I can't, Candy. Believe me, I just can't." He never said he didn't want to, he never hinted that he wouldn't enjoy it, it was just a simple, "I can't."

Later that evening they were playing Gin Rummy in Candy's cell. Hawk came in, and after Candy had introduced him to Skip, he politely asked Skip to leave. Hawk's politeness, for a tough con, was one of the traits that endeared him to Candy. To Candy, it made Hawk more of a man, not less of one.

Sex with Hawk was always one-sided. He was not a very responsive lover, but Candy always enjoyed doing him. Hawk removed his clothes and lay on the bunk, his legs spread just wide enough to allow Candy to crawl between them. Rarely did he have a hard-on when they started; it was one of Candy's pleasures to tease the limp penis into a proud erection. His hands glided along the hairy legs with a feather-light touch, as his head lowered, tongue extended, to Hawk's furry scrotum. The man's flaccid cock lay to the left side, thick and full even in its limber state.

Hawk was always clean, having showered earlier in the evening. The clean, fresh smell of his crotch never failed to excite Candy. On far too many occasions, Candy had coaxed someone into bed only to be turned off by the guy's lack of personal hygiene. Hawk used nothing more than state issue soap, no artificial scents, no colognes; yet the natural aroma of his masculine body was much more exciting.

As Candy's tongue toyed with Hawk's balls, the sleeping giant began to awaken. Candy continued his feather touch exploration up the length of his old man's body, coming to rest in the soft pelt of his chest. Slowly, tantalizingly, he began a slow ascent with his tongue from the base to the crown of Hawk's now fully erect cock. As his tongue darted across the reddish purple cap, the teased organ jerked, like a spoiled child in a tantrum, demanding more attention. Hawk's dick was not the largest that Candy had ever taken, but it certainly begged for no comparison. It was large enough to cause Candy to gag if he tried to take all of it into his mouth; thus he had gotten into the habit of gripping the base of it with two fingers.

Hawk, as a rather passive participant, demonstrated very little passion, except at the beginning and at orgasm. When Candy at last guided the rigid pole of throbbing flesh into his mouth, he felt an urgent upward thrust of Hawk's pelvis. This was when Candy got turned on by his old man. The feeling of that swollen dick in his mouth, pulsating and vibrating against his tongue and cheeks, was ecstatic—better only at the moment of climax.

He had tried numerous times to trigger a more passionate response from the body-builder, but he remained passive. He simply wasn't the demonstrative type. He preferred a straight forward blow-job, admitting only that it felt good when Candy fondled his body with his feather-like touch. Even though he felt that he was giving less of himself than he was capable of, Candy had settled into a fellatic routine which seemed to please the other man.

Urging Hawk's gorgeous tool toward ejaculation, Candy felt his legs tighten against his body. Another well recognized signal that he was about to cum was when his hands went to Candy's shoulders and began a gentle massage that accelerated as his body hurled into the throes of orgasm. The ordinarily controlled and reserved weight lifter writhed and moaned as his cock erupted into Candy's mouth; his body jerked and contorted; his legs wrapped around his old lady; his cock thrust as deeply as Candy could allow. Audible gasps, as though he was in great pain, escaped his throat; his head arched backward, exposing cords of muscle in his neck. Then, as suddenly as it had come on, the ecstatic moment of passion had passed. Immediately after orgasm, the crown of his cock was tremendously sensitive. Candy had to take his mouth away quickly, as soon as the cum had ceased gushing.

Sitting on his feet, his knees still between Hawk's legs, Candy looked at his exhausted and spent lover. "Hawk?" he asked softly. "Can anything be done to protect this new kid? You know as well as I do that he's much too pretty for his own good. I've already grown to like him, Hawk. I'd hate to see anything happen to him. There must be something we can do."

Hawk was silent for a minute, then said, "I don't think so, Candy. You know how these guys are. What's his name? Skip? He's up for grabs. He'll just have to learn how to take care of himself."

"Can't you make him your kid or something?" Candy persisted.

"No. These guys know that I've already got you as my ol' lady. Even if I put a claim on him as my kid, I'd have to put him out on the line. It would save him from getting raped, but he'd still get fucked. Talk to him, Candy. If he wants me as his old man, I can keep him from gettin' hurt, but make sure he knows he'll have to give up ass. That's the cold, hard facts of life, Candy, and you know it."

Candy knew that if anyone could, or would, have been able to help Skip, it would have been Hawk. Beneath that tough exterior, Candy knew there lived a tame pussy cat; but Hawk was a realist, a man who faced facts, a man who knew the rules of the game as well as anyone. Candy realized that Skip was in serious trouble. He had seen too many youngsters fall victim to sexual assault. He was growing weary of it. It would eat him up inside every time it happened.

The next day, he kept as close as possible to Skip. He told the young man about his conversation with Hawk, and about Hawk's limited offer to help with its frightful implications. Skip insisted he would be okay.

"Skip, you've got your head up your ass if you think you can survive without someone's help. You don't know the way these animals are. Most of them have nothing more to lose. And you're just too goddam pretty for them to ignore."

"Okay, Candy," Skip said at last. "I'm going to tell you my secret." After taking Candy into his confidence, he said, "So you see? I've got nothing to worry about."

Candy wasn't convinced it would work, but he wished the younger man good luck.

That evening, Candy was feverishly at work on a new story. Hawk and Gypsy, one of Hawk's workout partners, dropped in. Hawk, always abreast of Candy's literary output, asked him what the new story was about. He never took the time to read one of his old lady's stories, but he always wanted Candy to give him the *Reader's Digest* version.

"It's still rough," he began, "but I'm really enthusiastic about it. Right now, I'm calling it *A Kid with a Heart,* but I might change the title. It's about a handsome young guy who comes to prison at an early age. I'm going to make him eighteen. Most guys like him would get raped right away, but for some reason, he skates. In the meantime, he buffs up on the iron pile and learns how to box. A couple of guys know his secret, and after a while the truth comes out. The first time someone started to rape him, he warned the guy that he had the clap. Naturally the guy backs off. After that, it happened a few more times, but each time the would-be booty bandits back off. Pretty soon, the guy, I'm gonna call Mike, is buffed up real big and is a damned good fighter. He's a likable guy and has become very popular. With lots of friends for back up, he finally tells the truth. He never really had the clap. By now, even the guys he had lied to like him. In fact, they figure the kid's got a whole lot of heart."

Candy admitted that the ending needed a little work, but aside from that, he really liked his latest idea. There was no way he could have known that Gypsy would be the leader of the pack of animals that would rape Skip.

About an hour and a half before cell lockup, Hawk told Candy to come down to his cell at the far end of the tier. It was slightly unusual. Hawk always went to Candy's cell for sex, and it was rare for him to get down two nights in a row. It was only after he had given Hawk a blow-job and smoked a couple of joints with him that it occurred to Candy that the whole scene might have been a setup to get him away from his own cell—so close to Skip's.

On his way back to his cell, he saw several guys emerge from Skip's room. Gypsy was the last one out. His heart leaped into his throat, and he rushed past Gypsy into Skip's cell.

He was lying face down on his bunk, naked and sweaty. His cell was a shambles, his bunk was a mess; Skip had scratches and bruises all over his tender young body. He had apparently put up a fight, but to no avail against such overwhelming odds.

Candy sat on the bunk and said softly, "Skip. It's Candy. Oh my God, I'm so sorry." He heard stifled sobs and noticed that Skip was trembling. He ran a hand gently through the matted sandy hair. "Do you want to go to the infirmary? I'll call for a screw. They'll bring a guerney, if you want. Are you hurt bad?"

In a choking voice, Skip's only reply was, "They didn't believe me, Candy."

With sudden surprise, he remembered Gypsy. Gypsy had been there when he told Hawk about his new story. "Oh Skip. I'm sorry. My God, I'm sorry."

Skip insisted that he didn't want to got to the infirmary. "I'll be all right;" he said, crying softly now. "I just want to be alone, Candy. You know?"

Candy left the cell, unable to hold back his own tears. He was filled with outrage for what had happened, furious at himself for his own stupidity, and aching with grief for poor Skip. He went straight to Gypsy's cell.

Gypsy, Tex, and Lucky were watching TV as if nothing had happened.

"You fools!" Candy screamed at the three of them, catching them by surprise. "You stupid, fucking fools! He tried to tell you, but you wouldn't believe him." Under most circumstances, he would never dare to talk to any of them that way; Hawk or no Hawk, he would get his face beat in. But he couldn't control his mounting anger. "You and the other scum bags who did it better get to the infirmary, and fast. Clap can be harmful to your health, you know, You idiots! You fools!"

"Back off, Candy," Gypsy growled. "The kid way lyin' about that V. D. shit, and you know it. He got the idea from your story. He thought we'd go for the okey–dokey. Who's kidding who? The punk ain't got the clap, and you better watch your mouth, bitch."

"You fool! Skip didn't get the idea from me. I got the idea from him! When Skip told me he had the clap, I was glad he wouldn't let me suck his dick, but only later did I get the idea for my story. You fool. I made up the part about him lying about having it, just to make the story more interesting. You wanna know something else? Skip doesn't even know about the story yet."

Gypsy's smug air of self-confidence faded.

"What are you saying, Candy?" Tex asked.

Gypsy interrupted. "Get off it! That punk ain't got V.D. any more than I do."

"You're right," Candy seethed, "because you've got it now, you bastard. This is one time you let your cock overload your asshole, Gypsy. You can believe me, Skip's got the clap. And so do you and the other guys who fucked him. Have fun explaining to the doctor where you got it. I'll tell you this. Skip ain't gonna snitch on you guys. I just wonder how many of you—men—will turn snitch on Skip."

The next day, seven guys went to the infirmary for V.D. check-ups. Candy couldn't imagine how Skip had survived seven of them. He was feeling better, if painfully sore, when Candy confessed to inadvertently sabotaging his line of defense. Skip forgave Candy, and the two became the closest of friends.

Word spreads quickly in most prisons. Skip never again faced a rape situation. He took up body building and even became a boxer. And yes, he really did have V.D. and, soon after, so did Gypsy, Tex, Lucky, Joker, Cal, and Pineapple. For some reason, Jake remained immune.

PRISONERS

"THEY KILLED JOHNNY WRIGHT this morning on the yard. They're gonna lock us down." Rossi was trembling. Bobby didn't know why.

"What's the matter, Guy?" Bobby sat up and pulled the covers around his slender chest. "What has this got to do with you?"

Gaetano Rossi flopped onto his own bunk. Until now, the two-man cell had always seemed safe, a refuge from the creeps. This morning it was different. If they could get Johnny, they could get him. And if they got Guy, they might try to take Bobby, too. He had never really thought about it before; he suddenly realized that Bobby was more than just a jail-house queen. Without Bobby, Guy would be lost.

Guy had forgotten about Bobby's question. When Bobby asked it the second time, he wondered how he could answer it. How could he tell this sweet young kid that his "old man" was guilty of murder? No, Guy had not killed Johnny Wright, but he knew it was coming. He could have warned the punk, but he didn't. And Johnny Wright had trusted him. Dumb, stupid, wimpy lop!

"Guy! Answer me." Bobby was out of bed, dressed only in his satin bikini briefs, the ones Guy had bought for him through a mail-order house.

Guy took Bobby's hand. The blond youth sat down next to him, looking into his eyes searchingly. Guy knew he had to say something. Anything.

"Bobby," he began slowly. "There are some things you're better off not knowing. Trust me." *Trust me.* The words rang inside his head. Those were the words he had said to Johnny Wright not more than forty-five minutes ago. Now, Johnny was dead. *Trust me.*

Bobby was silent. Guy knew he would be. Bobby never questioned him.

"LOCK UP!" The sound of the guard's voice echoed down the tier. In a moment cell doors were slamming shut with loud clanging noises. Bobby leaned forward and lay his head on Guy's chest.

*   *

Derek stood under the running water, soaping his cock for the fourth time. The water was hot, adding to the warm sensation Derek was feeling as he stroked his rigid pole faster. He was almost ready to cum.

The shower curtain quietly opened behind him. Derek didn't know Norman Clayborne was watching as his round buns worked in time with his stroking fist. He reached for the bar of soap to add to the lather.

A shiver of terror shot down his spine as he felt someone grab his wrist. Suddenly he was spun around and rammed against the wall. He felt a hand tighten around his neck. He focused his eyes and recognized Clayborne. He wanted to shout but the big man's hand was constricting his vocal chords.

Clayborne was easily twice his size, broad and muscular. The man's hand felt like a tightening vise. Derek felt a shudder of cold fear race throughout his body. The heat of seconds ago had changed to ice.

"You can do this willingly," came the whispered threat, "or I can knock you out first. Which will it be?" There was no mistaking the seriousness in the man's voice.

Derek was too frightened to answer and wasn't sure he could force any response through his choking throat. Apparently no answer was necessary; the big man released his grip on the slender young man's throat and found his left wrist again. Derek's arm was wrapped behind him in a hammerlock.

Derek had always feared this moment. Nineteen-year-old men in prison don't stay virgins for long if they are as pretty and slender as Derek, unless they know karate or something. A thousand thoughts sped through his mind but the only thing he felt was icy fear.

He felt the bar of soap between his legs, then the rough probing of his ass by sausage-size fingers. Pressure on his arm forced him to lean forward. He tried to brace himself but didn't know what to expect nor how to prepare for it.

And then he knew. A sharp, thrusting pain into his rectum made him believe that his ass had been torn open. He gasped loudly and wanted to scream. Fear choked the scream and pain brought tears to his eyes.

*   *

Sweet Roger was having the best time he had had since coming to prison. Greg just had to be the best looking stud in the joint and here he was, naked as a jay bird, on Roger's bunk, his proud cock thrust upward like the George Washington Monument. Greg also had the biggest piece of meat on the yard, Roger was sure. And he should know if anyone did! Sweet Roger had probably sucked every piece of white meat on the yard. He had even been tempted to try some black meat, but it had been made clear to him from day one that he would be killed if he got down with any blacks.

Roger slid his mouth off Greg's dick, ran his tongue along the side of it, and sucked the balls into his mouth. He heard Greg let out a soft moan. He stroked the gargantuan dick with his hand as he ran his tongue along the inner thighs of the massive body-builder.

Greg's body was the smoothest, most hairless hunk of flesh Roger had ever had the pleasure of doing. Every square inch was solid muscle; not an ounce of fat anywhere. The mere sight of his body was ten times as exciting as any Roger had ever seen in any of his gay magazines. In fact, it was like having a fantasy come true. He was sucking on the cock of every body-beautiful ever photographed.

His mouth returned to the swollen head of Greg's cock as his hands found their way to his silky smooth chest with its rippling muscles. He couldn't remember ever having been so sexually aroused when doing someone. His own cock was ready to burst.

He barely managed to avoid gagging as he felt Greg's cock plunge deep into his throat. The spasmodic contracting of the magnificent cock erupting into him was too much. His own body shuddered and he was cumming in his jeans while the milky flood of Greg's juices flowed into his throat.

"LOCK UP!"

The sound of the guard's voice cut like a buzz-saw into Sweet Roger's moment of passion. Neither man could stop. Each man seemed desperate to finish the orgasm. But when a guard yells *lock up,* there is no time to waste.

Greg pushed Roger away from his still-gushing prick. "Jesus! I've got to get dressed!"

* *

Rumors spread through the cell house. Only three or four actually knew what had happened—and they weren't telling. Johnny Wright was a punk, a snitch, a dope-dealer, a homosexual, and a liar. It was amazing that he had lasted as long as he had. His body was found in the enclosed bathroom just off the main yard. He had been beaten, clubbed, and stabbed. But death had been caused by strangulation.

* *

Guy looked up as he heard the metallic clang of the cell door. Bobby came into the cell and sat beside him. Guy fixed two cups of instant coffee with tap water and handed one to his "old lady."

"How was it? What did they ask?"

Bobby was still for a moment, sipped some coffee, made a face, then looked into Guy's deep brown eyes.

"They think *you* did it! Or at least that you *know* who did it. I told them you were in the cell all morning, but they called me a liar. They know you were on the yard, Guy."

Gaetano Rossi felt his chest muscles constrict, his stomach tied into knots. He tried to look into Bobby's eyes, but had to look away. "You shouldn't have lied for me, Bobby. It can only make things worse."

"Guy, tell me. I've got to know . . ."

Rossi interrupted, "No, Bobby! You don't have to know nothin'." He heard his own voice sounding like a shrill screech. He cleared his throat and turned away from his blond lover. "Believe me, Bobby. What you don't know can't hurt you."

Bobby stood up and wrapped his arms around Guy's naked waist. "Guy, I love you. Nothing can change the way I feel about you. If I knew what happened, I'd be better off. I'd know what to say or not to say."

Guy slowly turned and enfolded Bobby in his strong arms. "I love you, too, Bobby. I didn't know it until today. Oh, I *liked* you, but I just thought of you as another prison queen. Now I know that I'd be lost without you. I don't know what you did to me, but I guess you made me fall in love."

The tier was quiet. There was still an hour till lunch. In spite of the murder of Johnny Wright, Gaetano Rossi had found something, and that something welled up inside him. He kissed Bobby on the lips, a long, lingering, warm, sensitive kiss.

*   *

Sweet Roger had taken off his jeans and thrown them in the corner. He was washing his genitals with a cloth, thinking back to Greg's gorgeous cock and the tremendous excitement he had felt when the guard had yelled *"lock-up."* Greg had jumped up so fast that Roger barely managed a swift glance at those fine, firm cakes of his!

Roger had always been a freelancer; no "old men" for Roger! He had liked the idea of doing *who* he wanted, *when* he wanted. But now . . . well, Roger had to admit that having a gorgeous hunk like Greg for an old man could be delightfully wonderful. Besides, most of Greg's friends were also body-builders. "Good grief, I could have a harem!" he thought aloud.

For just a fraction of a second his thoughts flitted away from Greg and his magnificent cock. "I wonder what this lock-up business is all about." He called to the guy in the cell next to him. "Mike, why are we locked down?"

"They killed some guy on the yard this morning," came the mildly disinterested reply. "Some guy from the second floor. A faggot and a snitch from what I hear."

"Who was it?"

The answer came from the other direction. "Johnny Wright."

Sweet Roger felt faint. He sunk to his bed, his head spinning, the feeling of nausea creeping throughout his body. Just yesterday Johnny had been in Roger's cell. "He can't be dead," Roger murmured. Those ever so soft buns, that silky flesh, those deep brown eyes. . . . Usually, Roger wouldn't get down with another queen, but Johnny Wright was so goddam sexy! He really knew how to throw a good fuck. DEAD!

Roger could still feel the swollen cock up his ass; he could feel Johnny's ass wrapped around his own cock. It was too unreal! That wonderfully warm body was now as cold as ice. Just yesterday. Not even twenty-four hours ago!

*   *

Derek sat on the shitter. His ass hurt painfully. So did his throat and his left arm. It was quiet now. The tier seemed like a morgue. It was not quiet inside his head. He could still hear the roar of the running water, the nightmarish sound of Clayborne's whispers, the distant almost unreal sound of the guard yelling "lock-up."

It happened. It was no dream, no nightmare. Clayborne had come into the shower and had raped him. Derek's mind still found it impossible to accept. Women get raped—men don't. But men *do,* apparently!

At nineteen, he had been sent to prison for armed robbery. He had heard stories of prison rapes, but even though he deeply feared it, could not begin to imagine that *he* would be the object of rape.

What should he do now? He knew that Clayborne would soon be bragging about his conquest to everyone on the yard.

He would be fair game for any tough guy who wanted to fuck him. And no one would give a damn about what happened to Derek Webster! He could get fucked twenty-five times a day, and the only question would be: who is next?

He would have to P.C. Protective Custody was the only escape route. The thought renewed his depression. P.C. was for snitches. He was no snitch! But he would have to do it unless he wanted to get fucked by every swinging dick on the yard.

Again his thoughts raced at random. Suddenly he shuddered with revulsion as he realized he was thinking about how it was *almost* pleasurable. Clayborne had reached around and taken Derek's cock in his right hand and had even fondled his balls. Derek had become aroused again, after the initial shock and terror had subsided. Clayborne had been rough at first, but he had become gentle as he went along. For a while it didn't even hurt.

"Shut up!" he heard himself say. *"What's happening? Am I turning into a faggot?"*

His face felt hot, his sinuses began to fill, and tears formed at the corners of his eyes. He sniffled a couple of times. Then he let go and let it all come out. He cried and cried.

*   *

It was one of the most wonderful times Bobby had ever had with Guy. Instead of role-playing, Guy had let it all hang out. They had kissed, felt each other's body passionately, and had abandoned themselves. The tier was locked down, there was no one in the corridor. No prying eyes. Down the tier, radios and TVs played, drowning out the noises of their love-making.

Usually, Guy liked for Bobby to start off by giving him head. Guy could never seem to catch a nut with just a blow-job. Bobby would toy with Guy's cock for a long time, sucking, stroking, running his hands over the curly hairs on Guy's chest and legs, licking his balls and thighs. When Guy could stand it no longer, Bobby got out the hand lotion. Guy loved to fuck!

But it was always one-sided. Guy was a *man*. Bobby was his bitch.

Today was different. It began the same way, but when it came time for Bobby to lay on his stomach, Guy turned him over. They kissed, then Guy began a slow, meandering nibbling across Bobby's hairless chest, lingering at the nipples. By the time Guy's tongue reached Bobby's pubic hairs, Bobby's cock was rigidly erect and pulsating like a captured butterfly.

"I want you to fuck *me*," Guy whispered. The words were so soft that Bobby wasn't sure that he had heard right.

Bobby knew that he had not misunderstood. Guy was all *man*, which is what Bobby liked most about him. The manly roundness of Guy's buns sent a thrill of excitement through Bobby's body as he prodded with his cock, found the opening, and slid gently into the moist interior of the man he loved so well.

It was the first time in over a year that Guy had seen to it that Bobby got his pleasure too. Not that Bobby cared. He was more than satisfied just being able to be with Guy and to experience and explore that masculine body and to feel him at the moment of climax. Bobby relieved himself in the shower but always with thoughts of Guy running through his mind.

When Bobby had finished, Guy had to admit that it was not as pleasant as he thought it might be, but he was glad that he had finally done something *for* Bobby instead of *to* him.

*   *

Lunch consisted of sandwiches and coffee served in the cell. Word was passed along that the lockdown would last until they found out who had killed Wright. Every man in the prison was interrogated by the staff of investigators called in from the Attorney General's office.

"All I can tell you is that I was in my cell sucking a man's cock when it happened." Sweet Roger was a flaming faggot and didn't care who knew it.

The two investigators exchanged quick glances. "Are you a practicing homosexual?" one of them asked.

"Practicing, hell! I'm damned good at it. I don't need any practice!" Roger had used the line so many times it was stale. But the investigators had never heard it, so the effect was not lost.

"Who were you with?"

"None of your business!"

"It will be to both of your benefits to tell us. In murder cases an alibi can be very important, you know."

Roger hesitated for a moment. Greg might or might not want someone to know what had happened in Roger's cell that morning.

"Mr. Sweet," one of the investigators said, "Johnny Wright was either raped before his death or had anal intercourse by consent. We know he was a homosexual. Any man known to have indulged in sexual practices with any other inmate is suspect. Unless you can provide an alibi, you, too, are under suspicion."

Sweet Roger debated for a brief moment, then answered, "I was in bed with Greg Spencer when Johnny Wright was killed."

The two investigators again exchanged glances.

*　　*

Four days had passed since Johnny Wright's death. Eddie Evans knew too much; he was scared to death. He had seen Johnny talking to Rossi that morning, which now seemed so very long ago. He had seen Johnny go into the yard restroom. He had seen Norman Clayborne, Harold Sharpe, and Gregory Spencer follow him in. Eddie hadn't paid much attention at the time; it wasn't unusual for people to approach Johnny on the yard and ask him to go into the restroom to turn a trick. The only thing that had struck Eddie as slightly funny was that Johnny never did more than one guy at a time. So Eddie had watched, thinking that maybe Johnny was going to set a new record or something.

Until his dying day, Eddie would never forget the looks on their faces as they came out of the restroom, though. How they hurriedly went toward the cell house and got the guard to let them inside. How they had signaled to Rossi who quickly followed after them. He remembered seeing Rossi argue with the guard who wouldn't let him in until yard recall.

He remembered seeing two other inmates go into the restroom and come out white as ghosts. Eddie had become nervous. He wondered what the hell had happened. He had wanted so often to go up to Johnny and ask to go into the restroom with him. Johnny was so appealing, so sexually irresistible. But Eddie was too shy. Eddie kept his homosexuality a secret because sex to him was intimate and private, a thing to be shared by two people who cared for each other. In prison sex was too open-market-place; there was no intimacy, no privacy, no beauty in the sex act; it was nothing but dirty, cruddy, make-jokes-about-it lust.

As much as Eddie desired the beautiful and desirable Johnny Wright, he couldn't bring himself to approach him. Now he would never have the chance, never know the feel of that body felt by so many uncaring inmates.

Eddie had found the body. He had found Johnny Wright lying on the cement floor, his jeans pulled to his ankles, his face caved in (that handsome, boyish face), had seen the blood and the gore in a pool around his head, had seen the obscenity of rape and murder, and he had vomited. He had staggered out of the restroom and had fainted dead-away in the sunlight.

In the preliminary round of questioning he claimed to know absolutely nothing about anything that had happened. He had merely gone in to take a piss and had found Wright's body. But four days had elapsed. He was wrestling with his conscience, struggling to put down the insatiable urge to tell all he knew. He knew that if he disclosed any information he would be taking his own life in his hands. He would be very lucky indeed to get out of prison alive if he told what he knew.

But maybe, just maybe . . . he might get protective custody. He doubted that P.C. would protect him; too many guys had gone into P.C. merely to come out in pine boxes. But he had heard that a man could get a transfer to another state; in some cases they were given early paroles, especially in murder cases.

However, he told himself, he really hadn't *seen* anything. In fact he could be wrong about the people he *thought* he saw; maybe other people went in and out that he didn't see.

Eddie was still struggling with his soul-searching when he heard his cell door open. It was his turn with the investigators. As he walked down the tier, he still didn't know what he was going to do.

*   *

Derek's eyes were streaming tears as he shut the door behind him. He bumped into Eddie Evans but didn't notice him. He staggered to the outer door of the custody office and followed the guard back to his tier.

He passed Clayborne's cell. The big man stopped him. "Did you tell them?"

Derek wiped his eyes and answered, "Yeah. I told them but they didn't believe me. They said I was lyin' to cover for you."

"Keep movin', Webster," came the guard's voice from behind.

As Derek started to move away, Clayborne whispered to him. "That's okay. Just stick to it, you hear me?"

Once in his cell he broke down completely. It had been the hardest thing he had had to do in his entire life. Before two complete strangers, two callous, hardened investigators, he had exposed the details of his rape. Two cold men who couldn't care less what happened to a convict behind bars; two insensitive men-of-the-law who ridiculed him. They didn't believe him! They called him a jail house punk, a queer, a homosexual.

He hadn't wanted to tell them; he had decided to quietly P.C. himself, to not tell anyone what had happened. But Clayborne had sent him a note telling him to tell the truth because he needed the alibi. Clayborne had promised to leave him alone if Derek merely told the truth.

*   *

Ten days after Johnny Wright's death, they came off lock-down. The investigation had proven inconclusive. The six o'clock news stated simply that no suspects were apprehended and that after a thorough search of the prison for weapons and other contraband, prison officials had lifted the lock-down status.

Sweet Roger was back in the swing of things. Greg brought his friend, Rod, to Roger's cell. Rod was not as handsome, nor as well built, but Roger found him more responsive to sexual stimuli than

Greg. Nothing official happened, there were no spoken promises, but Greg had become Roger's old man. To Sweet Roger's delight, there followed a steady stream of gorgeous young hunks. Kelly had a dope connection, so not a week went by without at least an ounce of grass, maybe some "T's," a few 'ludes, and whatever else they could keyster in the visiting room.

Sweet Roger never knew that his old man had killed Johnny Wright. He never knew that Harold Sharpe had fucked the boy just before Norman Clayborne had beat his head in with a 2 x 4. He never knew that Greg's strong hands, so sensitive with Roger, had held the garotte that had snuffed out the life of little Johnny Wright.

In fact, if you had told Roger that his tender, loving, gentle old man was a cold-blooded murderer, Roger would have called you a cum-drunk faggot.

*   *

"You did good, kid. It even worked out better than we thought." Norman Clayborne had moved into the lower bunk in Derek's cell. Derek was forced to take the upper. But Norman had not kept his promise. Derek's ass was too sweet and tender to let get away. The one thing he had done that had pleased Derek was to keep their little affair a secret. Derek didn't have to worry about being fucked by twenty-five people a day, just one: Norman.

It wasn't really that bad. Norman was gentle, used lots of lotion, gave Derek a hand job every now and then, and kept the kid in zu-zu's and wam-wams and cigarettes. There was the added feature that Norman was big enough to protect Derek from other would-be rapists.

Derek was pretty sure that somehow or other Norman must have been involved in the murder of Johnny Wright, but he would never talk about it and he would never know for sure. It was better that way because if he ever learned the truth, there was no telling how long he might live. Just three more years in that hell-hole and he would be out on parole. The nightmare of the rape was fading, and he was learning to live with the compromise he had had to make. The only thing that really bothered him was that he was actually beginning to enjoy it.

He wondered if he would come out of prison a screaming faggot like Sweet Roger. God, he hoped not.

*   *

"But *why?*" Bobby asked. "That's all I want to know. Why did he have to be killed?"

Gaetano Rossi stood naked at the side of the bed. In the dim yellow light from the corridor his body looked like a statue of a bronze Greek god. "Bobby, do we have to talk about it?"

Bobby reached out and took the young man's cock in his hand. "Guy," he said softly, "ever since the day of Johnny's death, something has been eating you. It's going to fester and turn rotten if you don't get it out." He tugged at Guy's dick, and Guy sat down beside him.

"Bobby," he sighed, "the sick thing about it is that there was no good reason! He had burned a few guys, that's all. Johnny Wright got himself killed over a few balloons of grass. Nothing more than that."

"I love you, Guy." Bobby's voice was almost pleading. "I don't want to know for *my* sake, I want you to tell me for *your* sake."

"All I can tell you is this: Johnny Wright was a snitch. He was letting one of the guards fuck him in his cell late at night. Have you seen officer Forrest around lately? No. He quit right after Johnny got hit. Johnny was getting fucked by Forrest and giving up information about some of the drug traffic on the yard."

Bobby ran his hand along Guy's leg, up to the crotch. "I believe that that's *part* of it, but it's not *all* of it. That's okay. You can tell me when you're ready."

"Let's fuck," Guy whispered into Bobby's ear. "Let's take all night long. Let's not hurry it. Tomorrow is Sunday, we'll sleep in till noon. Tonight I want to do everything with you. Everything."

Bobby felt Guy's warm breath near his cock. Suddenly, there was a moist feeling at the tip. Guy had let Bobby fuck him, but this was the first time that Guy had gone down on Bobby's cock.

It was crazy, but Bobby was almost happy—yes, happy—that Johnny Wright got killed. Ever since that day, things with Guy had gotten so much better. Now this! He felt his cock being vacuumed into Guy's mouth. Then the thought occurred to him that he would have to tell Guy to use more pressure.

God! Do you believe what you were thinking? Bobby couldn't believe that he had actually thought that he might be happy because Johnny Wright got killed. But Guy was sucking on his cock; the man he loved was actually putting his cock in his mouth. It didn't matter what happened to cause the change in Guy; all that mattered was that

Bobby was ecstatically happy.

* *

Eddie Evans was tortured. He simply couldn't stand it any longer. He *had* to tell someone. Each day that passed the memory of that day so long ago burned brighter in his mind.

He watched from the horse-shoe pits as Gregory Spencer and Sweet Roger walked into the yard restroom. Harold Sharpe stood point, trying to look casual, smoking a cigarette and talking to Rodney Stone.

It didn't matter anymore. Even if it got him killed, he had to tell someone. Eddie stayed to himself; he had no friends. It would be so nice if he could just get it off his chest by merely talking about it to a friend. He stood up and began to walk toward the custody office.

The voice from behind him was familiar. "Eddie!"

He turned and saw Bobby Jensen. Bobby came out to the yard so seldom. Bobby was the only guy in the joint who knew Eddie was gay; they had known each other on the streets. But every time Eddie saw Bobby, he was with Rossi, so the friendship had drifted apart.

Bobby smiled brightly, and soon the two were deeply engrossed in idle chatter. The conversation got around to Johnny Wright, and Eddie could keep it back no more. Even if Bobby was Rossi's old lady, Eddie had to tell someone. Besides, Rossi really had nothing to do with it.

Monday afternoon, Bobby invited Eddie Evans into the yard restroom to smoke some doobies. Before they killed him, Eddie Evans suffered the greatest indignity of his life: he was gang-raped.

Bobby stood point. He hated the thought of Eddie's murder, but at least Guy would be safe; there would be no one to point the finger. And if anyone ever tried to hurt Guy in any way, shape, or form, it would end up the same way.

CELLMATES

Barry was sprawled on the lower bunk, wearing only white boxer shorts which displayed his nineteen-year-old body to its best advantage. He had begun lifting weights when he was fifteen; four years later, he was proud of the massive physique he had developed. He looked up as his cellmate came into the room. "How was your visit?" he asked.

"Great!" Ron replied, flashing a mouthful of straight, white teeth. "The only problem is that Linda couldn't keep her hands off me. She got me hornier than hell, and naturally we couldn't do anything about it. On the way back to the cell, I ran into that faggot, Carla, who's always wanting to suck my dick. I was so fuckin' horny, I almost went for it!"

"Fuck that shit," said Barry, absently letting his hand slip into his shorts. "I ain't never letting no queer touch me!"

"Me neither," Ron hastily added. He covered the small window in the cell door with a piece of cardboard, then began to undress. "I'm only doing five years; I don't plan to turn queer in this place."

Having stripped totally nude, he sat on the toilet. He made a grunt; there was a soft splash. Standing up, he fished out the balloon of sinsemilla which he had keistered during visiting period. "Linda came through for us," he boasted. "I told you she would." He began to clean the balloon. "It's bigger than last time. I didn't think I would be able to get it up my ass."

"If you can take *that* in the ass," Barry teased, gripping his ample cock, "I'll bet you could handle *this* with no sweat."

"Bullshit! This balloon is tiny compared to that horsecock hangin' between your legs." As he pulled his bathrobe around his naked, almost hairless body, he momentarily fondled his cock. At twenty-two, Ron had been in prison for fifteen months; much of that time had been devoted to pumping iron. He and Barry had met in the gym, had soon become close friends, and eventually had gotten a cell together. Ron's body was one of those lithe, wiry ones that obstinately refused to develop the kind of beefy bulk that he so admired in Barry.

Stealing a quick glance at Barry's reclining body, with its rippling musculature, he sat at the writing table hung from the cell wall and began to roll the marijuana into generous joints. He stashed about eight or nine of them and kept two to smoke with Barry.

Ron moved the chair to the head of the bunkbeds and gave the first joint to Barry. They passed it back and forth in silence.

"That's dynamite stuff," Barry commented, as he fired up the second one. "Tell Linda she's all right."

"Man, that's good shit!" Ron exclaimed, as he finished the second joint. He spread his legs, slumping in the chair and let his robe fall open to reveal his cock and nutsack. The blond fuzz on his slender legs matched the golden-white tint of his curly hair. "The trouble is, I always get horny on grass."

"Me, too," Barry murmured, idly running his hand over his smooth, hairless chest.

"I tell ya, Barry," said Ron, fondling his half-hard cock, "Carla is beginning to look real good. You know, a lot of guys in prison let sissies suck 'em off . . ."

"Shit! I'll beat off before I'll go to bed with a faggot! Hell, I'd fuck *you* first."

"Knock it off, Barry. I never know when you're bullshittin' me. But see what I mean?" Ron gripped his semi-erect cock and shook it at his cellmate. "I get awful fuckin' horny!"

Barry looked at Ron's swollen tool, then pulled his own throbbing cock through the slit in his boxers. "You? Look at me. You're only half as hard as I am."

"I feel like jacking off," Ron said, more to himself than to his cellmate. He was already stroking his cock into a full erection. They had been cellmates for so long that mutual nudity was nothing new; but they had never been so bold as to masturbate in front of each other. The grass was causing him to drop all inhibitions.

"I gotta take a piss," Barry said, swinging his legs over the edge of the bunk and standing up too quickly.

Seeing Barry stagger, Ron bolted out of the chair. The rapid motion caused him to lose his equilibrium. The two young men fell into each other's arms, searching for balance against each other. For a brief moment, they held one another tightly, warm flesh against warm flesh, hard cocks pressing into firm abdomens.

"You okay?" Ron asked.

"Yeah," Barry whispered, pulling away.

The close body contact had sent an unusual thrill down Ron's spine, and his cock pulsated. He knew it was the grass—it always made him horny. He knew also that he should turn on the stereo and sit down in the chair; but he found his eyes glued to Barry's body, and his mind refused to dispel the memory of those few seconds when he and Barry were locked in their unexpected embrace.

Under the numbing effects of the grass, his eyes caressed his cellmate's body, with its perfect symmetry, smooth lines, firm muscles, and his meat pouring out a cascade of golden piss.

Suddenly aware that he was staring at Barry's cock, Ron shook his head, as if to clear it. He sat down, aware that his own cock was now at full staff, bobbing eagerly, demanding attention.

Euphoria flooded through his senses. *God, that's good weed,* he thought. His mind began to swim in a rapid torrent of disjointed thoughts, far away from the prison, from the cell and his cellmate. He closed his eyes and allowed the light-headed sensations to envelop him.

Slowly, peripherally, he became aware of the presence of his cellmate. Barry was standing between Ron's outstretched legs; hairless thighs brushed against fuzzy ones. Opening his eyes, he found that Barry had stripped off his shorts and now stood bare-ass naked in front of him. Barry's mammoth cock, almost at eye-level, was thrust outward and upward.

"Do you still feel like jacking off?" Barry asked.

"Shit, yeah! I'm so horny, I could fuck that mouse that comes in here all the time." He saw, as if in slow motion, his cellmate lean forward and felt Barry's hands on his broad shoulders. Looking into Barry's eyes, he detected something he had never seen before—a hungry, passionate look. For a split second, Ron sensed that Barry was going to kiss him. *That's stupid,* he thought. *Barry's not queer.*

"Let's jack each other off," Barry whispered.

An hour ago, that suggestion would have upset him. But now, the thought of handling Barry's huge, throbbing cock seemed like the best idea to come along in a helluva long time. Somehow, he knew that if it weren't for the grass, he wouldn't be thinking that way. The thought of touching another man's cock *should* have been repulsive to him.

Barry's voice penetrated his consciousness, hazy because of the grass. "Whaddaya say? It's not like turning queer or nothing. I mean, we ain't gonna do nothing but jack each other off."

At that moment, Ron didn't care whether or not it was like "turning queer." He wanted to feel Barry's cock, in spite of a nagging feeling that he shouldn't. However, he didn't want to seem too eager. This could be one of those games Barry was always playing. Barry might just be testing him.

On the other hand, the grass could have had the same effect on Barry that it had on Ron. All he could answer was: "I dunno, Barry . . ."

"Whatsa matter? You chicken?"

"It's not that. It's just that you're always talking bad about faggots. I don't want you to think I'm turning queer."

"Hey, Ron," Barry said in a soothing voice, "you and me—we're friends, right? We've been friends for a year. I jack off, and I'm sure you do too. We're in prison; there ain't no pussy for fifty miles. So! Since we both jack off, and since we're as tight as friends can be, what's wrong if I help *you* jack off, and you help *me?*"

He felt Barry's right hand leave his shoulder. It glided down his chest, across his erect left nipple, down his body, then come to rest on his cock. Responding to Barry's lead, as well as to the thrill which shot through his body, Ron reached out and took hold of Barry's rock-hard dick. For several moments, he let his hand glide firmly back and forth along its length.

"Get it wet," came Barry's throaty voice.

Ron didn't react immediately to the command. Barry must have been impatient, for suddenly Ron felt two hands on the back of his head, pulling it forward. His eyes opened wide in astonishment, as Barry's cock thrust itself toward his open mouth.

"No!" Ron cried out, turning his head away. The head of Barry's cock nestled warmly against his cheek.

"What's the matter?" Barry taunted. "Here. I'll even go first, you pussy. All I wanted you to do was to get it wet enough to feel good."

In an instant, Barry had sunk to his knees. Fascinated, Ron watched his cellmate's sensuous mouth wrap around his cock, bringing about a warm, moist sensation.

All of a sudden, it wasn't enough to just sit there passively. "Let's do it together," Ron whispered. "It'll probably feel better if we do it at the same time."

Barry pulled away and looked up. Ron could tell by the glazed look of Barry's eyes that his cellmate was as loaded as he. Wordlessly, Barry moved to the bunk and lay down, waiting for Ron to join him.

Ron stood up and let his eyes feast on the sight of Barry's beautiful, silky-smooth body. Until now, he had always admired and envied the nineteen-year-old's body; he had never seen it as an object of sexual lust. Barry's physique had been the ideal toward which Ron struggled. Yet, suddenly, his cock throbbed in eager anticipation.

"Put your head down there," Barry ordered, pointing to his cock. "And put your cock up here . . ."

Carefully, Ron positioned himself on the narrow bunk. His field of vision was soon filled with the sight of Barry's groin, his flat, hairless abdomen, and two beefy, smooth thighs framing a ten inch pole of hard, thick flesh. A small patch of black pubic hair and a down-covered scrotum completed the picture. His heart raced with excitement as he opened his mouth and leaned toward the huge head of Barry's swollen cock. For a moment he paused; could he bring himself to take another man's dick in his mouth?

As he hesitated, a warm wetness encircled his own cock. Then the powerful, long suppressed attraction to Barry and the desire to make love to him made themselves felt. Greedily, he vacuumed Barry's thick shaft into his mouth and experienced the thrill of soft flesh riding on a rigid pole gliding silkily over his tongue, filling his mouth with a completely new sensation.

Ron became aware of Barry's strong hands gliding gently over his buttocks. The erotically stimulating effect caused him to thrust his cock deeply into Barry's mouth. The suddenness of the action caused Barry to gag.

Almost simultaneously, Ron was also gagged by an abrupt plunge of Barry's cock. By unspoken agreement, the two friends refrained from further deep throating and settled down to a rhythmic back-and-forth motion.

Due to the effects of the marijuana, time slowed down. It seemed to Ron as if hours passed while he enjoyed the hot, wet feel of Barry's mouth sucking and milking his cock toward climax and the pleasure of Barry's tool in his own mouth. Unable to resist the impulse, Ron let his free hand explore the silky smooth texture of Barry's legs, hips and ass cheeks. He allowed his index finger to trace the outline of his cellmate's asshole.

A sudden thought crossed his mind. What would Linda think if she were to see him in this position? Or worse, what if a guard were to key-open the celldoor and catch the two cellmates in a sixty-nine? Neither eventuality was very likely, so he put the thoughts out of his mind. He wondered what was going through Barry's mind at this moment . . .

Is he thinking about me? Or is he thinking of his girl-friend?

Ron was still inexperienced and unable to anticipate Barry's rapidly approaching orgasm. Without warning, except for the unnoticed acceleration in the speed of his thrusts, Barry's cock launched thick cum into Ron's mouth.

Reflexively, Ron gagged. When the realization hit him that Barry was cumming in his mouth, his immediate reaction was to pull away. Within a split second, however, the taste registered, and he found it delicious—curiously sweet and tart at the same time.

Just as he was growing to like the taste of Barry's cum, a finger surreptitiously slipped into his ass. Within seconds, Ron, too, erupted into a warm mouth. Spasms of pleasure coursed throughout his body. Barry's orgasm had been relatively mild, but Ron's was explosive. His body writhed in the throes of passion, causing his stomach muscles to contract and sending shivers of pleasure to every part of his body. Ron's head seemed about to explode as a result of the upheaval radiating outward from his cock. Again and again, his cock shot loads of cum into Barry's throat, and the pleasure seemed endless. Gradually the sensations lost their intensity, and the pleasure began to subside.

After a while, Barry's voice penetrated Ron's consciousness, "I'm gonna go take a shower."

Ron waited until Barry returned before going for his own shower. Under the running water he thought about the experience and was surprised to discover that he felt no guilt or shame. *As a matter of fact,* he thought, *I'm glad it happened.* He found himself wondering what Barry's reaction and attitude would be.

When Ron returned to the cell, Barry was combing his long brown hair, still wrapped in his towel. He avoided looking directly at Ron. An ominous silence hung in the air. The shower had diminished the effects of the grass, and Ron wondered if Barry was feeling regret for what had happened.

"Barry, . . ." Ron began hesitantly, "what we did . . . I mean, that doesn't make us . . . *queer,* does it?" When Barry didn't answer, he continued, "I mean, we were both stoned out of our minds, right?"

"Yeah, I guess so . . ." Barry sounded unconvinced.

"It's not like we're faggots, or something. I mean, it's not like we like to wear dresses or nothing . . ."

"Shut the fuck up!" Barry snapped.

"Hey! What's wrong? It was *your* idea . . ."

"Fuck off!"

The sharp, abrupt profanity wounded Ron. He liked Barry, and he had enjoyed the afternoon's encounter. He couldn't let it end with hard feelings between them. After several moments of silence, he said in a whisper, "Barry, let's talk about it."

"It's chow time. We'll talk later."

Ron was three years older than Barry; yet Barry was the more dominant of the two. Ron usually acquiesced to Barry's will, but he wasn't just a spineless follower. He looked up to Barry and admired him, but he wouldn't let his cellmate walk all over him. For now, Ron decided to wait, but after lock-up, he would insist on talking about what had happened.

During the course of the evening, several of their friends came to the cell. Ron shared the joints with them, and he and Barry became stoned out of their minds. By the time the Housing Unit Officer called lock-up, only one joint remained.

There had been a cell full of people all evening, but now silence again fell between the two friends. Once the cell door was shut, Barry stripped down to his shorts and lay on his bunk brooding. Ron lowered the volume on the stereo, peeled off his State-issue and again slipped into his bathrobe. The scene was one routinely familiar to both of them. Any other night they would have played cards, or chess, or backgammon, or would have sat and talked before turning in. That night each man thought his own thoughts, and neither of them suggested a way to pass the time.

At length, Ron decided to speak. "I think we need to talk about it, Barry."

Before Ron could say more, Barry interrupted. "Break out that last joint. If we're gonna talk, I'd rather do it after we fire up the grass."

After smoking the joint, both men waited for the other to break the ice. Ron wanted to talk but didn't know where to start, nor how much of his inner emotions he should express. Finally, he let it come out in random order. Under the influence of the grass, he didn't give a damn whether he said too much or not.

"I want you to know, Barry, that I enjoyed what happened today. I know that some people would call us queers for doing what we did, but I don't give a fuck. A faggot is someone who likes to act like a cunt, like Carla and Dusty, and that creep Whittamore. You and me have been friends for a long time, right? Ain't nothin' wrong with helpin' a friend get a nut."

"Ron," interrupted Barry, "that's not the point, and you know it. I liked it, too, but it was *wrong!* Neither one of us is queer; neither one of us acts like a pansy. And that's why it's wrong. Only a fag would stick a man's whammer in his mouth, don't you see?"

"But it was the grass," Ron insisted. "We weren't in our right minds. When it started, all we was gonna do was jack each other off..."

"I think we ought to forget that it ever happened," Barry said softly.

Ron felt a sinking sensation. Secretly, he wanted to do it again. Smoking pot all evening had made him hornier than ever. He began to see his hope for a repeat performance evaporate. Looking at Barry's almost naked body, he thought: *Maybe I am queer! I want to do it again.*

Aloud, he said, "All I can say is—it felt good, and I liked it. And it wasn't like doing it with a faggot."

Barry was silent; his eyes were closed.

Disappointed, Ron removed his robe and climbed up to the top bunk. He always slept naked, but tonight would be difficult. He was horny again, he was loaded, he was naked, and Barry's body was more inviting than ever. But Barry was apparently going through some kind of guilt trip.

Barry got up, took off his shorts, turned off the light, and got into bed. The cell was quiet for a long time, yet both men knew that the other was still awake.

Just as Ron was about to drift off to sleep, he heard Barry's voice. "I've been thinking, Ron. What we did today could probably break up our friendship. It was a stupid thing to do."

"You're right," Ron said without conviction.

"As I see it, though," Barry went on, "there's only one thing to do."

"What's that?"

"Do it again," came the soft-spoken reply. "We both liked it, right? If we don't ever do it again, it will eat away at us and maybe ruin our friendship. If we do it again—and again, and again—we'll probably become closer friends than ever."

Ron threw the covers back and jumped down off the bunk. "Do you really think so?" he asked eagerly.

"Yeah, I really do. Crawl in, cellmate. Let's do it again. I've got a rock-hard whammer that needs lots of attention. But this time . . ."

"Yeah? . . ."

"Let's do *everything!*"

WHAT GOES AROUND

L OREN WORKED AT THE ISSUE WINDOW of the prison laundry. He was a "sissy," but you wouldn't know it to look at him. He was a full 6' tall, a body-builder, and athlete. His virile, rugged handsomeness destroyed all preconceived notions of what a joint-sissy was supposed to look like. It was well known, though, that Loren was gay.

He pushed a set of prison blues through the window opening to the waiting inmate, who walked away after scrutinizing them for missing buttons and unseemly rips or tatters. The next inmate in line was a strikingly handsome new arrival. As the only window worker in the laundry, Loren knew every man-jack on the yard—at least by sight, if not by name. Since he made it a point to learn the names of the good-looking ones, he knew that the guy who now stood before him was Blair Compton.

Loren took the dirty blues being turned-in and said, "Let's see: 30-32 jeans and size 15 shirt, right?" Before Blair could say anything, Loren continued: "Don't look surprised. Anyone as sexy as you are, Blair, I get to know their sizes real quick. Size 40 jacket, 9½ shoes, and X-LGE cock warmer, right?"

Loren's boldness brought a smile to Blair's eyes. "I wish I took an extra-large size in . . . those, but no such luck." Blair sighed. He paused then said, "It's true, then? What they say about you?"

"What? That I'm gay?" Loren winked at the good-looking, young con. "Yes, it's true. Queer as a three-dollar bill, as they say." Loren looked around to be sure his supervisor wasn't in the area. "And I want to suck your cock," he said in a sultry voice.

The brazen pass caught the young con off guard; his lightly tanned cheeks turned to a brilliant crimson.

"Your're sexier than hell when you blush," Loren teased.."How about tonight? Just tell me what dorm you live in and what time I'll find you in the shower. Trust me, no one will see me coming or going. I've had lots of experience."

Blair hesitated. "I dunno . . ."

"Are you worried about what will happen? Don't let my size scare you. All I want to do is to give you some screamin' skull; I'm not going to do anything crazy like rape you or anything. Ask anyone. I don't abuse beautiful boys like you. All you do is lean back, relax, and enjoy the best tongue in the joint."

The young man frowned. "Let me think about it. I just don't know . . ."

"Look," Loren urged, realizing Blair was backing off, "everyone does it. No one admits it, but they all do it. I don't drop names, but if there's eight hundred guys in this joint, then five hundred guys do it. And the only reason the other three hundred don't do it is because they're too ugly to get a sissy to give 'em a play. A warm mouth is the best substitute for pussy while you're locked up, Blair."

"Yeah, I know, but. . . . Well, let me think about it."

Unnoticed by either of them, Benny Fowler had come up behind Loren. "Hey, Blair! What's happenin'?"

He had startled Loren. "Goddamn you, Benny! Don't creep on me like that."

Benny put on a false smile. "Hey man, I wasn't creepin'. I can't help it if you didn't hear me comin'. I just happened to see my good buddy Blair here, and I come over to say hello, that's all. Don't get so up-tight, Loren."

Loren detected a change in Blair's composure at Benny's arrival. Blair was not a very good actor, and it was obvious that he and Benny were not "good buddies." Sensing that something was wrong, but not knowing what it was, Loren swept the dirty blues into a laundry bin and walked back to the shelves to get a fresh issue for Blair. He took his time, trying to find some relatively new shirts and jeans to give to the attractive young man. Returning to the window, he overheard Benny say in a whisper, " . . . you understand me?" There was a menacing tone in Benny's voice which was unmistakable.

Loren saw Blair nod in agreement, then Benny turned and left without another word to either of them.

Handing the clean issue to Blair, Loren asked softly, "What was that all about?"

Blair swallowed and shook his head. "Nothin'." He picked up the blues and started to turn away.

"Hey, Blair," Loren said in a reassuring voice, "if there's anything wrong . . . if there's any way I can help . . ."

"I gotta go," Blair muttered. "See you around." And he left.

Loren leaned his elbows on the counter and watched Blair leave the laundry. He then turned in the direction of the iron presses. He caught Benny looking away. Something was wrong; he could feel it in the air. He didn't know what it was, but he was going to make a point to find out. Blair was much too good-looking and sexy to be chased out of Loren's life by a guy like Benny.

On Saturday morning, Loren enjoyed sleeping late, which meant that he didn't get up until nine o'clock instead of the usual five-thirty. His job in the laundry left his afternoons and evenings free for going to the gym or for involving himself in the various sports which proved to be the only organized activities at that prison. In spring and summer, Saturday afternoons were devoted to baseball, at which Loren excelled.

He awakened slowly, pulled his nude body out of the bed, and slipped into a pair of cut-offs. He put a shot of instant coffee into his mug and walked the length of the ten-man dorm toward the rest-room area, where he ran hot water in a sink until the billowing steam told him it was hot enough to make coffee. He ran a comb through his hair, then stood in front of the urinal. Handling his cock reminded him that he had a date later that afternoon with one of his baseball teammates in the shower after the game.

Retrieving his coffee mug he turned to go back into the dorm. The door from the corridor opened, and Loren saw Blair coming into the restroom. His face brightened. "Well, good morning. What a pleasant surprise, Blair. Did you come to see me or someone else?"

Blair glanced over his shoulder, down the hall, before closing the door behind him. His expression was sober, worried. "Loren, can I talk to you? Privately?"

"Of course," Loren answered seriously. "Let me get dressed and we'll take a few laps around the athletic field."

The grass on the athletic field was a lustrous green. Puffy clouds drifted lazily in a baby-blue sky. The sun was warm. It was the kind of day that aggravated a prisoner's longing to be free, a day that fostered remorse for senseless, impetuous acts which had led to confinement.

Loren and Blair engaged in small talk as they walked toward the athletic field. Loren learned that Blair was twenty-three, a Libra, single, the third of five children, a highschool drop-out, a first-termer on an Armed Robbery charge, and was currently assigned to the prison kitchen for the mandatory three-months duty required of a fish.

Arriving at the gate to the vast, sprawling athletic field, Loren finally got down to brass tacks. "What's the problem, Blair? How can I help?"

Blair began slowly, searching for words. "I've only been here for two-and-a-half weeks. I don't know very many people, and I've got to talk to someone, and you're the only one who's been friendly toward me. You don't know me, and I don't know you, and I'm probably outta line to hit ya with my problems . . ."

"Let me make it easy on you," Loren said kindly. "First of all, you know that I'm gay and that I'm hot for your body. I'll never force that issue; when you're ready, you'll come around. In the meantime, I like you and would like to be your friend. Anything you tell me will stay strictly between us—unless it's something you want me to do something about. I've got a helluva lot of friends, here, and a lot of I.O.U.'s I can call in. But let me make it clear that if I can help you, I will—with no strings attached."

Loren looked at Blair to see if his point had sunk in.

"I don't know where to start," Blair said.

"Let me guess. It's Benny, isn't it."

Blair's affirmative reply was barely audible, but he said nothing more.

"Well?" Loren coaxed.

"It's not easy to talk about."

Loren stopped in his tracks and looked Blair squarely in the eyes. "Blair, either you trust me or you don't. I've done a lot of time. Nothing you say can surprise me or shock me. The best thing to do is just spit it out."

Blair held Loren's gaze for a moment, then looked away. "Several days ago," he began, "I was taking a shower. All of a sudden, Benny was there in the shower with me. Naked. I was surprised. I didn't know what to do. Until then, he had been my only friend in the dorm. He smiled at me and said, 'Let's fuck.' I tried to tell him that I don't play that shit. Before I knew what was happening, he slammed me against the wall. I slipped and fell. He grabbed me into a hammer lock. I couldn't break away. He's twice as strong as me, you know." He was silent, as though reliving that moment.

"Go on," Loren said softly.

"What can I say?" He looked into Loren's eyes; his own were moist with held-back tears. "Do I have to say it? He *fucked* me."

Anger welled up in Loren's chest. Blair's story was not a new one; it happened all too frequently in men's prisons. Scum like Benny got a perverse thrill from raping young men they could easily overpower. The sad part for Loren was that he could do nothing to stop it. Male rape had existed since the first time men ever caged other men together and would probably continue till the end of time. This pragmatic knowledge, however, failed to ease Loren's anger. He had never liked Benny, for some reason. Now he had concrete substance to his loathing.

Blair interrupted his thoughts. "He said he would keep it quiet and just between the two of us as long as I kept my mouth shut. He even promised not to bother me again as long as I said nothing to no one. Yesterday, in the laundry, he thought I was being too friendly with you. He told me to stay away from you. I told him that I didn't even know you."

"Has Benny threatened you? About hanging around with me, I mean."

"As a matter of fact," Blair answered, "yeah. I gather you two don't like each other. Anyway, last night he came into the shower again. I guess I didn't put up much of a fight—what's the sense? I can't beat him. After it was over, he said that if he caught me hanging around you again, he was gonna beat the shit out of me. But I have to figure it this way: he has already broken his word. I might be new to prison life, but I can see it coming—he ain't gonna leave me alone. But when he starts choosing my friends for me, I gotta do something."

Loren studied the young man's face. It was an open face, an honest face. Loren liked this guy as much as he detested Benny. And Benny himself had given Loren the excuse to butt in.

"We've got a saying in prison, Blair. It goes like this: What goes around comes around, which is roughly the same thing as the Golden Rule turned around. What you do unto others is what they're gonna do to you. We got another saying: Pay-back is a mother-fucker! People like Benny have a tendency to think that these rules apply to other guys and not to themselves. I've got an idea about how to handle this little problem. I think you'll like it."

After the baseball game that afternoon, Loren talked to Matt, the guy with whom he had the date. Once the plan was explained to him, Matt had to laugh about it. He agreed to go along with it, which meant foregoing the afternoon's sex-play. But he admitted that it was going to be worth it.

Part of the plan was for Blair to be prominently seen in Loren's company, by one and by all, especially by Benny. They went to the evening meal together and were seen by Benny. They went to the gym after supper and played ping-pong and were seen by Benny, who was playing basketball. They watched TV together in the dayroom and were seen coming out of the room by Benny.

They parted company for the nine-thirty count. Loren felt reasonably certain that Benny would not take any action until Blair went for his shower which, according to the plan, was to be at exactly ten o'clock.

At five to ten, Loren went to Blair's dorm, clad only in a towel and shower shoes. The restroom area was deserted, and Loren stepped unseen into the shower stall. He turned on the water and waited for Blair.

Moments later, Blair stepped into the shower. Old plastic curtains shielded them from view.

Blair looked sheepish and appeared to be about to say something. Loren put a finger to his mouth and shushed him. He then appraised the youth's body, finally being allowed to see it totally nude and in the flesh. Blair's body lived up to the promise held out by his handsome face. It was flawless and nicely sculptured. Not too muscular, not too skinny; youthful, but not adolescent. A small tuft of brownish hair grew between his pectoral muscles, and the hair around his nipples was just beginning to get long. A trail of fine hair led away from his navel and disappeared into a thick patch of curly, wiry pubic hairs.

Blair's abdomen was flat but fleshy, soft looking, and had a noticeable "cut" or line of demarcation at his hips, looking a lot like one of those old Roman bronze breastplates that defined a deep U in the lower abdomen. Loren's eyes traveled down the beautiful flesh to the hunk of sausage hanging between those slim thighs. Blair's cock was thick and definitely above average in length. It was soft, but Loren wasted no time resolving that problem.

Blair stepped under the running water, and Loren dropped to his knees. Gripping large, firm, meaty buns in his hands, Loren glided his mouth onto the as yet limp tool. Water sprayed all around them, dripping from Loren's forehead into his eyes. With practised expertise, Loren quickly got Blair's cock rock-hard. As the cock, gliding in and out of his mouth, grew into mammoth proportions, Loren could feel his own dick expanding with a burning fever.

Blair's body was sensuously smooth under the cascading water, and Loren allowed his hands to stray from the silky cheeks to the velvety thighs of the young man standing in front of him, then up along the narrow hips to the slender waist.

Gradually, Loren became aware of the fact that Blair's cock was losing some of its rigidity. He brought his right hand down to toy with the low-hung satiny scrotum with its large balls. Even this ploy failed to rearouse the subsiding organ.

He pulled his mouth away from Blair's dick and stood up. "What's the matter? Not enjoying it?"

Blair swallowed his embarrassment. "I guess I'm just too nervous about what's going to happen."

"Don't worry about a thing," Loren whispered, just loud enough to be heard over the running water. "It's all set. All we're waiting for is Benny."

No sooner were the words out of his mouth than the shower curtain opened, and Benny stepped inside. He had been so busy making sure that no one had seen him going into the shower, he had failed to realize that Loren was in it. When it hit him that Blair was not alone, he was both dumbfounded and angry. "What the fuck you doin' here, Loren?" he asked in a menacing growl.

"The question is, what are *you* doing here, Benny? Do you make it a habit to jump into the shower when a sissy's got a trick goin' on? Get the fuck outta here."

In order to assure the success of his plan, Loren gave Benny's shoulder a rough push. He didn't want this confrontation to reduce itself to a gab-fest. He fully intended to goad Benny into action.

"You get out, faggot!" Benny snarled, making an abortive attempt to push against Loren's shoulder. "You're fuckin' around with my kid, and I don't like it, see? So get your faggot ass outta here."

"Blair, are you his kid?" Loren asked.

"No."

Benny growled, "Why you little punk, I'll beat your ass."

"You'll have to beat mine first, Benny. You're outta line by coming into the shower when I'm sucking a man's cock, and you're outta line when you start fucking with my friends. So, *leave!*" Loren gave another, rougher shove, pushing Benny backward.

"You cocksucker!" Benny shouted, as he slipped on the wet floor and fought to regain his balance. He managed to spin to the left and brace himself against the shower wall. In a flash, he whirled around and swung at Loren, catching him on the shoulder.

Loren feinted with the blow, then delivered his own to Benny's stomach, doubling him over. He stood back, waiting for Benny to catch his breath. The plan did not call for the fight to be over with so quickly. Loren was slightly amused at how easy a match this was turning into.

Loren watched as Benny straightened up then flexed to throw another punch. He moved in on Benny and grabbed him around the waist, pinning both arms to his sides, and carried him forward with the momentum out past the shower curtains and onto the floor of the restroom area.

Benny's naked body took the brunt of the fall as the two men came tumbling out of the shower stall onto the cement floor. Loren glanced around quickly and saw Matt coming through the corridor door, followed by several curious convicts. Within seconds, the restroom was crowded with onlookers.

Benny rolled to his side, shaking Loren loose. He tried to struggle to his feet but slipped and slided and could gain no purchase against the slick floor. Loren grabbed Benny's right arm and forced it into a half-Nelson, but he, too, was finding it difficult to gain traction as his slippery feet slid out from under him.

Suddenly, the position was reversed, and Loren found himself on bottom, with Benny trying to force his arm into a hammerlock. Loren became aware of the fact that his cock was throbbing with excitement as their two bodies slapped against each other. He was also aware of the fact that there were dozens of men watching as he and Benny wrestled totally naked, bodies still wet from the shower. He was on his knees, bent over with his head nearly touching the floor, his arm slowly giving way to the pressure being applied by Benny, who had apparently rediscovered his strength. Loren could feel Benny's cock nudging against his thigh. Benny, too, was firmly erect. *What a picture this must make,* Loren thought. Then, with a forceful effort, he broke away and twisted to the side, breaking loose from the hammerlock.

The move was greeted by cheers of approval from the crowd of cons, all of whom apparently were rooting for Loren. Matt's voice was the loudest: "Come on, Loren! Fuck him! Bone him down!"

The two combatants wrestled for a while, jockeying for position. At one point, they faced each other, on their knees, bodies upright, cocks jutting out stiffly before them. Benny lunged at Loren, hoping to gain the upper hand, but Loren merely rolled with the momentum and succeeded in unbalancing him. With deft movements, Loren swung around on top of Benny, who had managed to fall flat on his face.

Loren pushed against the back of Benny's head, pushing his face into the concrete while twisting his arm into a hammerlock. Benny's fall had left his buns up in the air, his knees scraping against the rough floor. Loren landed a solid left to Benny's kidney, evoking a gasp and a moan of intense pain.

He pulled the left arm around to meet with the hammerlocked right one and pushed roughly against the wrists, causing an even, fiery pain to shoot across Benny's shoulders and forcing his face even harder against the concrete. Benny's legs gave out, and his buns were no longer suspended in mid-air.

Loren quickly mounted the prostrated form of his adversary to a roar of approval from the enthusiastic crowd.

"Fuck him!"

"Get that ass!"

"Dick 'im down!"

"Ride 'im, cowboy!"

Loren's cock was hard as steel and ready for action. He rammed it ferociously against the unyielding buns while he continued to apply the pressure against the two wrists, assuring the effectiveness of the double hammerlock. With his knees, he forced Benny's legs agape, then swiftly and surely drove his cock into the unwilling ass. Tearing past the reluctant sphincter muscles, Loren's cock felt as though it were being shredded by sixteen razor blades. Benny was a punk, but he had still been a virgin up to that moment. As Loren's cock penetrated deeper into the hot, moist abyss, the thought raced through Loren's mind: *He ain't a virgin no more!* A roar of approval swelled through the ranks of the fascinated spectators.

Excited by fucking a guy with dozens of voyeurs in attendance, Loren began to pound feverishly against Benny's hairy buns, his cock thrilled by the torture of the tight ass. Pumping the·virgin ass with a driving passion, Loren could feel the uniquely sensual sensations coursing through his body. It was as erotic mentally as physically, and in a short while he felt orgasm rushing onto him. Pressing his knees together and tightening his muscles, he let the flood of sexual release crash through him. His body convulsed in spastic tremors as the eruption exploded, and his cum shot into the hot virgin ass. He writhed and squirmed until the climactic moment had finally passed.

Once his wad had been entirely shot, he released the pressure against Benny's wrists and eased his body off the one he had just raped.

Loren got to his feet to a resounding ovation. He was clasped into Matt's strong arms and was then bounced back and forth between the convicts, as though no one noticed he was naked.

"I'll kill you!" came a guttural growl from the floor as Benny struggled to his feet.

Despite the uproar, everyone heard the threatening menace from the floor. Loren was quickly unhanded, and once again the two antagonists were squared off in front of each other.

In a blind fury, Benny swung out against Loren. But his arms were too stiff and his shoulders too sore; the swing was too wide.

Loren stepped into the punch and landed three powerful blows to Benny's solar plexus, sending the battered con to the floor. He landed roughly and rolled over onto his back, his mouth wide agape.

Loren stood over his defeated opponent and grabbed his now limp cock in his right hand. As soon as the revelation of what Loren was about to do dawned on the onlookers, a murmur of disbelief mingled with admiration spread throughout the assemblage.

"That's too cold!" Matt exclaimed.

"Oh, Jesus!" came another voice.

"I don't believe this!"

At first Loren was afraid he was not going to be able to do it; his urine wouldn't flow. Then, a slow dribble to start with, his golden piss started to gush forth. The spray arched up toward Benny's open mouth. Before the defeated man could realize what was happening, he had a mouth full of warm piss.

Gasping and sputtering, he turned his head to one side, and the spray splashed all over his head and face as it came in a more forceful torrent.

"Six-Five!" someone yelled. It was the signal that a guard was in the area, a universally used code meaning: "Alert!"

"Six-Five!" the alarm was repeated.

As if previously choreographed, Matt and another man picked up the supine form laying on the floor and carried him into the dorm area. Loren called to Blair to get out of the shower and to get to his own bunk. Loren quickly stepped into the shower stall and adjusted the curtain. The crowd dispersed slowly, so as to draw no attention, some of the men disappearing into the dorm, some down the corridor, some even remaining behind—the restroom being a common congregating place.

The "Six-Five" had come from farther down the corridor; by the time the guard walked into the restroom area, nothing appeared to be unusual or out of place. The guard did not look into the shower; he poked his head into the darkened dorm but, seeing nothing unusual, went on his way.

Later that night, after the eleven-thirty count, Loren was relaxed on his bunk in his own dorm. The door to the restroom area opened, and Loren saw Blair come in.

The young man sat down on Loren's bunk. "He did it, just like you said he would. He locked-up. When the guard came through at count, he jumped up and demanded protective custody. I kinda feel sorry for the guy; they really gave him a bad time after you left. He didn't say anything about me, though—that kinda surprised me."

"It shouldn't surprise you. After what happened to him, in front of twenty witnesses, there was nothing he could say. If he tried to tell them what he had done to you, they would have shouted him into silence. And don't feel sorry for him. The next time you think about feeling sorry for him, just remember what he did to you. Earlier today I told you about an expression we use a lot here in the joint. Do you remember? 'What goes around comes around'. It's not a cute little jingle, like 'Out of sight out of mind', you know. It's a very real fact of life. People usually get what's coming to them. And speaking of that—you still owe me the pleasure of your company in the privacy of our dorm shower."

Blair blushed and smiled widely. "That sounds good to me. Now that it's over, I probably won't be nervous. Are you ready?"

"I'm *always* ready," Loren smiled.

Inside the shower stall, Loren resumed where he had left off earlier. This time, Blair's cock not only remained rigid and hard as steel, it seemed to grow even larger than before. Loren's cock, even though he had caught a nut earlier, was again throbbing with greedy lust. Blair's body was delightfully sensuous to touch, silky and fleshy. Loren slurped and sucked on the thick pole as it slammed into his open mouth.

Blair was considerably less inhibited this time, and he let himself fuck Loren's face with abandon. Soon Loren tasted the metallic flavor of Blair's cum.

Then, much to his utter amazement, Loren watched Blair sink to his knees before him and felt his cock being sucked into the inexperienced mouth. There was almost no pressure, but the sensation was curiously pleasurable. "You don't have to do that, you know," Loren said.

Blair pulled his mouth away. "What goes around comes around. Isn't that what you taught me?"

Somehow, the phrase seemed out of context, but Loren wasn't about to argue. He closed his eyes and let his body flow with the joys of sexual contact.

Abruptly, Loren realized that this fish con had just taught him something. Loren had always thought about the negative connotations of that expression. Blair had simply put it into an affirmative sense.

These thoughts dissipated as quickly as they formed, for he was rapidly reaching climax. Blair was inexperienced, but Loren had lots of time to teach him the tricks of the trade.

And who knows? Perhaps Loren could even learn a thing or two from Blair. After a shattering orgasm, the two men went to their own dorms.

Loren fell asleep with a contented smile on his face.

"THE HOLE"

CRAIG LEWIS, TWENTY-THREE YEARS OLD, lay atop his bunk in the darkened cell, wearing nothing but his short, blue, terry cloth bathrobe. The 7:30 PM count had just cleared, and he was waiting for Mel, who regularly came to Craig's cell on Tuesday nights.

Mel was one of the many young studs who constantly sought Craig's favors. Craig was the most attractive sissy in the joint: slender, attractive, boyishly sexy, and very, very popular among the hundreds of supposedly "straight" guys (like Mel) who had decided not to let their terms of confinement restrict their natural sex drives.

Getting caught in a sex act with another inmate, however, was definitely against the rules and was cause for immediate lock-up in Punitive Segregation, or "the hole," as the cons called it. After two and a half years in prison, Craig's attitude was: If I get caught, what are they gonna do? Throw me in jail? He had been gay for as long as he could remember; he certainly wasn't going to let one tiny little prison rule inhibit his sex life, not when he was surrounded by gorgeous studs twenty-four hours a day!

He heard the soft rap on the cell door and saw Mel's strong, handsome face framed in the 9 x 12-inch window. He got up and opened the door. "Hi, come on in."

"Were you expecting someone?" Mel teased. "It's dark in here." He pulled the door closed behind him and slipped his arms around Craig's slender body. As was his custom, Mel was wearing nothing but a t-shirt, prison blue jeans, and shower thongs—enough to look like he was dressed, but little enough to take off without too much trouble. He was a thirty-year-old body-builder, whose physique looked as though it were made of cast bronze, but which was also delicately soft to the touch. His eyes were the color of ice, but they burned with a lively, humorous glow.

Craig pulled away from Mel's bear-hug embrace. "Let me cover the window," he said, grabbing the piece of cardboard specially cut to fit the 9 x 12 opening. After setting it in place, he turned to face the muscular weight-lifter. Mel was taking off his t-shirt and simultaneously kicking off his thongs. Before he could remove his jeans, Craig's hands were fondling his hairy chest.

Mel tugged on Craig's bathrobe sash, spread the robe, and wrapped his arms around the youthful waist, allowing his hands to glide down and cup the small, firm buns.

The feel of Mel's powerful arms and hands sent shivers of excitement racing through Craig's body. His cock began to throb and to press against Mel's jeans. He kissed Mel on the neck, wanting to kiss him on the lips but knowing better than to try. With Mel, sex was a one-way street.

Mel pulled away and quickly removed his jeans. His cock burst free from its confinement, and Craig sank to his knees. He began by darting his tongue over the throbbing, expectant piece of swollen flesh while his hands clasped Mel's large, muscular buns. Although not a huge cock, it *was* slightly more than average length, and definitely thicker than most. He let his tongue tease the anxious cock, making it moist and ready but not yet going down on it.

"Lie down," Craig whispered. Mel complied and stretched his tall, muscular body out on the narrow bunk, spreading his legs to allow Craig to crawl between them.

Carelessly dropping his robe, Craig eased his smooth, nearly hairless body onto the bunk between Mel's hairy, beefy legs. As he lowered his head toward the pulsating cock, he felt Mel's hands glide gently onto his shoulders. Craig ran his hands along Mel's thighs, up to his hips, along the flat expansive abdomen, and up to those well-developed and well-defined pectorals covered by a mat of curly black hair. He timed his actions so that his thumbs and fingers lightly pinched the already erect nipples just as his mouth wrapped around the head of Mel's dick. Over the months, Craig had learned how to stimulate Mel's erogenous zones. At first, Mel had seemed to have no sensitivity on his tits, despite Craig's numerous attempts to excite them. Finally, Craig had stumbled on the idea of creating a mental association for Mel between the pleasure of having his cock sucked by a hot mouth and the simultaneous pinching of his tits. It had worked. Now even Mel had to admit that he liked it when Craig played with his tits.

Mel thrust his pelvis upward, driving his rock-hard cock into Craig's eager mouth. He pounded frantically; his fingers dug deeply into Craig's soft shoulders. Craig allowed Mel to pump away at his mouth for a while. He let his left hand glide away from the erect nipple and gently slide down the length of Mel's tightly muscled body. Then his hand moved further down the curve of the lower abdomen, and came to rest fondling Mel's soft, downy nutsac. Thereupon he gripped the thrusting cock under the balls, like a cockring, and forced Mel to stop fucking his face. The body-builder relaxed and allowed Craig's hot mouth and tongue to do the job they were made to do.

With long, slow movements, Craig's mouth moved up and down the length of Mel's thick cock. It lingered on the head; Craig ran his tongue over the sensitive flesh and probed into the slit, driving Mel wild. Craig's hand loosened its grip, and surreptitious fingers made their way to Mel's ass.

During the early days of their relationship, Mel had been defensive about fingers getting too close to his ass. He was a man, all man, and men didn't take anything in the ass. It was a typical prison concept of the macho man. It had taken Craig a long time to get Mel past that old-fashioned concept of masculinity. When he finally lost his inhibitions, Mel had to admit that anal stimulation was, indeed, highly pleasurable. Now he had progressed to the point of letting Craig insert his index finger to the hilt.

Mel writhed at the treatment his cock received from Craig's skillful mouth. Craig seized that moment to insert his finger. Mel moaned softly; his strong fingers gripped Craig's shoulders.

A jangle of keys startled both men: they froze. The keys sounded very close. Craig's heart, already beating rapidly in the heat of passion, began to race furiously at the sound of the keys.

Sure enough, a key was being inserted into the lock.

"Oh, shit!" Craig cried, pulling his finger out of Mel's ass and jumping off the bunk. He searched frantically for his robe.

"Oh, shit!" Mel echoed, leaping from the bed.

Suddenly the cell was bathed in light; the door opened wide, and two officers came into the cell. "Busted!" officer Mayer exclaimed gleefully. "Busted bigger than shit. Both of 'em naked as jaybirds, and both of 'em got hard-ons."

Officer Lowe glared at his partner. *Sick bastard,* he said to himself. Aloud, he said, "Okay, you two. You're invited to a come-as-you-are party. Nothin' but bluejeans. Get dressed."

Craig and Mel were allowed to put on jeans, but nothing else. They were escorted to the Watch Commander's office. A report was made and both men were given write-ups.

"Since you were caught in the act," the Commander said tonelessly, "you go to the hole, pending action by the Disciplinary Committee." He yawned and waved them away.

Officer Mayer escorted the two of them to the Punitive Segregation Unit, where he delivered them to the Unit Officer, Mr. Moore. "Coupla fags for ya," Mayer snarled.

Moore accepted the copies of the write-ups and told Mayer he could leave. When the escorting officer had left, Moore looked up at the two men standing before his desk. "Which one of you is the sissy?"

"I am," Craig quickly answered.

Moore looked like a linebacker, except better looking. "Okay. Sit over there," he said to Craig, pointing a finger to a chair located at the left of his ancient wooden desk. "I'll take your jock to a cell. Stay put and don't give me no headaches, and I might let you have a blanket."

Craig was shivering from the cold and from the embarrassment of getting caught. He obeyed instructions and sat quietly while Moore locked Mel in a cell.

When Moore returned, he sat down at his desk. He looked at the slender, boyishly handsome young man in silence for a minute, then said, "You like suckin' dicks, huh?"

Craig glared at him but said nothing.

"Shit, boy! Look at you! You're freezin'. Do you want to spend the night naked? Or do you want to cooperate and have a nice warm blanket to sleep under?"

"I'm gay," Craig replied petulantly. "And I'm proud. But what I like to do in bed is none of your business."

"Hold on, now, boy. This is a prison, not a boys' camp. I can make it easy for you, or I can make it hard. Rule book says I can put trouble-makers into strip-cells. You a trouble-maker?"

"No, sir," Craig whispered.

"You like suckin' dicks? Or do you like to take it in the ass? Or do you like it both ways?"

Craig knew that Moore wasn't bluffing; if he didn't play the man's game, he would sleep naked and freeze his balls off—he knew the strip-cells were specially equipped with air conditioning to make them even colder. "I go both ways," he answered softly.

"Hey, kid, loosen up!" Moore's tone was solicitous, kind. "You like men, don't you? I'm a man, right? I'm not bad lookin', am I?"

Craig had to admit that the man was, in fact, quite handsome, in a rugged sort of way.

"I'll see to it you get a t-shirt and *two* blankets. You'll be snug as a bug in a rug, kid. What say?"

Craig slowly nodded his head.

"Come with me, then." Moore led him off in a different direction. Mel had gone to the corridor on the left; Moore took Craig to the right. When they came to the last cell, Moore keyed it open and motioned for Craig to go in. "This is a special cell, kid. Ain't just a mattress on the floor; it's got a real *bed* in it. Take off your jeans and get comfortable."

Craig removed his jeans and sat on the edge of the bed. He watched the officer take off his uniform, everything but his socks. Beneath his khakis, he seemed fat and stocky; undressed, he wasn't all that bad to look at. His gut was a bit flabby, but his chest, arms, and legs were in good condition, and his body was as smooth as a baby's ass. Craig judged him to be in his late twenties; he had been to bed with worse than this, he thought. He tried to psych himself up to enjoy what was coming.

"What do you want me to do?" Craig asked.

Moore's cock was already semi-erect from expectation. He was stroking it to full rigidity. "Lay down on your stomach and spread them skinny legs of yours, boy. You ain't never been fucked till you been fucked by me," he boasted.

Craig did as he was told, determined to get it over with as soon as possible. He spat on his hand and ran it across his ass, just in case the guard failed to lubricate him. The he felt the tremendous weight of the massive guard on his back; he felt the inept prodding of Moore's cock, trying to find the hole. Craig lifted his pelvis and pulled his cheeks apart to provide an easier target. When the head of Moore's cock nudged against the knot of muscles around his ass, Craig relaxed and let it glide in.

At first, Moore's cock thrust in roughly. Craig realized that the man had probably fucked very few assholes in his life—if any at all—and that the boast had been idle. Moore didn't know what he was doing. Craig gritted his teeth and made up his mind to suffer through the punishing pounding to the best of his ability.

Despite Moore's ineptitude, however, Craig began to enjoy the man's warm body caressing his own, while the swollen dick moved in and out. As he got into the swing of it, Moore slowed down and made his strokes longer, less jabbing. Craig discovered he was getting a hard-on; he began to enjoy the thought of this prison guard fucking him. His body began to move in rhythm with Moore's gradually increasing speed. Then he noticed that Moore was passionately massaging his shoulders, neck, and arms.

Just as Craig was getting to the point where he was no longer resentful, where he was being swept up in the tide of physical lust, he felt Moore's hands tighten around his shoulders. Then the deep-thrusting cock erupted in orgasm. Moore's body trembled on top of him, writhed and jerked in sexual fulfillment. The powerful guard collapsed on top of Craig's frail body, almost suffocating him. It had taken less than five minutes; Craig was now fully aroused.

Without warning, Moore withdrew, causing Craig to wince in unexpected pain. The guard got to his feet. "Turn over and sit up," he commanded.

Craig rolled over and swung his legs over the edge of the bunk. To his amazement, Moore dropped to his knees in front of him. Pushing Craig's knees wide with his hands, he lowered his head to Craig's crotch. Moore took Craig's dick in his mouth (which was as inexperienced as his cock). The big man's teeth scraped against the skin of Craig's cock as it plunged deeper into the moist, wet interior of Moore's mouth. But there was very little sensation, no pressure, no suction. The big man was doing nothing to stimulate the youth; so Craig began to work the muscles of his groin in time with the up-and-down motion of Moore's mouth. Craig closed his eyes and ran his hand over his own smooth, slightly muscled chest, playing with his own nipples. In this way, he managed to work himself toward a climax, the orgasm which he had been so rudely deprived of earlier.

When he came, his body jack-knifed forward with uncontrollable jerking. Then he leaned back on the bunk as his cock shot the pent-up sperm into Moore's mouth. Surprisingly, Moore took it all. He even swallowed it. Craig figured this wasn't Moore's first blow-job.

As his cock grew limp, he felt Moore's mouth pull away. He opened his eyes and saw the guard get to his feet. As if nothing had happened, Moore began to get dressed. "The Disciplinary Committee won't meet till Friday morning, so you got three nights in here. That was real good, kid. I'll be back tomorrow night. And the night after. . . . Oh, by the way, I lied about the t-shirt, but this bed does have two blankets on it. Sleep tight."

With that, he was gone, and the cell door was locked behind him.

Craig lay back on the bunk, staring at the ceiling. *Unreal,* he thought. *It's against the rules to have sex, but even the guards do it!* "Fuck the rules," he said aloud. "What can they do? Throw me in jail?"

GOING HOME

A T LONG LAST, the day of Mickey's parole board appearance had arrived. It had been a restless, sleepless night during which he had played over in his mind the numerous possible answers to the numerous possible questions the board members might ask him. At one point or other, he had finally dozed off, only to awaken at five thirty. He pulled his naked body out of bed, thrust his long, hairless legs into a scrubby pair of jeans, and walked out of the ten man dorm into the adjoining "shitter," which was what the cons called the large room containing the wash basins, urinals, toilets, mop closet, laundry sink, and shower stall—all in one.

He pissed, then went to a basin and splashed cold water on his face, realizing too late that he hadn't brought a towel. He looked in the mirror and decided to shave, even though he didn't need to. At twenty-two, Mickey still managed to sprout only the finest of peach fuzz. Through the mirror, he saw the dorm door open.

Wearing only white boxer shorts, Ned walked over and stood directly behind Mickey, rubbing his groin into the scrubby jeans, and wrapping his arms around Mickey's slender, naked torso. "What's the matter, Mick? Can't sleep?"

Backing into Ned, Mickey reached around and cupped his hands on firm buns, encouraging Ned's actions. "I'm just nervous about the board. Today's the big day."

"Let's jump in the shower while everyone's still asleep," Ned suggested.

They both crept back to their bed areas for towels and toiletries. It would be an hour yet before most of them would get up, not that Mickey cared. The whole joint knew that Mickey was gay, just one of at least a dozen sissies (not counting the closet queens). No one ever said anything to him about his sex life, unless they wanted to be a part of it. Once, fat old Kelly had bitched about "the shower never being available." Ned had told the old fart he could move if he didn't like it. Ned was not Mickey's "old man." Mickey liked sex too much to be tied down to just one guy, but Ned was his favorite. Mickey liked his hairy, muscular chest, with nipples that stood out like baby pacifiers, his flat, rippled abdomen, those powerful, fleshy buns, that seven-and-a-half-inch cock . . .

An old, musty woolen blanket substituted for long lost shower curtains and afforded complete privacy to a man taking a shower, or to the men doing more than showering together. It was an unwritten law that you never looked into a shower when the water was running. It was more than simple, common courtesy. A man like Ned would just as soon slit your throat if you peeked into a shower when he was fucking a sissy. Even the screws observed the rule—for the same reasons.

With the hot water cascading down on them, the two men soaped each other's bodies. Ned was one of the few jocks Mickey had found who didn't feel he was compromising his own masculinity by fondling a homosexual's cock. Ned was straight; that is to say, he wouldn't take it in the ass, and he wouldn't suck dick. But he was a good lover to a sissy. Mickey found that most guys would hold on to his waist or his thighs while fucking, but Ned would feel his balls with one hand and jack him off with the other while he fucked. And so it was with foreplay. Ned would get him throbbing hard while he lathered his silky smooth body.

That morning was no different from the innumerable times before. The only extraordinary thing was the time of day. It had been sixteen months since they had done it in the morning. Both men discovered they were hornier than usual. Ned pulled Mickey's body close to his own in a tight embrace. Their rigid cocks pressed against their stomachs, hands glided feverishly over soapy backs and buns, Ned's mouth nibbled along Mickey's neck, across his chin. Then, unexpectedly, their lips found each other in an open mouth kiss.

Mickey greedily sucked Ned's tongue into his mouth, and suddenly a tongue was insufficient. He pulled away and slid to his knees, turning Ned's body into the spray of water, rinsing the soap away from his erect staff. His hands reached up to the massive, furry chest and gently pinched rock-hard nipples as his tongue darted, snakelike, across the swollen head of Ned's mammoth sex. He felt strong, thick hands tenderly stroke his neck and shoulders as the cock bobbed in eager anticipation at his teasing tongue. He slid his tongue down the right side of the pulsing organ. Even under the warm water, Ned's scrotum was tight, his testicles large and anxiously awaiting release. He sucked them both into his mouth as he dropped his right hand down to grab hold of the thick hunk of meat.

Ned's fingers wandered frantically through Mickey's thick, wavy, sandy brown hair. An involuntary moan escaped his lips.

Mickey stood up, kissed him again, then reached for the Irish Spring. Ned turned his back to the running water as Mickey relathered his cock. Ned then took the bar away from him. Mickey turned away as Ned ran the soap between his legs.

Bending at the waist, he backed into Ned and felt the tip of his cock nudge against the knot of his rectum. He felt Ned's hands find their customary position, the right one touching the fleshy helmet of his cock just as his ass was parted. Ned knew to penetrate slowly at first, allowing Mickey to back into him at his own pace.

Mickey held his breath until the entire length of Ned's beautiful tool had found shelter in the deep, warm, moist recesses of his ass. Then he exhaled with a soft cooing noise of pure pleasure. "Oooh! Fuck me," he pleaded as Ned began a simultaneous stroking of his sphincter muscles and his cock. Mickey loved to be jacked off while being fucked, and no one did it better than Ned.

The rhythmic in and out motion of Ned's rod began to accelerate while his hand moved more rapidly up and down Mickey's pole. The other hand played with the downy smoothness of Mickey's balls.

Mickey knew it would be over too soon, but he couldn't help it. He gyrated his pelvis in syncopation with Ned's thrusting and retracting cock, while urging his own cock to orgasm. He felt a tightening sensation in the muscles around his eyes, then a contraction in his testicles, a hot feeling throughout his body. The pleasure in the head of his dick was too overwhelming, and he jerked forward with the first convulsion of climax. The jerking motion drove Ned's cock deeper inside him and served to heighten the ecstatic sensation. He squirmed and writhed as his cock erupted into Ned's hand.

Conforming to Mickey's wishes, Ned stopped the stroking motions of his hand at the first spasm and wrapped around the head of the gushing penis. He also stopped his pelvic motions for

Mickey's orgasm, burying his cock as far into his ass as he could shove it. Everything had to stop for Mickey's climax. It was the only way he could get full enjoyment of the erotic pleasure flooding through his body.

Mickey's body continued to convulse for well over a minute, and the feel of his body, racked in passionate, feverish ecstasy, worked its own magic on Ned's deeply embedded organ. As soon as Mickey's orgasm had subsided, Ned began pumping with renewed frenzy, and within seconds his own cock exploded. Unlike Mickey, Ned worked his cock round and round as it spurted its load of cum into Mickey's ass. He pounded away at the delicate buns until the last drop had seeped from the head of his dick, until his body's passion was spent, until his contracting muscles were exhausted.

Like a record, slowly revolving after the turntable has been shut off, coming ever so slowly to a stop, the two writhing bodies finally grew still. Rapid breathing and heart rates eventually returned to normal.

When his penis was limp, Ned withdrew.

Mickey turned to face him and put his hands on his broad shoulders. All he could say was, "Wow."

Ned kissed him on the nose and said, "Good luck at the board."

* *

They had asked all the wrong questions, and Mickey had given all the wrong answers. They had asked him to step outside while they deliberated. When the screw held the door open for him to go back into the board room, Mickey felt certain the outcome would be bad news. He sat down, trying not to look nervous to the board members, staff members, and flunkies sitting behind the three long tables arranged like a horseshoe around his solitary chair. The words "star chamber" flitted into his mind, quickly dispelled by the sonorous voice of the board chairman.

"Michael Edgar Dewey," he began. "After careful consideration, the Board of Paroles and Pardons has decided to grant your request for parole. In addition to the standard terms of parole, which you'll be given a copy of, the Board stipulates two Special Conditions. One, you are to maintain steady employment, and two, this parole is contingent upon acceptance by the State of Colorado." He looked up from the papers and spoke directly to Mickey. "As I'm sure you know, out of state paroles must be approved by the receiving state. We cannot give you a specific release date. The effective date of your parole will be determined by when the paper work comes back from Denver. Do you have any questions?"

"No Sir."

"Good luck to you."

"Thank you."

*   *

"I'm going home," he called out to Tina, as he emerged from the Admin. Building, waving his copies of the board results. Tina, whose real name was Alvin Baker, was Mickey's closest friend. She had been waiting expectantly, hoping to hear Mickey's good news.

"Oh girl!" Tina squealed. "I'm so happy for you, child!" She threw her arms around Mickey right there on the yard, in front of God and everybody. After a moment, she asked, "Where's home, girl? I thought you didn't have any family, except for a brother."

"I'm going to Denver."

"Good grief, girl. Why did you pick Denver? Why not New York or San Francisco? As pretty as you are, you could have an old man takin' care of you in no time."

"I've got a friend who'll let me stay with him and his lover till I get back on my feet. Besides, Tina, Denver's a swingin' place too."

But Mickey wasn't all that positive, deep inside. It had been three years since he and Lee had been lovers. It had been shortly after they broke up that Mickey had robbed that liquor store, acting on an impulse prompted by a feeling of loss and futility. Lee had written regularly for about six months, then after a three-month silence, wrote to tell about Kevin, a thirty-five year old oilman he had met in Houston but who lived in Denver.

When Mickey was twenty, thirty-five seemed ancient. He was sure that Lee, only three years older than himself, would eventually abandon the wealthy old fossil. But it hadn't happened. What had started out for Lee as a gravy train, had, by slow degrees which showed clearly in his letters, turned to love. Mickey was sure there was no place for him in Lee's life anymore—not the way Mickey wanted it anyway. The Parole Board wouldn't let a man just walk out of prison with nowhere to go, so Mickey had accepted Kevin's offer of a room to himself in their spacious home and the pledge to help him find a job. What bothered Mickey was whether or not he could again live so close to Lee without disrupting his affair with Kevin.

There had been many affairs in prison, but they were nothing more than sex and expediency. Lee had been his only real lover, and Mickey felt that he still loved Lee. The bitter words and harsh feelings at the time of the breakup had evaporated over the past few years. Nineteen-year-old Mickey had been immature and self-centered. Twenty-two-year-old Mickey had done a lot of growing up. Prison does that. It makes you or breaks you. The maturing process, behind bars, had been hell. His cute, little turned up nose had been broken, two ribbons of (thank heavens, almost undetectable) scar tissue crossed his stomach, and three ribs had been cracked during that first year. A spoiled, pampered Mickey had said no to the wrong people, had refused to face the hard, cold facts of prison life.

The second year had been a time for deep soul searching. All the fight had been taken out of the impertinent youngster. He had had to make more compromises than he believed possible, merely to stay alive. Several times, it seemed his sanity would be the price of survival. To say it had not been easy was to make a mockery of the hell he had lived through. It had been almost humanly impossible. He had to fight because he was gay. He had to fight because he sometimes said no. He had to fight when he sometimes said yes. He had to fight to remain a human being, to avoid becoming an animal, to avoid becoming someone's property

When he finally decided it was prudent to have a protective old man, he had let his loins make the choice instead of his brains. Ronald Horn had been a veritable Greek god, but he had no "juice" —no pull, no influence among the tougher cons. Mickey had stepped between Ronny and Joe Kemper just as Joe had pulled his shank. Kemper was going to take Mickey away from Ronny. With the words, "Sit down, bitch. Speak when spoken to," Joe had inflicted the superficial knife wounds on Mickey's stomach. As it turned out, Ronny turned snitch on Joe. Ronny went into P.C.— protective custody—and Joe got locked up in Max—maximum security. That was when Ned took over.

Now, at last, he was going home. He could put behind him forever the living nightmare of prison. To get that chance at parole, he had had to accept Kevin and Lee's offer. At first, he had hesitated. He wrote to his brother, Eugene, to ask for help with his parole plans. Gene's reply was a vicious slap in the face, hurting worse than any pain he had suffered during the past three years. Gene did not want a criminal in his home, and he didn't want a homosexual around his young sons. There was no one else, no friends, no family—just Lee.

"Come back to the living, honey," Tina was saying. "I know you're in seventh heaven about getting out, but don't put your friends on the shine, girl."

Mickey apologized, admitted he had been spacing out, but said he needed to be alone with his thoughts. Tina understood, of course, and walked with Mickey to his dorm in silence.

After imparting his good news to the guys in the dorm (Ned had been overjoyed for him), he lay on his bunk, put on his headphones, and listened to a Moody Blues tape.

I'm going home. The phrase played around his brain. *Going home. At last I'm going home. Where is home?* he wondered. He knew it wouldn't be easy. For three years, his life had been regulated for him. He wondered what it would be like to be free again, to be away from the assholes, the cruds, the chicken shit screws. For sure he would miss Tina, Ned, Mark, Tim, Dave, Bob, Kurt, Bill—all of them. Except for Tina and Ned, he was sure he would soon forget them.

There were good times to remember. They weren't all bad. Gary had turned him on to his first hash. He and Gary were a lot alike: tall, good looking, slender, sandy brown hair, young. If Gary had only been gay. He had sucked Gary's dick right there in the dorm, in Gary's corner bunk, in the middle of the night. It had taken more than forty-five minutes, but it had been pure heaven. His head had been floating because of the hash. At first, Gary just lay there like a dead fish, but soon the two of them had been thrashing around in the throes of sexual bliss. They had woken at least two guys in the dorm.

And could he ever forget Jim Steed? Steed was a closet queen; he had to protect his masculine image as the joint's champion weight lifter. Whenever they showered together, Steed insisted on sucking Mickey's dick; sometimes they sixty-nined on the rough shower floor; and sometimes Mickey fucked him. It was a wild head trip, fucking the biggest, strongest man in prison. Mickey had kept his secret. To this day, the only ones who knew that Jim Steed was gay were the sissies who had showered with him.

There was the time when he and Tina were talking together on the yard, and Eric Rasmussen had come up to them and said, "You girls would have better luck if you stood on different corners." They had laughed till their sides ached and tears streaked their faces. It had been all the funnier because Eric was such a sweet, naive, innocent type. The statement had almost sounded sincere. Even now, Tina would occasionally say, whenever they parted, "Time to go stand on different corners, girl."

Wonderful, loveable Tina. He would never forget her.

*   *

Ned had woken him for lunch, but he preferred to sleep. He had come down from the "high" of getting his parole. There were still at least forty five days before he could go home. It would take that long for Colorado to process the paper work. He wished he could sleep straight through it.

He got up around two-thirty. Ned wasn't around, so he went to look for Tina. He was stopped outside Tina's dorm by Carl Halley.

"Don't go in there, Mickey."

"I'm looking for Tina."

"She ain't here right now. Come back later."

The sound of Tina's voice coming from the shitter gave the lie to Carl's statement. Tina sounded like she was arguing with someone.

"That's Tina. What's going on, Carl?"

"Get lost, Mickey."

"No! I'm gonna see what's going on." He yanked the door open and pushed Carl backward when he tried to bar the way.

"I ain't suckin' your dick" Tina was saying, "and I ain't lettin' you fuck me. Now let me go!"

Tina had her back to the mop closet and was surrounded by three shirtless tough guys. "Just 'cause my old man's in lock-up, don't mean I'm up for grabs. He'll be out any day now, so just get out of my way."

"Let her go," Mickey heard himself say. He had been in too many fights to back away from one now, and Tina was outnumbered.

The three of them turned to look. The one on Mickey's right said, "Fuck off, Mickey. This ain't none of your business."

"If it has to do with Tina, it's my business," he stated flatly.

The one in the middle said, "He told you to fuck off." He swung at Mickey. Mickey blocked with his left arm and hit the guy square in the gut. The first guy caught Mickey with a slam to the kidney.

Mickey grunted loudly, spun around and hit the guy in the face.

Carl had followed Mickey into the shitter. He had pulled a shank and now stood in a threatening stance. "Get the hell out of here, Mick, before I have to use this."

Tina took the opportunity to kick the third guy in the nuts. "We ain't doing shit. It's you guys better get the fuck out of here."

The one Mickey had hit in the face shoved him from behind. Mickey was propelled forward, into Carl's shank. It happened too quickly for Carl to avoid the impact.

Mickey felt the sharp pain in his chest and saw Carl's expression change from malice to shock, then to horror. At first, Mickey didn't believe he had been stabbed. For one terrified second, Mickey and Carl stared at each other, frozen in panic and shock. Then the pain registered in Mickey's brain and seared through his body. He gasped for air and felt a raspy rattle in his left lung.

Carl backed away. "I've stabbed him!" The words came out in a hoarse whisper. He turned and ran from the shitter.

In a blur, Mickey watched as Carl and the three others dashed out of the room. His head was spinning and his chest hurt real bad. From somewhere in the distance he heard Tina call his name.

He suddenly felt very tired. He wanted to lie down. As if in answer, his legs buckled under him and he crumpled to the floor. Something had softened the fall. Then he realized it was Tina. He was lying with his head in Tina's lap, looking up at her. Her face was upside down, and it hurt his eyes to look at her that way. As he closed his eyes, he heard Tina telling someone to find Ned.

"Yeah. Get Ned," he heard himself say in a raspy whisper. Ned would help him to his bunk where he could be comfortable. He was terribly, terribly sleepy—and cold. He had a funny taste in his mouth, kinda like, yeah, kinda like blood. Then he remembered he had just been stabbed. It couldn't be too bad, he thought; the pain was going away. He opened his eyes, once again looking up into Tina's upside down face. "I'll—I'll be all right."

"Of course you will, girl." Tina sounded like she was crying.

"Really," Mickey insisted. "I'm okay now. Just a little tired. Tina? Where's Ned?"

"He's comin', Mickey."

"I want to go lay down, Tina. Tell Ned to help me."

He felt a hand on his knee. "I'm here, Mick. My God, what happened?"

He heard Tina telling Ned that Carl had shanked him. "He was stickin' up for me, Ned. And look what it got him. Oh, dear God, don't let him die."

Die? I'm not gonna die. Mickey tried to get up. The stabbing pain returned to his chest. Oh God, it hurt so bad. He gasped from the pain and felt the raspy rattle in his lung again.

"Don't move, Mickey," Ned pleaded. "We'll get you to the infirmary. Just lay still." Then he heard Ned say to Tina, "The kid just got his parole. I don't believe this. This can't be happening."

There were so many things he wanted to say, but he couldn't concentrate. His eyes kept getting blurry. He couldn't see Ned. *Maybe I am gonna die. People do die from knife wounds, ya know.* A panicky chill raced through him. He tried to focus on Ned.

"I don't wanna die," he sobbed aloud. "Ned! I'm scared! Help me!"

"Shhh. Be still. You'll be okay, Mick. Just lay still."

The taste of blood was stronger now. With something like relief, he suddenly *knew* that he was going to die, and it didn't matter any more. He was no longer afraid.

"Ned? Tina? It's okay. I'm not afraid. I'm all right." The words came out slowly and painfully. He wanted to let them know that he was dying, but it was okay now.

"I'm going home," he whispered.

"Of course you are," Ned consoled. "You'll be okay, Mick."

Then, just because it seemed like the right thing to do, he looked up into Tina's tear filled eyes and said, "Time to . . . go stand . . . on . . . different corners . . ."

He felt Ned take his right hand in both of his own. A profound feeling of love for Ned flooded through him. *Why didn't I see it before now?*

Ned let go of his hand, and Mickey focused his eyes again. The medics, in their pale green tunics, had arrived with a gurney. He felt Tina's lap recede, hands wrap under his armpits and around his ankles. He knew he was being lifted because the ceiling was coming closer. A fiery flash of pain shot through his chest, and everything went black. He died before he reached the gurney.

Mickey had gone home.

NO ONE EVER WINS

A Novella

I. LARRY

FRANK WAS ASLEEP. Larry, sitting cross-legged on his own bunk, gazed fondly at the sleeping form of the man he loved, noticing how the beads of perspiration on Frank's body glistened in the reflected, relentless light of the sun, which baked the concrete walls of the eighty-year-old prison. It was a hot afternoon in August. Both Larry and Frank were stripped to their prison-issue boxer shorts.

While watching his lover's muscular, hairy chest slowly rise and fall with the slow rhythm of peaceful sleep, he was once again amazed to think that he, Larry Jonas, was actually in love with a man. For the first twenty-six years of his life, he had thought of himself as straight. He could easily remember the times when he had beat the shit out of guys who had made passes at him. He used to hate faggots.

Now he found himself so deeply in love—with a *man*—he would kill anyone who tried to harm Frank. To Larry's way of thinking, Frank wasn't a faggot. Faggots were effeminate, limp-wristed sissies. Frank was a man—all man. There was nothing feminine about him. His body was a weight-lifter's ideal: rock-hard muscles under soft, bronzed flesh. His face was ruggedly handsome, with soft-blue eyes and surfer-blond hair, a cleft chin, and an almost white moustache that accentuated his full, sensuous lips. Frank's tan was deeper and richer than Larry's; but Frank had done more time, and what else was there to do except pump iron and lay around in the sun?

He thought about the events leading up to their relationship:

Busted for sales of cocaine, Larry had decided to use his ten-year sentence to build his body. He met Frank on the weight pile. He offered a hand with some weights, and they soon became workout partners. When he was told that Frank was a queer, he didn't believe it. He thought that the guy who had told him that piece of crap had been bullshitting him. He decided that Frank should be told that someone was spreading some shit. But Frank simply said: "Yeah, I'm gay. Everyone knows it. I thought you did, too."

Frank never made a pass at Larry, saying only, "When you're ready for some screamin' skull, you'll let me know." So Larry felt safe and comfortable around his new-found friend. At first, he was slightly disgusted when he saw Frank slip into another man's cell. It took a while for him to become accustomed to the things that went on in prison. His aversion to homosexuality eroded slowly and was replaced by a growing curiosity. He decided that if he ever let a sissy suck his cock, it would have to be Frank, because he just couldn't imagine letting one of those freakish, wanta-be-women types touch him. On the other hand, it gave him a funny feeling to think about getting a blow job from his best friend. For this reason, it took him longer to come around than it might have otherwise.

They both lived on the first floor of the cellhouse, which consisted of two-man cells. Larry's cellmate was a quiet, older man who worked in the laundry. Frank's cellmate was a guy named Steve Brackman, a member of the only white gang at the prison, the Nazis. Steve had been Frank's "old-man" for over a year. Each of the sissies had an old-man, even the macho, masculine types like Frank. For most of them, an old-man was a protector. Frank needed no one to protect him nor to fight his battles, but Steve's association with the Nazi was a fringe benefit. The relationship between Frank and Steve went from sexual lust to friendship to dislike for each other. Steve eventually moved out of the cell and now lived in one of the single cells on the second floor.

In June of that year, when Larry had been in prison for over eight months, he finally broke down and let Frank know that he was ready. After a particularly strenuous workout, they jumped into the shower together, and Larry lathered his cock into a throbbing hard-on. Frank, of course, noticed but took no action in the shower—the curtain had been removed on the orders of the cell house sergeant, and Frank preferred as much privacy as possible, especially since privacy was such a precious commodity in prison.

After the shower, they went to Frank's cell. Frank lit up a joint. Larry was no longer amazed at how much pot there was inside prison; Frank always had some. Nothing was said about sex as they toked on the joint, but both men had known that the time had come.

Larry was nervous as hell. Letting a man suck his cock was still an alien concept to him, despite the fact that he had finally resolved to "take the plunge." If there had been any discussion on the subject, Larry would probably have backed out of the situation.

Frank was sensitive to this part of Larry's nature. He knew that Larry was ready, but that kid gloves were needed in the handling of the matter. He told Larry to kick back while he hung a blanket over the cell door. Still wearing nothing but a towel around his waist, Larry lay back on Frank's bunk, letting the excellent grass take its effect.

Frank sat on the edge of the bunk, smoked the joint down to a roach which he had hidden in the false bottom of a can of tobacco, and then gently placed his hand on the towel, directly over Larry's crotch.

Larry tensed, then slowly relaxed, determined not to fight it. He and Frank had been friends long enough so that he didn't experience the revulsion he had anticipated. To his surprise, his cock responded to the feel of Frank's hand, even with a towel separating them. Feeling light-headed and euphoric from the grass, he closed his eyes and swam in a pool of delightful anticipation. When Frank's fingers loosened the towel, it was as though it were happening to someone else, in Larry's drugged state of mind. Then, he had the feeling that, no, it was happening to him, but as if in a surrealistic dream.

He felt Frank's hand come to rest on the flatness of his stomach between his belly-button and his pubic hairs. The hand was warm, soft, gentle—not feverishly racing toward his cock, as he had imagined it would. He not only enjoyed the feel of Frank's hand, but he no longer felt that his masculinity was being threatened. As Frank allowed his hands to glide over Larry's muscular body, Larry suddenly realized that he had never been felt up before. With women, it had always been Larry that had done the feeling. The sensation of having his body felt up by gentle, caring hands was more pleasurable than he could have imagined. Frank's hands, floating over his naked body with the lightness of a feather, stimulated his sexual awareness and caused his cock to swell to rigid hardness—and Frank had not yet even touched it.

With graceful fluidity, Frank glided onto the bunk and positioned himself between Larry's legs. Fingers, delicately exploring the sensitive areas on the inside of his thighs, sent shivers of delight racing through Larry's body. Suddenly, there was a warm wetness where his legs met at his groin. Slowly, Larry became aware that Frank's tongue was bathing his nutsack; then it found the base of his majestic tool.

By that time, Larry's cock was begging for attention—bobbing and jerking like a child throwing a tantrum. Frank's hands traced a caressing course along the lines of Larry's body while his tongue licked up the length of the palpitating shaft. Larry was surprised to hear himself moan with pleasure; he had never been vocal or noisy in sex. His sighs escaped involuntarily from somewhere deep inside. Realizing that they were his body's natural, uninhibited responses to these never-before-experienced sensations, he decided not to suppress them.

Frank's tongue reached the tip of Larry's dick and began a flicking, darting, teasing action across the crown. Larry knew from the times he had masturbated that the head of his cock was super-sensitive, yet none of the women who had ever gone down on him had ever thought to do what Frank was doing, and none of them had ever given him reason to believe that a blow-job could be so thoroughly enjoyable. "Blow-jobs are okay," he had once said to a friend, "but it'll never replace fucking." He was no longer quite so sure, because Frank obviously knew what he was doing, and it was rapidly becoming more enjoyable than any piece of ass he had ever had.

He shuddered with delight when Frank's mouth closed around the cap of his prick. At that same instant, he became aware (also for the first time) that his tits were sensitive. He knew, as every boy learns in his early teens, that women were sensitive on their tits; he never thought that men might also be sensitive there. Frank ever-so-gently pinched Larry's nipples as he sucked the head of his cock into his mouth. It aroused Larry and prompted him to thrust his cock forward, meeting a tight, constricted resistance which was more sensual than the tightest cunt he had ever fucked.

The hesitations of a lifetime evaporated. He wondered why he had waited so long. He cursed the months he had wasted since coming to prison; yet he knew that the moment had probably been all the more pleasurable because it had taken so long in coming. Without thinking, he placed his hands on Frank's muscular, fleshy, soft shoulders and began a feverish exploration of his workout partner's body. When he realized what he was doing, he stopped, but instantly continued. He had to admit to himself that he liked the feel of Frank's body—especially while Frank's mouth was milking his cock toward a frenetic climax.

In those moments, he felt a deep bond with Frank. More than a partner, more than a friend, it was a lot like . . . like love. He rapidly dismissed the unbidden thought from his mind.

By then, his whole body was becoming responsive to Frank's expert manipulations, which miraculously converted Larry's entire body into one massive, uninterrupted erogenous zone. No one had ever shown his body so much attention. This was the first time that a man had ever made love to his body, and the only thing he could compare it to was the women he had been with—he had never before known such total involvement; never had his entire body been so turned-on and tuned-in.

His cock pumped furiously into Frank's eager mouth. It seemed as though Frank had a dozen hands: they were everywhere, generating previously unknown delights and wild sensations. Just as Larry was getting ready to explode, one of Frank's fingers found his asshole. Larry was about to "draw the line" and tell Frank to leave his ass alone, but it was too late. From deep inside, the eruption commenced. He felt his stomach muscles contract and the muscles around his eyes tighten. Then the first surge of cum raced from his testicles into the shaft of his swollen cock and gushed, with an explosive fury, into Frank's mouth. Larry wrapped his legs around Frank's torso as his body convulsed and writhed in spastic tremors. Frank's index finger popped into Larry's virgin ass and probed deeply. To his astonishment, Larry had to admit that the finger heightened the total sensuality of the orgasm. His ass squeezed tightly on the finger as his cock continued to shoot loads of stored-up cum.

Once again, that unbidden thought—*I love you*—flitted into his mind. In the heat and passion of orgasm, he let the thought linger. For a brief instant, he recalled his first orgasm. At twelve, he had discovered that by rubbing the head of his dick long enough he could experience a remarkable and enjoyable sensation. He had never forgotten that first orgasm. This first time with Frank had been like rediscovering one of the most memorable moments of his life.

Now, sitting in the cell that they had shared for little over a month, quietly enjoying the sight of the man he had come to love so intensely, the memory of that first time was as fresh in his mind as that morning's workout. Less than two months had passed, during which time Larry had slowly broken down the barriers. At first, he had been unable to reciprocate sexually; but he had wanted to. Frank had not tried to get him to—it was all Larry's idea. And it hadn't been easy to overcome society's bigoted brainwashing against man-love. The thought of putting another man's cock into his mouth had been an abhorrent concept, overcome only by his deepening love for this guy. When at last he had done it—forcing himself to go down on Frank's cock—he had discovered that it hadn't been repulsive at all; in fact, it had been exciting and unlike anything he had imagined in his wildest dreams.

Yes. He truly loved this guy. He had never really known what love was until Frank had come into his life. *Funny,* he thought, *I had to get busted and come to prison to find what happiness is really all about.* A year ago, he had thought that homosexuality was probably the sickest thing on earth. Six months ago, he had come to tolerate it. Seven weeks ago, he found out that he had been a narrow-minded bigot. Today, he knew what "Gay Pride" meant. If loving Frank more than anyone or anything else on earth meant that he was gay, then he was gay—and damned proud of it.

Frank stirred, yawned, and stretched his powerful muscles. To Larry, there was nothing more beautiful than the wildly seductive poses Frank struck when stretching. He uncrossed his legs and moved to Frank's bunk. The two men pressed their sweaty bodies close together and gently kissed. "Have a good nap?" Larry asked.

"Mmmmm," Frank replied affirmatively. "Did you get any sleep?"

"No, I sat on my bunk watching you most of the time. I love to watch you. I was remembering the first time we had sex together, and I was thinking about what a helluva lucky guy I am."

"What time is it?" Frank got up and went to the little basin at the rear of the cell. He splashed cold water into his face.

Larry looked at his watch. Ever since Frank's watch had been stolen five months earlier, Frank had constantly had to ask Larry for the time. "Ten to three. It's almost time for Yard Recall. Which reminds me, Baby Jim came by. He said he would be back after Recall."

"Oh, good!" Frank began to dry his face. "Hand me the roll of toilet paper under my mattress, will you?" Since the prison issued no pillows, it was common for the inmates to put a roll of tissue under the head of the mattress, to elevate the head.

Taking the roll from Larry, Frank carefully removed the wrapper and withdrew a ten-dollar bill. He handed the bill to Larry. "This is for Baby Jim; he's bringing a balloon. Now that you're officially my old-man, I want *you* to pay for it when he brings it."

"You never cease to amaze me, Frank. I haven't seen a ten-spot since I got busted. Where did you manage to get green money?"

"I've had it for a long time, Lare. Frenchy used to always give me a ten whenever I . . . never mind. Hey! Get that hurt look outta your eyes. I haven't turned a trick since you moved in. That's the last of the wine. You don't want me to turn any more tricks, so I haven't. I love you, too, Larry; your love for me ain't a one-way street. Once you pay Baby Jim for the grass today, that's all there is until we figure out some other way to make money."

Larry felt as though he had been slapped. He knew that Frank had not intended it that way, but Larry suddenly realized that his lover had been paying for all the grass and that he, Larry, had not contributed a dime. Something had to be done. It was his turn to chip in for the few niceties; one way or another, he would do it.

II. FRENCHY

The few men who had dared to brave the oppressive heat and go outside to the exercise yard were beginning to wilt and to seek the precious little shade to be found against the west wall of the enclosed area. The only men without shirts were the ones who had already sun-ripened into deep, dark tans. All others, even the usually semi-nude weight-lifters, were covered against the merciless sun.

"Frenchy" Lefebvre, leader of the White Power Nazis, and a handful of Lieutenants in the white supremacy gang, which exercised control over most (if not all) of the white inmates, stood against the concrete wall. To his right was "Shotgun" Willis; to his left stood Wayne Carver. Most of the members of the gang took on nicknames, such as Moose, Whitey, Zapper, and so on. But Wayne needed no other handle than his own last name—he was noted for his expertise with a knife.

"It's gotta be Weasel," Frenchy said with finality. "He's the only mule that didn't get skin-shook yesterday. Three mules get popped with the shit on 'em. Weasel don't even get shook down."

"Yeah," said Moose, "but ya gotta admit, he delivered the shit."

Shotgun interrupted. "Yeah, but to who? To Dakota, that's who! And whose cell got shook down last night?"

"We know, Shotgun," said Frenchy. "It was a good thing that Baby Jim connected before chow. Fuckin' pigs tore Dakota's cell to shreds lookin' for the stash."

Zapper, the quietest of the group, said, "I think we oughta be real sure before we waste him. Weasel's been a damn good mule . . ."

"Maybe too good," Shotgun interrupted again. "It's funny he never gets caught when mules right and left get busted."

Frenchy raised both hands, palms outward—the sign that discussion had come to an end. "Carver?"

"Dust him."

One by one, Frenchy polled his lieutenants. The verdict—and the sentence—was unanimous: *Dust him.* Even Zapper, after a moment's hesitation, concurred. Weasel had been found guilty of being a snitch; his sentence was death.

"Who wants it?" Frenchy asked.

Carver answered, "I'll take it. It'll give me pleasure to carve up that snitch's ass."

Frenchy shook his head. "No, Wayne. The way I've got it figured, I want you in the cell house when it happens. I'll run that past ya later. Who else?"

"CLEAR THE YARD. YARD RECALL. ALL MEN RETURN TO YOUR CELLS." The loudspeaker, suspended on the wall twenty feet above Frenchy's head, blared through their conversation.

The announcement was repeated. When the speaker was silent, Shotgun spoke. "I'll take it. I'll get a nut cuttin' the punk."

"Okay. Me and Shotgun will work out the details later. But the rest of you guys, get this: When Shotgun wastes Weasel, that'll be the signal to cut loose. I want this joint torn apart. I mean, we're gonna make Santa Fe and Attica look like picnics. Got it?"

"YOU MEN BY BUILDING: CLEAR THE YARD. LOCK-UP."

"Fuck you, screw!"

"Don't push it, Reynolds!"

"Hold on to your cock, pig!"

Frenchy gave a sign, saying, "Knock it off! Let's not blow it for tomorrow." He led his lieutenants across the yard to the entrance of the cell house. After the pat-down, Frenchy said to Whitey: "Weasel lives on the second floor, north side, right?" When Whitey confirmed this, Frenchy continued, "Get word to Steve Brackman. Tell him to send Weasel to see me tonight. Eight-thirty. Make sure Steve don't go scaring the punk, neither."

III. STEVE

A lot of guys who never thought about body-building before coming to prison find that the long, idle, empty hours behind bars provide the ideal opportunity to devote themselves to the development of powerful, impressive physiques. Moreover, physical strength is an asset in an environment where the strong subjugate the weak. Steve was one of those rare individuals who knew both sides of the coin quite well.

At seventeen, he had been sent to prison for armed robbery. He had been totally unprepared for the living nightmare which he was forced to live for the next two-and-a-half years. Steve had been a "pretty boy"—one of those unfortunate teenagers who was much too pretty for his own good. He had been brutally raped during his first week, and for more than two years had been forced to submit to every imaginable sex act. He had been *turned-out,* made into a punk, and he suffered every indignity that hardened cons can heap onto the weak. That particular prison had had no such thing as Protective Custody—a man either survived or he didn't, depending on no other factor than his own mettle. Only by swallowing his pride, along with a lot of cum, and by making the best out of insufferable situations did Steve manage to survive. He was twenty when he got out.

For five years, he avoided getting into trouble. He moved to one of the western states, met a girl, got married, had a daughter, and had put the past out of his mind. Then had come the divorce, precipitating long periods of depression. He soon found himself in prison again, for robbery. He had developed into a strikingly handsome man, and years of hard work as a laborer had developed his once-frail body into a hardened, lithe physique. Even so, he had set to work immediately upon arriving at the prison, pumping iron every day with a zest that bordered on fanaticism. He was determined to never again be turned-out and made into a punk.

He had met Frank on the weight pile. Frank was openly gay, but not a punk, not a turn-out. Steve had been flattered by Frank's attentions, and when he realized that he, Steve, would not have to reciprocate sexually, he entered into a relationship with Frank. In time, he had been taken into the White Power Nazis. Unlike his first time in prison, Steve was now counted among the strong, not the weak.

But Frank had stirred some long-suppressed emotions deep inside of Steve. He wasn't introspective enough to delve into those emotions, nor did he try to understand them. The relationship between the two men had finally disintegrated. He did not realize that his antagonism toward Frank was a subconscious transferral of his own self-hate for having been a punk his first time in prison; nor could he have understood that the hatred he felt toward Larry Jonas was actually sublimated jealousy.

A psychologist could have written an entire text book based on Steve's case history. Steve's move to the second floor of the old cell house—superficially a move to get away from Frank—was actually motivated by the fact that most of the younger, prettier cons were celled there. Steve would never have admitted this to himself, of course. To his way of thinking, his developing interest in Tommy, a nineteen-year-old "fish," was nothing more than the strong exerting power over the weak. Despite the hell he went through at Tommy's age, Steve felt no remorse for what he was about to do. To Steve, it was a simple matter: The strong take from the weak. He had once been weak and had had to suffer the consequences; but now, the shoe was on the other foot.

That's just the way things were—when you're a freshman, you take the hazings of the upper-classmen; when you're a senior, you're in the position to dish it out.

Steve was lying on his bunk, planning his moves against Tommy, when Whitey appeared at his cell door. He was suddenly aware that he had developed a hard-on, thinking about the nineteen-year-old, and that his cock had poked its way through the slit in his boxer shorts. Seeing Whitey, he swung his legs over the edge of the bunk and sat up, tucking his cock back into his shorts.

"It's Weasel," said Whitey, a twenty-two-year-old Nazi who owed his nickname to his almost white blond hair. "Frenchy, Carver, Shotgun, and the rest of us figured it out. Shotgun'll hit him tomorrow. The hit will be the signal to cut loose."

Whitey had entered the cell and was sitting on the bunk next to Steve. If Whitey had not been a Nazi, he would probably have been a punk—he was very good looking. Luckily for him, his older brother had been a Nazi, which had automatically made Whitey eligible for membership in the "brotherhood."

"Frenchy wants you to tell Weasel that he wants to see him, but he said not to scare him. Don't let on about what's comin' down."

"Why me?" Steve asked.

"He didn't say. Just told me to tell you. Just make sure you don't scare him. Make it casual-like." Whitey got up and left the cell.

Steve watched the movement of Whitey's buns as the younger man walked out. When he was out of hearing range, Steve muttered softly, "If you weren't a brother, I'd fuck you!"

IV. TOMMY

He looked up as Whitey passed his cell. Tommy had spoken to the blond-haired guy just once, and he was hoping to become friends with him. He knew that he was going to need friends, and as a brother in the Nazis, Whitey would have been a valuable ally. Unfortunately, Whitey had shown no inclination to establishing a friendship with a non-brother.

Tommy let out a long sigh. He had never felt so lonely in his entire life. And scared. Yeah, he had to admit it: He was afraid. He was completely alone; and the stories he had heard about what happens to good-looking youngsters in prison—stories he had once scoffed at—now seemed amazingly close to reality. He had already over-heard too many comments made about his "pretty ass," and he had been unnerved by that guy Steve Brackman.

For four days, he had not taken a shower, for fear of what might happen. Washing in the sink had been okay, but he knew that he needed a good shower. Sooner or later, he would have to overcome his fears. So far (he reasoned), no one had actually done anything, and Steve had actually been friendly toward him—so what was he getting up-tight about? When he thought about it, he realized that he had overheard a lot of sex talk. But it had all been just a bunch of guys kidding each other.

"Fuck it," he said aloud. He stripped to his shorts, grabbed his towel and soap, and went to take a shower.

After an uneventful, but invigorating, shower, he returned to his cell, his towel wrapped around his waist because he didn't want to put his dirty shorts back on. He stood in front of the polished sheet of stainless steel which served as a mirror and combed his thick, wavy black hair. He smirked at himself for having been afraid to take a shower. He thought to himself: *all that rape crap is just a bunch of bullshit.*

Before pulling out a clean pair of shorts, he unwrapped the towel and began to give himself a once-over dry-off. His body was smooth, almost hairless. He had been jealous of those guys in high school who developed hairy chests and legs at early ages. Hell, he hadn't even grown any pubic hair until he was almost fifteen. And even though he shaved a couple of times each week, he couldn't seem to cultivate anything but peach-fuzz on his handsome, boyish face.

Tommy was strikingly handsome, a beautiful young man. He had soft brown eyes, with long lashes, a small, turned-up nose, sensuous lips, flawless complexion, and a body which he knew attracted homos. But he was miserably unhappy about the length of time it was taking his body to ripen into manhood.

"Hi, kid."

Tommy looked up to see Steve Brackman standing at the open cell door. "Oh, hi, Steve. I'm just about to get some clothes on; come on in." He noticed that Steve was wearing nothing but his shorts.

"Don't bother. For what I've got in mind, you don't need any clothes, kid."

Tommy froze. A cold shiver shot up his spine. His knees felt weak, and his stomach turned queasy. He hoped that Steve was joking, but one look at those steel-gray eyes told him that this was no joke.

"Wha . . . what do you mean, Steve?" The words came out in a hoarse whisper.

Steve took a few steps into the cell and snapped the towel out of Tommy's hands. "It's initiation time. I'm gonna fuck you, kid."

V. WHITEY

He had forgotten to tell Steve to tell Weasel that Frenchy wanted to see him at eight-thirty. Walking back to Steve's cell, he noticed the new fish, Tommy, in the shower with his back turned. Whitey had stopped for a few seconds to admire the slender legs topped by fleshy mounds of silky-smooth skin. Whitey had never fucked another guy before, even though he had let the sissy, Stella, suck his dick several times. Watching the water glide over those soft-looking buns, his cock had gotten excited.

Hurrying back to Steve's cell, he wondered what it would be like to be able to fuck someone like Tommy in the shower. Steve had told him of his plans to turn-out the nineteen-year-old. So after delivering the balance of the message from Frenchy, he told Steve that Tommy was in the shower.

Steve asked Whitey to come along to stand point. "Once I've fucked him," Steve said, "I'll stand point while you do it."

There was no one walking along the tier as they arrived at Tommy's cell. Whitey watched as Steve grabbed the towel and slapped the kid, knocking him back onto the bunk. Tommy struggled, but he was no match for someone as strong as Steve. Watching the naked teenager attempt to wrestle the almost naked Steve gave Whitey a throbbing hard-on. He wondered if raping a woman would be just as easy—and just as exciting.

Remembering his duty as point, he looked up and down the length of the tier. No one was in sight. He returned his attention to Steve and Tommy. Steve had flipped the young man onto his stomach; his cock (*a huge thing,* thought Whitey) was protruding from the opening in his shorts, just as it had done earlier when Whitey had delivered Frenchy's message the first time. Steve drove a fist into Tommy's back, knocking the wind out of him. He then slid his shorts to his knees. Whitey was even more amazed at the size of Steve's cock, seeing it fully erect and no longer hidden.

He watched Steve spit into his hands, then smear the spit on his cockhead. Unaware of his own actions—he was so engrossed with watching the rape scene inside the cell—Whitey rubbed his hand against the pulsating cock in his jeans, just as Steve rammed his cock into Tommy's ass.

Tommy let out a cry of pain, and Whitey again looked around to see if anyone was coming. One guy was approaching from the other end of the tier. He had a towel around his neck, so he would stop at the shower, located at the midpoint of the forty cells; the guy would not come as far as Tommy's cell.

Whitey looked back into the cell. Steve was pumping away at that beautiful ass. The kid was gripping the edges of the mattress. Whitey could hear him crying quietly, with an occasional "Stop. Please stop." For a brief instant, he felt sorry for the kid; but he quickly repressed that feeling and began to wish that Steve would hurry. Whitey wanted his turn.

Finally, with a deep thrust of his cock into Tommy's ass, Steve reached his climax. Watching him in the throes of orgasm was a new experience for Whitey. He had never been a voyeur—in fact, he laughed at guys who liked to watch. But he had become so excited and sexually aroused while watching Steve fuck the struggling kid, that he almost creamed his jeans. He knew it wouldn't take him long to shoot his load once he climbed on top and stuck his throbbing cock into that sweet ass.

Steve withdrew, pulled up his shorts, and crawled off the bunk. Whitey overheard him tell the sweaty Tommy, "Lie still, kid. You've got one more customer. And unless you want us to beat the shit out of you, you'll stay right where you are." Tommy looked up into Whitey's eyes, then buried his head into the blanket again.

Steve took Whitey's place outside the cell and Whitey hurriedly took off all of his clothes, including his socks and shorts, because he liked to be totally naked for sex. His body was almost as hairless as Tommy's, but weight-lifting had given him beautifully symmetric definition. His cock had lost none of its hardness.

As he crawled between Tommy's legs, the sight of that slender, delicate body and those plump buns sent a thrill surging through Whitey's loins. His cock, wet from pre-cum, slid easily into the ass that Steve had already loosened up. He lowered himself onto Tommy's hot body and felt the heat from both of their bodies become more intense.

God! He's so smooth. Just like fuckin' a broad, Whitey thought, as his hands began to feel the body of the boy beneath him. His cock glided in and out of Tommy's ass with deliberate slowness. Despite Steve's earlier use, Tommy's ass was wonderfully tight. The kid had not yet learned how to relax. Whitey could feel the tension in every one of the kid's muscles.

He pulled his cock back, all the way to its head, then slowly shoved it back into the hot wet interior, forcing it as deeply as it would go. He was trying to prolong the pleasure, but it didn't work. He could feel the cum ready to erupt. It was too quick. So he vowed to himself to come back later that evening. There would be no opportunity to come back tomorrow, but he was determined to fuck this kid when he could take his time and enjoy it.

He was ready to cum. So he accelerated his strokes, his body slapping feverishly against those oh-so-soft buns. With a violent shudder, he rammed his cock deep and felt his cum spurting through his cock. *Oh, God! It feels so goddam good.* His body jerked and trembled with pleasure.

Steve came into the cell, just as Whitey crawled off Tommy. "That was real good, kid," Steve said, tugging on Tommy's shoulder to make him look up. "From now on, you belong to me and Whitey. Do you understand? Whenever either one of us wants to fuck, you'll fuck. On the other hand, kid, we'll take good care of you. You need anything, just let one of us know. If anyone gives you a bad time, just tell us; we'll take care of it. You're gonna be around for a couple of years. Me and Whitey will also be here for a long time; so let's be good to each other, okay?"

Whitey wanted to correct Steve: Whitey was going to be one of those guys in on the escape tomorrow during the riot—he would not be here for a long time. But he couldn't say anything. Steve was not one of those guys who had been let in on the escape plans. As far as Whitey was concerned, after tomorrow the kid belonged entirely to Steve. So he merely stood there and agreed with Steve as he spelled out the rules of the game to Tommy.

None of the three men gathered in that tiny cell on that hot afternoon knew what the next day would bring. Tommy had no idea that a riot was being planned. Steve had no idea that an escape was being planned to coincide with the riot. Whitey knew about both the riot and the escape.

What none of them knew was that each of them had less than twenty-four hours to live.

VI. WEASEL

Fifteen years was a lot of time to take out of a man's life for one simple, stupid mistake. Mike "The Weasel" Weaver had broken down and cried when the judge had imposed the heavy-handed sentence. Everyone had assured him that a simple strong-arm robbery was considered a "lightweight beef." Everyone had told him that court would go easy on a twenty-year-old. Everyone had told him. And everyone had been wrong.

Weasel, who had been given the unattractive nickname because of his resemblance to the furry animal of the same name, had become an easy "mark" for Lieutenant Ramos, Chief of Investigations at the prison. The Lieutenant made it a habit to interview all new inmates, carefully judging them as to their potential use to Staff. Ramos quickly assessed Weasel as a man who could be manipulated, threatened, bribed, coerced, and scared into doing anything Staff asked of him. Ramos, promising Weasel that he would get early action at the Parole Board, had easily recruited the young man as an informer.

A thousand times, Weasel had regretted having acquiesced to the easy promises of the overly-friendly Ramos. "A lot of good it's doin' me!" he had often mumbled in the privacy of his cell on the second floor. "I've got to do four years in this hell-hole before I even get to see what a Parole Commissioner looks like. Will I live that long?"

Weasel knew that Frenchy and his gang were not stupid, nor were they blind. It was just a matter of time before they put the finger on him as a snitch. When that happened, would he be able to get to Ramos before Frenchy got to Weasel? He had managed to survive for two and a half years, so far; but what about the next year and a half before he could get to the Parole Board? Just last night, the "goon squad" had tried to bust Dakota, based on the information Weasel had given to Ramos. The bust had failed. Dakota's cell was clean. But why? Why had the grass and dope been moved out of Dakota's cell? Did Frenchy already suspect Weasel?

And now, Steve Brackman had just come by to tell him that Frenchy wanted to see him later. Steve had been friendly enough, but Weasel's guilt was beginning to play havoc with his imagination. He was scared to death to go up to the third floor to Frenchy's cell. He could get himself killed before he had the chance to go to

Control. Ramos worked days, but he had told Weasel to see Lt. Averill if anything ever happened on the third shift. Lt. Averill stayed in Control, except in the case of emergencies. It was impossible for an inmate to get to Control on the third shift unless that, too, was an emergency. And if Frenchy knew that Weasel was an informer, Weasel could be dead before he could reach help. Lieutenant Averill would then have an emergency on his hands to break up the tranquility of the third shift, and he would have to come out of Control into the cell house. But by then, it would be too late for Weasel.

Looking at his watch, Weasel wondered if he would suffer a nervous breakdown during the hour he still had to wait before going up to the third floor. Nervously grabbing his coffee cup, he left his cell and walked quickly along the tier to the mop closet where he ran the hot water until it was steaming hot. He filled his cup and returned to his cell. As he was stirring instant coffee into the cup, someone passed his open cell then stopped abruptly.

"Hi, Weasel," an effeminate man called out. "Can I come in?"

"Sure, Stella. Come on in."

Stella was in his mid-thirties. With plucked eyebrows, eye liner, and lip rouge, Stella was typical of many joint sissies who played the feminine role to the hilt. There was a time when all out-front gay men had been expected to play this role. More and more gay men, like Frank, were maintaining their manly images. Stella's type, though, was still common enough because a lot of straight men were simply unable to accept men like Frank as gay. They could understand the Stella types, but not the Frank types. A lot of men, like Weasel, felt more comfortable around the effeminate types—it somehow made the homosexual experience seem like less of a threat toward their own masculinity. To Weasel, Stella was more woman than man. In fact, it was difficult to think of Stella as a man. There was nothing masculine about him.

Stella swished into the cell. "Feel like some screamin' skull tonight, Weasel?" she asked. "It's been over a week since I wrapped these hot lips around your gorgeous tool."

Weasel was about to decline the offer but changed his mind. "Yeah," he answered. "That sounds great, Stella. I think that's exactly what I need, in my present frame of mind."

VII. STELLA

She had been around prisons since she was eighteen; she had been a graduate of juvenile homes and youth centers before that. She was one hundred percent gay and loved every minute of it. Prison brought her no terrors: she was at home behind bars, comfortable in other men's cells, delirious between men's legs. She was, at heart, a chicken queen. She loved and adored guys between the ages of fourteen and twenty-six because the first loves of her life had been those sweet, hairless, smooth, adolescents she had grown up with. So even now, in a men's prison, where the youngest was at least eighteen, she still found lots of young men to suit her tastes. As a matter of survival, she naturally gave herself up to older men—when she had to, but *only* when she had to.

Weasel was just her type: twenty-years old, boyish, sexy as hell, hairless, and hung like a stud horse. Actually, she had no type. She loved men. As long as they were young, smooth, and hung, it didn't matter what they looked like. A stringy, pimply-faced kid with an eight inch cock was just as gorgeous to her as a beefed-up Adonis with only five inches.

She wasn't at all like that faggot, Frank. To Stella, Frank was a snotty, holier-than-thou queen who thought she was too good for the likes of Stella simply because Frank was straight-acting. Even so, she was glad that the Franks of this world existed—Frank took a lot of the older-guys' pressure off Stella, leaving her free to enjoy as many of the younger types as she could persuade to crawl into bed with her.

With expertise, she grabbed one of Weasel's blankets and hung it across the cell door opening. Turning to face Weasel, she extracted a marijuana cigarette from her shirt pocket, tossed it to him, and told him to fire it up. "This is some of the stuff that you brought in just yesterday," she said. "It's dynamite. But I guess you already know it."

"Yeah," Weasel admitted. "It's good shit. Did you have to buy it?" Weasel, naturally, still had his own personal stash left over and would have smoked some of it with Stella, had she not brought her own.

"Oh, no! Not me!" she insisted. "I haven't *bought* grass in years. I always make those Nazi guys pay me. Like Whitey. God, I'm such a slut. I actually charge him to suck his dick. Are you kidding? I would eat a mile of his shit just to smell his asshole. But a girl has to do things to get ahead in this world."

"Who do you like best?" Weasel asked, through choked breath, as he passed the joint to Stella. "Me or Whitey?"

"There's no comparison," she insisted. "Whitey is built better than you are—and I must admit that I like muscles—but he's got a snotty attitude. Thinks he's better than everyone else, just because he's a Nazi. Big fuckin' deal! I enjoy sucking him off, and I enjoy feeling his body, but otherwise I can't stand to be around him. But *you!* I like you because you're so sweet to me." She passed the joint back to him. "And you've got a bigger cock."

"Do you like it when a guy's got a big cock?"

"Only if he knows what to do with it. And you, Weasel, you know what to do with it." She put her hand on his crotch and felt the young man's rod stirring beneath the denims.

They finished the joint and Weasel stripped. Stella watched as he removed his shirt, revealing a slender, ripening body. There were tiny tufts of hair in his armpits, but otherwise his body was as smooth as a baby's butt. Even the area between his belly-button and his groin was devoid of hair. His forearms had the slightest hint of downy fur. Until Weasel removed his jeans, Stella was able to enjoy the highly erotic visual aspect of his flawless body. When the jeans came off, Weasel's cock jutted out from a small patch of pubic hairs. His thighs were as hairless as his chest, and only on the young man's calves was there any hint of the type of pelt which covered more mature bodies and which were definite turn-offs for Stella.

She sank to her knees while Weasel was still standing. She let her hands grip his small, firm buns as she licked the boy's shaft. Weasel's cock was maybe seven inches or so, but sticking out from his slender, smooth body, it seemed much longer. Stella had seen eight inch cocks growing out of such thick patches of pubic hairs that they looked smaller than Weasel's.

Her tongue glided over the silky smooth instrument as one of her hands reached between Weasel's thighs and gripped his testicles firmly. *I love the silky feel of those hairless balls,* Stella thought. She pulled on Weasel's nutsac, forcing the upright cock down, then slid her mouth over the slick cock which she had prepared with her tongue. As her lips wrapped around the swollen tool, Weasel thrust his cock deep into her throat and tightened the muscles of his buttocks. Stella squeezed his testicles and his bun in response to the tightening. Weasel let out an audible gasp of pleasure.

Stella pulled away and stood up, running her hands along the smooth contours of his lithe, lean body. Weasel's tits were almost perfectly round—the same size as a nickel—and his nipples were tiny erect dots, set squarely in the center. She leaned over and sucked the left tit into her mouth and rubbed her groin against his.

She nibbled her way up his chest to his neck, then whispered, "Lie down." She pulled away, and Weasel lay down on the bunk. Of all the guys with whom Stella would occasionally get down, Weasel was the most seductive in his poses. Just lying there on the bunk, he looked to Stella like a young Greek god waiting to be worshipped.

She crawled between his legs and licked the insides of his legs. Her hands reached upward to caress his flat, silky smooth chest. Then her mouth found and sucked the youth's nuts while his cock bobbed with eager anticipation. Weasel's hands found Stella's shoulders and began a gentle massage, just as Stella's tongue began to lick its way up the length of his rigid cock. When her tongue reached the crown of Weasel's dick, her tongue licked across the top of it, teasing and toying with it. Weasel moaned with delight.

"Suck my dick," he murmured. "Suck that big piece of meat."

Stella loved the way Weasel talked while they were having sex. It excited her to have him tell her what to do, when to do it, and how to do it.

"Play with my nuts," came Weasel's command, and Stella's right hand gently tugged on the young man's nutsac. Weasel moaned. "Oh, yeah! God, that feels so good." He then lifted his legs and wrapped them around Stella's body. She felt her shoulders pressing against the backs of his slender, muscular thighs. She opened her eyes and drank in his baby-soft stomach, a sight she loved when his legs were in the air. It gave his youthful body a roundness at the waist that she delighted in.

"Play with my ass," Weasel insisted.

Her right hand slid away from his nuts. At first, she simply let the palm of her hand massage the area near his rectum, then slowly her index finger began to probe the rosebud of muscles around Weasel's ass.

Stella knew that Weasel was one of Frenchy's "mules"—that he often keystered grass and other dope and brought it in from the visiting room. Stella had surmised that the regular practice of putting something up his ass had become an erogenous stimulant. The first time she had tried to toy with his ass, he had objected strenuously; but slowly he had given in. Now, whenever they had sex, it was Weasel who always asked Stella for the anal stimulation. *One of these days,* Stella mused to herself, *I'm going to fuck this boy. He likes me to play with his ass too much.*

Stella felt her own cock throbbing wildly as she inserted both her index and middle fingers into Weasel's rectum. Weasel responded by thrusting his cock deeper into Stella's mouth and by squirming pleasurably.

"Eat me, Stella!"

She knew that he didn't mean: suck my cock; he meant: lick my ass.

She pulled her mouth away from his cock and pushed against his thighs, motioning him to lift his legs even higher. He complied as her left hand reached around his right leg and grabbed his pulsating dick. She licked his balls, then even lower. Her nose nudged that nameless area between the bottom of his scrotum and his ass, then pushed even harder against his thighs. Weasel eased his butt even higher.

Her tongue now found the anal orifice. Having satisfied herself that he was clean—she had taken a good smell before permitting her tongue to venture too close—she licked around the tight opening, as her left hand stroked Weasel's cock firmly.

She heard him moan with delight as her tongue touched, then forced its way into his tight ass.

"Oooh," Weasel murmured. "I'm going to cum!"

Stella quickly retreated; Weasel lowered his legs. Her mouth quickly found his swollen organ and descended on it with a feverish zeal. She then felt his thighs pressing against her, his hands clasped around her neck, and his body arched forward. Suddenly, Weasel's body lifted from the bunk, hanging onto Stella like a sloth hanging from a tree branch. His pelvis pounded away at her face as he exploded with a fury. His young body shot load after load of hot, delicious cum into her mouth.

One of the things Stella liked about Weasel was that he seemed to take forever to shoot his wad. Time and time again, his cock ejaculated into her; his body was like a jackhammer. He seemed to have an almost inexhaustible supply of sperm, and it was never bitter.

Gradually, he loosened his grip on her and let his body slowly sink back to the bunk. For a long time, she continued to suck on his cock; it seemed to stay hard forever, even after multiple orgasms. When she was in the mood to do him more than once in an evening, she knew exactly how to keep him aroused. One afternoon, she had actually sucked him off four times in a row, and his cock had never gone soft. Tonight, however, once was enough. She had already decided that she was going to pay a visit to the new fish, Tommy, and see if she could get anywhere with him. She doubted if she would be successful immediately, but she had to break the ice sometime, and tonight would be the night.

She crawled from between Weasel's legs and sat on the edge of the bunk, running her hand over his slight chest.

"Hey, Weasel," a voice came from outside the cell. "You in there?"

Weasel responded with something that Stella had taught him to use on just such an occasion. "I'm on the shitter."

"It's me, Frenchy. You don't mind if I come in while you're on the shitter, do ya? It won't take but a minute."

Without waiting for Weasel's answer, Frenchy drew the blanket aside and walked into the cell.

Stella hastily stood up and said, "Frenchy Lefebvre. Shame on you! How would you like it if someone had just walked in on you and me when we were having sex?"

Frenchy flushed. "Oh, hey, man, I'm sorry. I really thought the guy was actually on the shitter. I'm sorry if I busted you two in the act." He smiled sheepishly.

"Naw, that's awright," Weasel answered. He got off the bed and wrapped a towel around himself. "We was through, anyway."

Stella, who had been in bed with Frenchy often enough to be able to say things to him that other guys wouldn't dare, continued, "But what if we had *not* been finished? I think you're very rude, Frenchy . . ."

"Shut up, Stella," Frenchy said evenly. "I just came down to tell ya," he said to Weasel, "that you don't gotta bother to come up to my cell tonight. I had to come down to the second floor to see Steve. So what I had to tell ya, I can say it quick."

Frenchy patted Stella on the ass, then sat on Weasel's bunk. "I've got another mule job for ya, tomorrow. I'll meet you on the yard after breakfast and run the details past you. It ain't no biggie; just another keyster job—some grass. Ain't no big deal. I'll meet with you and Shotgun tomorrow mornin' on the weight pile. I just wanted to tell you not to make plans for tomorrow afternoon." He stood up and went to the cell door. "Be there. After breakfast."

"Sure thing, Frenchy," Weasel answered.

Frenchy reached into a back pocket and brought out two joints. He handed them to Stella. "Here, sweet cakes, you and the Weasel go ahead and smoke these, okay?" With that, he was gone.

VIII. BABY JIM

The hot water cascaded over his youthful physique as he lathered his body one last time before rinsing off. Baby Jim was the youngest of the Nazi "brothers" and had managed to become a "prospect" for the group at the age of seventeen only because he had met several tests, one of which had been that he had been the victor in three separate fights against some of the gang's toughest members. Baby Jim was no one to fool with. Standing only five-feet seven-inches, his body was a compact mass of tight, taut, powerful muscles. He was now twenty but still looked no more than seventeen. He had been sentenced to life in prison for the murder of his own mother, whom he had caught in bed with a strange man. His father had been out of town on business, and Jim was supposed to be at school.

He had come home early, had seen a strange car in the driveway, had sneaked into the house, and had overheard his mother and this guy talking about Jim's father in such a way that made him furious. Jim loved his father with an idealistic fervor, and it had hurt to realize that his mother had not only given his father "horns," she and this creep in bed with her were ridiculing the old man. He had gone out to the garage, found a tire wrench, and had gone back inside. By that time, the creep was dressed. When he barged into the room, wielding the tire iron with murderous intent, the creep had escaped. His mother had cringed on the bed, shouting at him, yelling, begging him to stop.

Suddenly, he had been overcome by a tremendous calm. With cold-blooded deliberation, he took his mother by the throat and strangled her to death, refusing to release his iron-like grip until she had given up the ghost with a terrible death spasm.

He had never told anyone the truth; he couldn't bring himself to let his father wear the horns his mother had placed on him. His father would never know that Jim had killed her in order to redeem his honor. Jim had steadfastly refused to give any reason for the murder. The case had taken on a great deal of notoriety which had preceded him to prison. Even the hardened cons couldn't understand why or how a guy could kill his own mother; so Jim had been forced into several fights. His many victories and his steadfast refusal to give up any of the details of his crime made him an excellent candidate for membership in the White Power group.

At seventeen, his only future was life behind bars. He learned quickly how to manipulate things for himself, both people and circumstances. He recognized the fact that membership in the Nazis would be to his distinct advantage. He proved to be correct in his judgement.

And now, freedom was just around the corner. Frenchy had decided that Baby Jim should be one of the few allowed to escape with him. As he rinsed the soap from his body, Baby Jim smiled, thinking about the plans for tomorrow. After three years in prison, he knew he couldn't bear the thought of spending the rest of his life there. The smell of freedom was in his nostrils; and now, it was so close.

He dried off and walked down the tier to his cell, which he shared with a sissy named "Brandy." Baby Jim was not the type to allow the opinions of others to interfere with his pleasures. Some guys weren't strong enough to stand up under the teasing of their fellow inmates, but Baby Jim, looking at a lifetime deprived of women, had readily fallen in with a homosexual who would take care of his sexual needs. The first sissy to bed him down had been Frank. He had been followed by a succession of others, until Brandy had come along. Brandy was more to Baby Jim's liking. Brandy was fairly young (twenty-four) and rather effeminate, without being too flamboyant (like Stella). What's more, Brandy kept her mouth shut and asked no questions, a trait that Baby Jim appreciated.

Walking into the cell, Jim saw Brandy standing in front of the mirror, combing her long blond hair. Brandy was an excellent complement to Baby Jim: She had fair skin to Jim's swarthy dark looks; she was tall, to Jim's shortness; she was slender to Jim's massive bulkiness. To Jim, Brandy looked feminine enough to allow his imagination to run wild when they were in bed. Frank had been too masculine, Stella too much like a faggot, and the rest of them fell somewhere in between.

He walked up behind Brandy and wrapped his arms around her waist. He felt the sissy push backward into his groin, gyrating her pelvis in a seductive dance.

"Let's fuck," Baby Jim whispered in a brutish tone.

"Not now," Brandy's husky voice teased, "I've got a headache." She turned around, still wrapped in Jim's arms, a smile playing on her lips. "But I've heard that sex cures headaches." She snuggled her head into his neck-shoulder area and began to nibble where she knew Jim was especially sensitive.

Baby Jim covered the cell door with a blanket while Brandy stripped out of her blue denims. She always wore black bikini briefs, because Baby Jim liked them. She shaved her chest daily, because otherwise the manliness of her body would have been too apparent for Jim's tastes. It wasn't much of a bother, since it only involved shaving around her tits and a tiny patch in the center of her chest. She also shaved her lower abdomen area, which also grew only a trace of hair from the navel down. She had learned early that the more like a real woman she was, the looser Baby Jim would get.

She lay on her bunk, her cock strategically hidden inside the bikini, so that when Jim looked at her, she could easily have been a real woman, except for the lack of breasts. Brandy was pitifully flat chested—even her pectoral muscles were underdeveloped. But with only the littlest amount of imagination, Baby Jim could envision a sexy chick lying on a bed waiting to be seduced.

He sat on the edge of the bed and began the foreplay they both liked so well. Despite the fact that Brandy had too little flesh on her chest to give the impression of breasts, Jim would grip her there anyway and pretend as though he had a handful of titty. He would then begin to lick and nibble his way along Brandy's smooth body to that ever-so-feminine navel. Many was the time he had been so caught up in his own fantasies that he licked his way down her entire body and covered Brandy's crotch with his mouth—the black bikini, with cock neatly tucked out of the way, seemed just like a broad's.

In the meantime, Brandy would let her hands rush feverishly all over Jim's magnificent physique. Jim enjoyed being felt up. He liked it when he was the object of body worship.

He felt Brandy's hand on his cock just as he reached the edge of the bikinis, his tongue enjoying the delightfully smooth feel of her silky body—so much like a woman's. Then he allowed his tongue to penetrate deeper into the bikini, using his nose to nudge it lower. Soon, his tongue was darting amid Brandy's pubic hairs. Her legs were pressed tightly together—her cock tucked between them—and it was like muff-diving. His hands slid into the bikini and began to push it down over the slender hips, then down her thighs. In doing so, Brandy's cock sprung into view, nearly touching Jim on the face. Jim had never really paid a great deal of attention to Brandy's cock. It was usually out of sight, but even when it was in view, Jim was not what they called a "peter gazer."

This time, however, Brandy's cock was close, obvious, near his face, demanding his attention. Baby Jim couldn't help but notice how large the sissy's dick was. By comparison to his own, it was positively huge. The swollen head of Brandy's cock loomed largely in front of him, and for a moment Jim felt an urge to lick it. He fought against that wild impulse; but another thought was also traversing the depths of his brain: *What the hell! I'm gettin' outta here tomorrow. Who's gonna know? And even if Brandy says anything to anyone, what the difference does it make?* On an impulse, he let his tongue touch the fleshy piece of meat. It felt even smoother than the rest of her body, and he was curiously aroused by the sensation.

For a second, he struggled against the urge to put his mouth onto the head of Brandy's cock. Then his macho, virile self-image took over, and he pulled away. He stood up, dropped his towel, and crawled onto the bunk between Brandy's legs. Baby Jim's cock was not a large one: It was exactly six-and-one-quarter inches long, but it was thick.

He pushed against Brandy's legs, pushing them up, exposing her round, hairless buns and her rosy ass, surrounded by downy tufts of almost invisible blond hair. He rarely looked at her cock when he was in that position: on his knees, ready to penetrate. But now he noticed that her cock lay on her stomach like a mammoth tool of pleasure. Even Brandy's balls looked so curiously edible. He couldn't understand it. He had never experienced these emotions before.

It wasn't love. He liked Brandy a lot, but love had never entered the picture. It was lust, pure and simple. But why was he beginning to think about doing things that he had always assumed were unmanly?

Jim's ego was strong, and he managed to put the unwanted thoughts out of his mind. He reached for the jar of vaseline, which Brandy always kept under the mattress near the wall in the center of the bed—just handy enough for Jim to reach without having to interrupt their sexual episodes. He smeared the thick jelly over his pulsating cock and put a dab against Brandy's asshole, rubbing it around erotically. He then scooted closer to her buns and guided his cock into her waiting ass. This was the moment of greatest joy for Jim. Nothing beat the feel of penetration. Even orgasm rated only a second place compared to that initial feel of his cock gliding into that hot, sweet ass.

The head of his cock nudged against Brandy's ass, pressed, then slipped gently into the warm, moist interior of her body. He let a flood of sensations inundate his body, savoring the exquisite feel before slowly gliding his cock deeper. The tight muscles of Brandy's ass offered a controlled resistance to the penetration of Baby Jim's thick, rigid shaft. He then allowed his body to fall forward against her thighs, contorting her body like an acrobat's. He nestled his head in the hollow of her shoulder as he slowly began a rhythmic pumping.

The delightful sensations of bodily fulfillment washed over him, and for a while he was lost in the ecstatic pleasures of the moment. His entire body seemed to tingle with a renewed feeling of being vibrantly alive. He enjoyed the warm contact with another body.

From somewhere in the hidden recesses of his brain, a thought began to emerge, slowly coalescing into an urge. He wanted to make sure that Brandy reached an orgasm, this time. He had never before been concerned about how or when Brandy got a nut—that was her business, not his. Sometimes, it seemed, Brandy would reach an orgasm during sex simply by the sheer pleasure she derived from having Baby Jim fuck her. More often than not, Jim simply assumed that she beat-off in the shower or when he wasn't in the cell. With thoughts of freedom, precious freedom, invigorating him, he was beginning to feel expansive, generous, even considerate. Without retracting his cock, he pulled his body up and was again balanced on his knees, Brandy's legs around his shoulders.

Tentatively, he felt down the length of her body. When his hands came to her groin, he hesitated. Then he went ahead and took a firm grip of Brandy's cock. Surprisingly, the gesture was not repulsive; in fact, he found that the feel of her cock was immensely pleasurable—

it was so much bigger than his own, and he had always wished his cock were bigger. Fondling Brandy's huge organ was a little like being able to imagine that he was feeling his own cock and that it had grown to the size he had always wished it were.

He coordinated his back and forth strokes in Brandy's ass with the up and down strokes of his hand on Brandy's cock. He heard her moan in delight and was glad that he had thought to make it more pleasurable for his prison-lover.

Brandy seemed to come alive, more so than ever before, and the heat of her passion transferred itself to Baby Jim. He could feel her ass tightening more than ever and tugging on his cock as if trying to make him penetrate more deeply than he was capable of. He began to ram his cock as hard as he could, simultaneously increasing the speed with which he was jacking her off.

It didn't take long for Brandy to approach the moment of orgasm. Baby Jim could feel her body writhing and pitching to a climax. Then suddenly, Brandy's cock was jerking spasmodically and shooting out white creamy cum. It shot up onto Brandy's chest, some even hit her face while Jim watched with childlike amazement —as if he had personally invented something new and was now watching the successful results of his invention.

The sight of Brandy's ejaculation was a mental and visual turn-on. Within seconds, Baby Jim felt the stirring in his own groin. He then reached his own climax, shooting his wad into Brandy's ass, as his body convulsed.

Their bodies had become sweaty and slippery. It had been a hot day and was still a very warm evening. Baby Jim knew he would have to take another shower, and he still had to go see Frank and Larry before lock-up. He, therefore, cut short their post-coital period of relaxation when they would usually lie together, snuggled against each other, enjoying the feel of each other's body.

Standing up, he said, "I've got to take a paper of weed to Frank and Larry, Brandy; then I've got to talk to Zapper before lock-up. So I better get movin'." Then, as an afterthought, he said, "That was pretty good, Brandy. I think that was one of the best sessions we ever had." He almost added, *I'm going to miss you,* but held his tongue.

After showering for the second time within an hour, he got dressed and went down the tier to Frank's cell. He looked in and saw Frank and Larry playing a game of chess.

"Who's winning?" he asked as he stepped into the tiny cubicle.

"Oh, hi, Baby Jim," Frank said, looking up from the chessboard. "Were you able to get that weed for us?"

"Got it right here," Jim replied, pulling out a tiny piece of folded paper from his right rear pocket. A paper of grass consisted of the contents of a chapstick lid filled with the ground-up buds of whatever type was currently available. The miniscule amount of grass was then folded into a piece of paper. The amount of grass sold for ten dollars wouldn't have made a decent "street-size" joint; but in prison it was a precious commodity that commanded outrageous prices.

Taking the paper from Baby Jim, Frank remarked, "That's a nice looking watch, Baby Jim. Where'd you get it?"

"Oh, this? I bought it from Steve Brackman a couple of months ago. I bought it from him when you two were still together. I guess he never told you, huh?"

Jim noticed the funny look on Frank's face. "Why?" he asked. "What's up? You know this watch?"

"It belonged to Frank," Larry commented.

"Yeah," Frank said. "It was my watch. One day it came up missing. Steve told me that he looked around for it but couldn't find it. The creep apparently took it himself, then sold it to you."

Baby Jim suddenly realized that he had snitched-off a brother, but it was too late to backtrack. "Yeah. But he told me it wasn't hot. I guess he lied to me." The fact that a fellow Nazi had lied to him began to rankle him. "So what you're telling me is that a brother not only stole a watch from his sissy, he also lied to a fellow brother when he turned around and sold it, huh?"

"That's what it looks like," Frank said evenly.

Baby Jim didn't like the situation. It put him in a cross. Frank had been a brother's sissy, but was not himself a brother. Even so, it was an unwritten rule that a brother was supposed to watch out for his sissy. It was also an unwritten rule that one brother did not lie to another. Steve Brackman had broken two Brotherhood rules. And Baby Jim was having to answer to someone for it.

"Here's what you do, Frank," said Baby Jim after thinking about it for a moment. "Talk to Frenchy. Tell him what happened. It's my understanding that Frenchy's gonna hold a Brotherhood Council tomorrow. You can file a grievance against Steve. And with me as your witness, you gotta win."

Larry asked, "But tell me, Jim; even if Frank wins, what does he win? I mean, he can't take the watch away from you, can he? After all, you paid for it, right? I mean, what can Frank really do about it?"

"A couple of things. To begin with, Frank will state his complaint in front of the Council. Then Steve will have a chance to give his side of the story. Then both sides call witnesses. Then the Council decides who's in the right. They always find in favor of a brother, if it's a brother against a non-brother and nothing can be proved. But if you can prove that the brother did something against the rules of the brotherhood, then you got some play coming. They might, like, make Steve pay Frank for the cost of the watch."

"Or something else," Frank said enigmatically.

Baby Jim didn't know what he meant, so he dropped the subject. "Do you still want this paper?"

Larry stood up and handed him the ten dollar bill that Frank had given to him. He gave it to Baby Jim and took the paper of weed.

Frank then said, as Baby Jim was about to leave, "Will you tell Frenchy that I intend to file a grievance at tomorrow's Council? You can tell him what it's about, if you want to."

"Will do," Baby Jim answered, leaving the cell and heading for Zapper's. *Tough shit,* he thought. *I've never really liked Steve anyway. I don't give a fuck what happens. I'm leaving this place, tomorrow!*

IX. PAWNSHOP

Hiram Little was in his mid-sixties. He had been doing time, in and out of prisons across the country, since his early twenties. He knew no other way of life. As an orphan, he had grown up unloved and unwanted, shunted from one orphanage to another, from one foster home to yet another, from one Juvenile Home to another, and eventually from one Youth Authority prison to another. He had never married and had never made any close friends. His had been a lonely life—unproductive, unmeaningful, and ultimately worthless.

He had been an ugly child—a homely, gangly, awkward teenager —and a plain, nondescript adult. Over the years, alcoholism had taken its toll, and his face was a landscape of scars, blemishes, and puffy flesh, lined with visible veins. His fingers were stained yellow-brown from cheap tobacco and from smoking cigarettes too close to the end.

With everything in the world stacked against him, he had had to struggle all his life. There was no one on the outside to send Hiram money in the mail, so he had to make his living the best way he could. Many years earlier, he had learned that he could act as a fence for stolen property, in prison and on the streets. Fencing stolen goods in prison was riskier than it was outside; the victims of the thefts were still in close proximity. But Hiram had learned his trade well over the years and had earned the nickname "Pawnshop." In fact, more than half the cons in the joint were unable to tell you his name; he was known simply as Pawnshop to one and all.

Not all of the merchandise he sold was stolen. He often managed to buy items from guys who needed money, for one reason or another. He would buy cheap and sell expensive—or for any price he could get. All in all, he did rather well for himself. It had been a hard life, but these days he rarely did without those things in life that meant something to him.

The night before the riot, Zapper had come to him to tell him that it had been decreed by the Nazis. Zapper had been fond of the old man and had wanted to make sure that he stayed out of the way when the shit hit the fan. Zapper also knew that Pawnship could be trusted to keep his mouth shut. As a matter of fact, Pawnshop was more aware of what was going on around him than most people realized. Pawnshop observed, noted, made mental records, and kept his own counsel.

He had been in so many prisons that he had seen it all. He had been in too many riots to count. Whenever a disturbance broke out in his youth, he had been in the front lines of the fray. As age began to creep up on him, he began to take a back seat and let the youngsters get into all the trouble. Pawnshop was not distinguished by a gift of higher intelligence, but he knew one thing for certain: No one wins in a riot! He had seen his share of young men killed or maimed; he had seen guards become sadistic beasts; he had seen the anguish of the innocent victims; he had, in short, seen it all. And this he knew: No one ever wins!

Riots rarely changed anything. After a riot, the food continued to be terrible; conditions remained deplorable. In fact, the prison itself was usually an almost uninhabitable wasteland for months after.

The public, instead of being aroused to sympathy for the plight of the convicts who were rioting to draw attention to conditions, inevitably took a hostile attitude toward the animals who were running rampant behind bars and felt that they deserved whatever they got.

No, Pawnshop knew that the only thing ever accomplished by a riot was that the young bucks were able to let off a little steam, and sometimes people got hurt.

Thinking about riots made him uncomfortable. Something was nagging at his memory. A face. But it wouldn't focus. Somewhere, someplace, he had been in a riot that stirred memories. And he had a disarming feeling that someone right here in this prison had been with him in some other prison, some other time. And whoever it was, it had been when a riot had occurred. It couldn't really be important, but it bugged him that, with his facility at names and faces, he couldn't pin-point this guy. Intuitively, Pawnshop knew that his inability to bring all of these thoughts into clear focus meant something.

He found it hard to get to sleep that night. That indistinguishable face kept popping into his mind. Five years ago? Ten? And since he could see that face, why couldn't he put it with a face in this prison? Why wouldn't they coalesce? And why was it bothering him in the first place?

May he was just getting old. Old age had been creeping up on him; maybe now it was making an all-out frontal attack!

Breaker. The word shot into his consciousness. It wasn't right; he was sure of it. Breaker was not the word—or the name—he was looking for. But he knew he was getting close. He turned over onto his side and tried again to put the thought out of his mind.

But he couldn't. His psyche was trying to tell him something. And he had a funny feeling that it had something to do with Zapper. Zapper had been the only one in the prison to ever take any kind of personal interest in Pawnshop. To everyone else, he was just an eccentric, uninteresting, ugly, and old derelict. Zapper had been the closest thing to a friend that Pawnshop could ever recall having had. If these thoughts that he couldn't shake had anything to do with Zapper, he felt he should put everything into trying to figure it out.

Eventually, sleep overtook him, before he could solve the enigmatic puzzle tormenting him. Pawnshop slept restlessly that night.

X. FRENCHY

The third floor of the cell house consisted of four-man dorms, one of which was occupied by Frenchy, Shotgun, Moose, and a sissy nicknamed Rhonda. Theirs was the first dorm on the north side, the closest one to the grillgate which opened onto the landing where the stairwell, leading up from the lower floors, yawned its cavernous mouth before continuing up to the fourth floor.

The night before the proposed riot, Frenchy had sent for Baby Jim. The Nazi leader had personally called on each of his lieutenants earlier in the evening. He had arrived at Baby Jim's cell during the younger man's interlude with Brandy and had left word with Zapper that Jim would be expected at Frenchy's dorm after the 9:30 count.

Rhonda had been sent off to "service" a few of the brothers, while her cellmates, joined now by Baby Jim, smoked a few joints and began to firm up the plans for the next day's events. "I want everything to run smoothly in the morning," Frenchy insisted. "I want everything to be normal-like, right up to the point where Shotgun makes the hit on Weasel. Then I want all hell to break loose! We're gonna time it to take place right at morning yard recall. The cell house guards will be totally unprepared. Us guys on the yard will storm the cell house; you guys inside will take over the guard-shacks on each floor. Me and Shotgun will take over the sergeant's office. Brackman and Whitey'll run things on the second floor. Moose and Carver will handle the action on the third floor. You and Zapper," he said to Baby Jim, "will organize the first floor. Our business on the fourth floor will come after the whole cell house is under our control. Make sure that no man stays in his cell, got it? Anyone who don't take part in the riot is to be treated like a snitch." He drew his right index finger across his throat to add emphasis.

"What about some of the old men?" Moose asked. "Like Pawn-shop and old man Meyers?"

"There's gonna be two or three who we'll let sit it out," Frenchy answered. "But no one else. If some lop thinks that this ain't none of his business, slap him around. Now listen to me good. Anyone caught trying to kick-back and not take part is to be brought to me in the sergeant's office. We're gonna set a few examples. I'm gonna hold a Council."

Shotgun jumped to his feet. "What the fuck for?"

Frenchy glared at his lieutenant. "For lots of reasons," he answered icily. "Only a handful of us know that we're making a break. By holding a Council, I can make it clear to all the brothers who their next leader is without actually telling them straight out."

"That reminds me," said Baby Jim. "That faggot, Frank, wants to bring charges against Steve Brackman." He went ahead to explain the circumstances surrounding Frank's watch. "Brackman not only pushed a hot watch onto me, he lied about it. He lied to one of his own brothers. I'm pissed."

"Okay," Frenchy sighed. "But I don't want a lot of bullshit taking up too much time. In fact, Baby Jim, if this didn't involve you, Frankie could go fuck herself for that watch."

"But what about the escape," Shotgun blurted out. "We can't go pissing off too much time. Dusting Weasel is a murder rap, you know. We gotta get outta here."

"Keep your fuckin' pants on." Frenchy's exasperation with his right-hand man was clearly beginning to show. "I'm gonna keep the Council short; then we break into the plumbing chase. The stairs to the basement are right off the sergeant's office. The keys to the plumbing chase door should be right on the sergeant's key ring."

"I don't understand," said Baby Jim. "What's in the plumbing chase? What is it, a sewer pipe or something?"

Moose took up the explanation. "This joint was built in the 1870s. The builders used the same idea for sewers that they used in Paris—a man can walk upright, down there. It runs all the way out to the sewage treatment plant, three and a half miles from the prison. In the 1920s, they blasted out a lot of rock and built ten isolation cells down there, right along the walkway of the sewer. In 1931 some guy was being taken to isolation; he made a break for it. From what we know, he got clean away. After a couple more breaks, they built new isolation cells on the fourth floor. Since then, they've never used those cells down there; but the sewer still exists. Nobody ever goes down there anymore unless they've got plumbing problems that can't be fixed from inside the cell house."

Frenchy cut in. "Most people don't even know about it. Shit! Even the warden probably don't know. He never worries his little head about sewers and plumbing and things. There's only one problem we don't know about: We don't know what we'll run into at the treatment plant. It might be wide open with a clear shot to freedom, or it might be sealed off, in which case we'll have to swim through shit and piss to get free. But I'll tell ya—for myself, I'd wade neck deep in shit to gett outta here."

"Who all is going?" Baby Jim asked.

Frenchy answered: "Me, Shotgun, Moose, Whitey, and you. Zapper could've come, but he's only got a year left to do and he says he wants to walk out of here. You can bet that a hundred others would go along for the ride if they knew about it, but we don't want no fuckin' army to bust outta here. By the time they get the riot put down, we'll be long gone."

"Sounds good to me," said Baby Jim enthusiastically.

"What about the money?" Shotgun asked.

Frenchy pulled out an unused roll of toilet paper, opened it, and withdrew a fistful of bills. "There's over five hundred bucks here. We each get a hundred. It ain't much, but it's enough to get us going. We can steal a car, but we gotta pay for food and clothes and other things. We can't go around holding up hamburger joints every time we get hungry. We'll make a couple of hits on liquor stores to put more cash in our pockets, but we'll play all of that by ear when we come to it. Right now, get everything ready for tomorrow. I want everything to come off without a hitch."

XI. TOMMY

The hydraulically operated cell doors came shut with a loud clang; then one at at time, forty deadbolts slammed into place, and the cells on the tier were locked for the night. For Tommy, the locked door represented safety, security, and a retreat from the horrors to which he had so recently been subjected. His body still ached from the strenuous use of seldom-used muscles when he had struggled against Steve so ineffectively. His rectum was sore from the misuse it had received four times in the brief span of eight hours.

He had been raped by Steve, then taken by Whitey without a fight. He had mistakenly assumed that he would be left in peace for the rest of the day. When the two men returned after the 9:30 count, Tommy thought that they were simply coming back to talk to him—they brought marijuana and were friendly. The blanket went back up over the cell door to give them the privacy to smoke the joints, Steve said.

Tommy had observed that most of the cons dressed rather skimpy, especially in the uncommon heat they were experiencing, even late into the night. It was not uncommon to see men walking up and down the tier wearing nothing but shorts and shower shoes. Seeing Steve and Whitey come into his cell dressed only in shorts gave him a fright at first. Their friendliness and the grass dispelled his fears, but only momentarily. All too soon the conversation came around to sex, with heavy emphasis on how good it had been that afternoon.

Tommy, fully dressed despite the heat, was asked to take his clothes off. When he hesitated, the request became an order. He complied too slowly. Steve slapped him and said, "Take 'em off or we'll rip 'em off."

While he quickly stripped, Steve and Whitey stepped out of their shorts. All three of the young men were then stark naked. Tommy noticed that Steve's cock was already fully extended, jutting out from his body like a pole, as thick as a tennis racket handle. Whitey's dick was gradually getting hard, as the young blond fondled himself. Tommy's had shrivelled up because of the icy fingers of fear which gripped his body.

For a brief, awkward moment, the three of them stood there, almost motionless. Whitey and Steve were lewdly admiring Tommy's boyish body; Tommy simply awaited instructions.

He nearly jumped out of his skin when Steve placed a hand on his shoulder.

"Relax," Steve said, as his hand glided down Tommy's back to his soft, round, firm buns. "Whitey and I have decided to teach you how to suck dicks. We figured it might be easier on you than getting fucked every time." He then sat on the edge of the bunk, his legs wide apart, his huge piece of meat rigidly erect.

Tommy's eyes were drawn to Steve's crotch. The sight of the blood-engorged dick and the low-slung, smooth-looking nutsac prompted a deep-seated revulsion. His head began to swim and his stomach revolted at the thought of putting a man's cock into his mouth.

Steve apparently misinterpreted the teenager's fixated stare. "You like what you see, kid?" he asked. Before Tommy could answer, he snapped his fingers, imperiously. "Get on it, then!"

Whitey put his hands on Tommy's shoulders, applying an unmistakable downward pressure while allowing his now fully erect cock to brush against Tommy's buns.

He sunk to his knees but tried to avoid looking at Steve's huge shaft, the tip of which glistened with pre-cum. Suddenly, Steve grabbed his head with both hands and forced it down into his groin. Tommy felt his facial muscles twitch as the hard, yet curiously soft, piece of rigid flesh glanced off his cheek.

At Steve's command, "Open your mouth!" he obeyed. The huge cock was then abruptly thrust into his throat. His stomach's rebellion manifested itself in a surge of bile. He gagged violently, and his mouth was filled with an extremely bitter taste. Afraid of vomiting, he jerked his head back.

"Fuck this!" Steve exclaimed, pushing Tommy away. "It'll take all night to get a nut."

They then made him lie on his back with his legs in the air. Steve crawled on top of him and roughly pushed his rock-hard dick into Tommy's ass. As soon as Steve had settled into a steady rhythm, pounding Tommy's ass unmercifully, Tommy felt Whitey tug on one of his hands.

"Play with my dick," Whitey ordered.

He complied with Whitey's command and cautiously took hold of the silky-smooth sex organ. While Steve's cock hammered away, tormenting his already unbearably sore rectum, he found it difficult to concentrate on Whitey's.

After Steve reached his ass-tearing climax, Tommy released his grip on Whitey's tool; the muscular stud then climbed off him, and the handsome blond youth took his place.

Whitey was gentle, almost tender, almost loving. For some inexplicable reason, Tommy found it difficult to harbor any hate for the attractive young man. He felt a deep hatred for Steve. When he lay on his bunk later, reviewing the events of that afternoon and of that evening, he felt something almost approaching affection for Whitey. He couldn't understand it and didn't try.

The second episode seemed to last forever. In actuality, it took less than forty-five minutes, including the time spent talking and smoking joints. When they had gone, he had remained prone on his bunk, with the light off, and only his shorts on.

Barely five minutes passed when, through the closed lids of his eyes, he sensed a shadow at his cell door. Looking up, he saw Steve and groaned inwardly as Steve came back into the cell and re-hung the blanket.

Steve's voice had a gentle ring to it. "Hey, kid, don't get uptight." He sat on the bunk next to Tommy and lit up yet another joint of marijuana. "I didn't come back to fuck you again. Christ! I'm not superhuman."

Tommy accepted the joint and took a deep drag on it. Passing it back, he suddenly felt one of Steve's hands come to rest on his chest. Steve gently tweaked his left nipple.

They smoked the joint, and Tommy felt Steve's hand gliding over the sensuously soft contours of his torso. He then became aware of the roaming hand coming to a stop on top of his shorts, just over his crotch. Without any warning, Steve slipped his fingers into the slit of the white boxer shorts and began to feel his cock.

"No, Tommy pleaded. "Don't."

"Pull down your shorts," Steve coaxed gently. "And that's an order. Take 'em all the way off." The viciousness had gone out of the voice, but there was no mistaking the fact that Steve was serious and would enforce his will.

Tommy lifted his butt, slid the shorts to his ankles, and kicked them off his feet. The grass had taken effect, making him even higher than he had been. He was confused about Steve's intentions, because Steve had promised not to fuck him again. Why, then, was he ordered to take off his shorts?

"That's more like it," Steve whispered. From his open pack of cigarettes, he shook out yet another joint, fired it up, and insisted that Tommy smoke it, despite the youth's insistence that he was already higher than he had been in his entire life. "I want you to loosen up, kid. Believe me, I'll take good care of you. Hey, look, Tommy, I'm not a one-way guy, see? Take this grass, for example: The amount we've smoked just today would've cost you thirty bucks at joint prices.

While he talked, his hand continued to caress Tommy's body, feeling his chest, his stomach, his thighs, and lightly brushing over his dick.

"I like looking at your naked body," Steve continued, "and I really like feeling you up. You remind me of someone else when that someone else was your age." After a moment's silence, during which Tommy sensed that Steve had been remembering another time and another place, he went on to say, "There ain't nothin' wrong with a little sex between two guys, Tommy; especially when those guys are locked up away from women."

Either because of the grass, or in spite of it, Tommy became more acutely aware of Steve. He realized that Steve had been extremely nervous, as if he had been building up his courage to do something—but what?

The answer came to him a split second before the beefy stud apparently solidified his resolve. *He wants to suck my dick!* The thought flashed into his mind an instant before Steve made the move to crawl onto the bed between his legs.

Before lowering his head to Tommy's crotch, Steve whispered, "It's my turn to make *you* feel good. Lay back and relax, kid. I'm gonna show you how to give a real good blow-job."

For what seemed like a long time, Tommy's cock refused to stiffen. He felt Steve's hands caressing his body as a hot tongue licked his flaccid cock, followed by a warm mouth sucking on it. Then the wet tongue began to lick his balls, the junction of his thighs, that nameless area between his nuts and his ass, then back to his balls, and up to the head of his cock.

At first it took no effort to avoid getting a hard-on. But slowly he began to feel a tingling sensation somewhere in his loins, spreading to his cock, nuts, legs, and even to his stomach, and up to his tits, which Steve was paying attention to with more frequency. Soon, he was unable to resist Steve's persuasive mouth, and he felt his cock growing, swelling, expanding, hardening. His entire body, all of his senses, swimming euphorically, responded to Steve's sexual urgings.

In spite of himself, Tommy admitted that it felt good—oh, so very, very good. Still a virgin, Tommy had never experienced sex at the manipulation of another human being. All he knew was masturbation. Approaching orgasm, he warned Steve that he was about to cum—certain that he should not shoot his load into his mouth—but Steve paid him no attention, except to increase the frenzy with which he sucked on the explosive shaft.

Suddenly, an immense orgasm racked his body. Time after time, his body convulsed in ecstatic pleasure. The ejaculations seemed endless; the sensations were excruciatingly pleasurable.

That had all taken place before lock-up. The memory of it was still fresh, his body was still flushed, residual pleasure still coursed through his every nerve fiber.

So much had happened in so short a space of time; his unsophisticated mind was incapable of coming to grips with it.

The noise on the tier abated slowly. Convicts called out to their friends, and the bawdy jokes of caged men rang out along the tier. Tommy heard none of it. When silence finally descended over the second floor, he was still wide awake, lost in deep thought. His confused state of mind would not allow him to concentrate on any single thought for more than a fleeting second. One thought kept recurring: He could not go on like this; he could not accept being used as a substitute for women.

Although the sexual aspects played an important part in his unwillingness to tolerate that which had been forced upon him, he could probably learn to put up with it, possibly even learn to like it—as Steve had tried to make him believe. He thought of Whitey and forced himself to admit that he could, indeed, learn to enjoy having sex with him.

But sex alone was not the issue. He bridled at the thought of being a slave. Yes, that was the problem. His ego could not allow him to suffer the degradation of being another man's lackey. Was he to permit himself to be the unwilling servant of Steve? Was he to give up his own free will to be at the beck and call of an overbearing convict? Was he to sacrifice his pride and self-esteem?

His brain tumbled down a grass-induced waterfall that seemed to go on forever. Slowly, one thought began to edge out all others.

Suicide.

What did he have to live for? At nineteen, he felt that his life was over. There was nothing left. Not only was he in prison—when a man his age should be free to enjoy his youth—he had been humiliated and degraded. He would no longer be able to look himself in the miror and still retain any degree of self-esteem. He had been left with only one self-assertive course of action.

Suicide.

He swallowed the tears of self-pity that were welling up inside, but they were too overpowering to contain. Unable to check the flow, he cried for several hours, silently, uncontrollably, unashamedly. He was dimly aware of the passing of time. He knew when the footsteps of the guard sounded quietly in the catwalk that the 2:30 a.m. count was in progress.

His tears eventually ceased and were replaced by a dull ache in his stomach. The horror of facing death slowly gave way to the detached, objective, impersonal matter of the logistics of death. How would he kill himself? He thought of hoarding enough aspirin over the next few weeks until he had enough to do the job.

No good. He didn't want to live any longer than necessary.

He considered slicing his wrists with a razor blade. No.

Abruptly, he caught sight of an overhead plumbing pipe. Yes. He would hang himself. It would be simple: rip some sheets into strips, make a noose, and jump from his bed. The noose would first hinder then stop altogether the flow of blood to his brain; he would black out and simply never wake up.

In the quiet peacefulness of the sleeping cell house, the sound of sheets being torn seemed abnormally loud to Tommy; but if anyone was awakened by the noise, Tommy never knew about it.

By the 5:00 a.m. count, the noose was ready, its strength had been tested. Tommy himself was ready. His emotional strength to follow through was all that remained to be tested.

The black of night had given way to the gray light of dawn. The noose was securely in place. Tommy stood on the edge of his bunk. He felt ancient, tired, weary, and sick of life. Disconnected thoughts came and went. He wondered, for the last time, if there were any other way out of his intolerable plight, other than death. After a moment, he answered his question.

"No," he said aloud to the three walls of the pitiless, uncaring cell. With one last look at the cold steel bars across the front of his cell, he stepped off his bunk and into nothingness.

XII. STEVE

He didn't know what it was that had driven him to return to Tommy's cell. He really hadn't planned to give the kid a blow-job; it had just happened on the spur of the moment. It had been a dumb thing to do, even though he had thoroughly enjoyed it. If it were ever to get around that he, Steve Brackman, liked to suck cocks, he would be finished as a member of the White Power group.

It had been more than five years since he had sucked a cock. He thought he had put all of that behind him. He was not the type to think too long or too hard about his actions, nor the motivations behind them. As far as he was concerned, he gave Tommy the blow-job to keep him happy, and most of all, quiet. He didn't want the kid to go crying to Lt. Ramos that he had been raped.

Overpowering Tommy had been easy, just as he himself had once been so easily overpowered. That's just the way things are in prison, he told himself. The strong rule the weak.

Leaving Tommy's cell, he had noticed the red-haired kid who lived on the south side of the second floor cell block. He had seen the kid before—Donald Stuart was his name—but the kid was a quiet guy who never drew attention to himself. He wasn't nearly as cute as Tommy, and for various reasons, Steve had never thought about Don in terms of sexual dominance until he had seen him walking on the tier without a shirt just before lock-up.

Steve had stopped him and said, "What's happenin'?" and the two of them talked about how hot it was that day. The simple conversation was meaningless, but Steve had begun to look at Don in a new light. The kid was almost ugly, as far as his face was concerned, but his body was a lot like Tommy's. Steve discovered that his cock was beginning to come to life while he talked with the young man so close to his semi-naked body.

He had fallen to sleep fantasizing how he and Whitey would make a new conquest the next day. In the middle of the riot, they would drag the red-headed kid into an empty cell—it didn't matter whose cell it was because all of the cells had better be empty.

As keyed-up as he was about the coming riot and about his new plans for sexual conquest, he slept restlessly. He was awake before the 6:00 unlock, a raging hard-on tempting him to jack-off before the cell doors came open. But he controlled his urges by telling himself that he wanted to save it for Donald Stuart.

It had been a warm night, and it promised to be another scorcher of a day. Already, with the first rays of the sun, the air was sultry and still. Apparently, several others hadn't slept well in the heat, for Steve could hear toilets flushing, water running in sinks, the morning hacking of cigarette smokers, and the numerous other sounds of men stirring in the confines of their cells. Steve realized that most of them didn't know that the Nazis had planned a riot in order to cover the murder of the snitch, Weasel, and that several other guys had been fingered for severe beatings for various infractions against the Brotherhood. The guys in this prison were getting too loose, and today the Nazis were going to reassert their mastery.

The shattering sound of deadbolts being released hydraulically brought Steve to his feet. After pissing through his semi-erect cock, he ran water in the sink and splashed his face. He decided not to shave. Still naked, for he always slept nude, he got down on his hands and knees, fished a cardboard box out from under his bunk, and pulled out a clean pair of shorts. He started to put them on. Thoughts of Donald Stuart came into his mind, and he decided against wearing any underwear that day. He was tucking his cock into his jeans just as Whitey appeared at his cell door. The look on Whitey's face made Steve freeze.

"Je-Jesus!" Whitey stammered. "He, he's killed himself!"

"What the fuck are you talking about?" Steve asked, zipping up his jeans.

"Whitey swallowed hard. "The kid. Tommy. He hung himself. Come on and see for yourself. We've gotta do something."

The two men walked hurriedly down the tier to Tommy's cell. In the doorway, Steve once again froze, mesmerized by the limp, naked body suspended a foot from the floor, twirling ever-so-slowly at the end of the make-shift noose.

Whitey's voice seemed to be coming from miles away: "I got up feeling horny. I was gonna come down here and fuck him again this morning, as soon as the doors came open, before he had a chance to get dressed." His voice was trembling: "I found him like—like this."

Repressing an urge to throw up, Steve quickly took control of the situation. "He musta done it less than an hour ago; he'd have been seen hanging there at the five o'clock count if he'd done it any earlier. We gotta cut him down. We don't want no screws up here this morning. Cover the bars while I get my shank."

Steve moved quickly to his cell and withdrew the knife he had fashioned from a piece of metal stolen from the Maintenance shop. The metal had been honed to a sharp edge by hours of rubbing on the concrete floor. Such weapons, of course, were illegal—possession of a shank would bring a man six more years—but all the White Power members had at least one apiece, as did several of the other inmates, hidden in the most unlikely places, but readily available for immediate use.

On his way back to Tommy's cell, Steve noted with gratification that no one had yet come out of their cells. He and Whitey were the only ones who knew about the suicide.

Ducking through the blanket into the cell, Steve noticed that Whitey had his back turned to the dangling corpse. His face had drained of all color, and he was swallowing rapidly as if to avoid vomiting. Without hesitation, he slapped the blond viciously.

"Come out of it!" Steve said through clenched teeth. "This ain't no time to behave like a cunt! Move his blanket off the bed. Okay. Now, hold him by the waist while I cut him down."

When the knife cut through the improvised noose, Tommy's lifeless body crumpled to the floor. Whitey hadn't been prepared for the shock of the feel of a still-warm dead body. The meaning of the term "deadweight" hit him like a ton of bricks.

Steve swore. "Goddamn it, Whitey! Get ahold of yourself. It's just a stiff. Gimme a hand and let's get him onto the bunk."

Once the body was on the bunk, Steve covered it with the blanket. He took a quick look around the cell to see if there was anything of any value. Finding nothing, he turned to Whitey. "Shit! The punk was so poor he couldn't even afford a bottle of shampoo. Let's get out of here. But leave the blanket on the bars."

They went to Steve's cell and made cups of instant coffee. Steve pulled out a paper of grass, rolled four pin-joints, and smoked two of them with Whitey. While they waited for the seven o'clock chow release, Steve told of his plans to get into Donald Stuart's pants. He noticed that Whitey was not as enthusiastic as he had been about Tommy; he was beginning to see his blond brother in a different light.

A scared young punk, Steve thought. *I could probably fuck Whitey as easily as I fucked Tommy. Just wait until I tell the other brothers how Whitey almost shit his pants when we cut Tommy down.*

Then the idea began to formulate in his mind: *I'm gonna fuck his blond ass before this day is over.*

XIII. ON THE YARD

The rectangular prison yard was totally enclosed by buildings of concrete, and stone, and brick. The northern wall was the four-storey cell house; the western wall was the Admin. building, site of the warden's office, Control, the armory, the secretarial pool, and the numerous offices housing counselors and other parasitic, useless bureaucrats. These perpetuated themselves by fucking-over the inmates, while justifying their existence to the Legislative Budget

Committee by creating "programs" for inmates. Taxpayers and legislators never seemed to question one little paradox: There was always enough money to pay the salaries of these self-styled "program administrators," but there was never any money in the budget for the programs themselves.

The chow hall, the two chapels, the education building, and the maintenance shop formed the southern wall of the yard. The gym, the laundry, the inmate store, and the mail room formed the eastern wall.

From the cell house, the inmates had an unobstructed view of the mountains which rose cliff-like behind the prison. This was the only view of the outside world to be seen. Once a man entered the "Reception" area (which the cons called the "fish-tank"), at the northwest corner of the prison, abutting the cell house, he saw no further sign of civilization until the day of his release. The yard and three of the buildings surrounding it comprised the inmates' entire world.

The yard itself was nothing but hard-packed clay covered by a fine layer of sand. Over the decades a path had been worn near the buildings, forming an irregular circle where men walked or jogged. The weight pile was the only athletic or recreational "program" available. Balls of any sort, frisbees, and other equipment had long ago been proscribed and banned as too dangerous.

For most of the inmates, then, the yard was nothing more than a place to get some fresh air and some sun, to talk, walk, or jog. Even on days when the sun was unbearably hot, the yard offered the only break from the tedium of the cell house.

Frenchy was glad to see so many men on the yard, and especially around the weight pile. The more men pushing iron, the more bodies there were to conceal Shotgun's movements when the time came to stick Weasel. By the time the guards in their towers at the four corners of the yard realized that there was a dead body on the weight pile, the riot would be under way.

Many of the White Power brothers were on the yard that morning. They were needed to help storm the cell house. Moose and Carver had remained inside, as had Zapper, Baby Jim, and Brackman. But Whitey had stayed on the yard after breakfast, against Frenchy's express orders.

Frenchy moved away from the weight pile and approached Whitey who was leaning against the wall next to the closed window

206 / SEX BEHIND BARS

of the inmate store. Before Frenchy could express his indignation at the flagrant disobedience of his orders, Whitey spoke.

"I've gotta talk to you, Frenchy. It's about Steve . . ."

"Brackman's in the cell house where you're supposed to be."

"I know, I know, but listen. Yesterday, Steve raped a kid on the second floor . . ."

"Big fuckin' deal!"

"Last night the kid hung himself. Steve and I found him this morning. Steve made me help him cut him down. Don't you see? We've got a dead body on the second floor."

Frenchy considered the situation for a moment. Rape was no big deal, and people were always committing suicide in prisons. But it was imperative that the body of this kid not be found until after the riot. If the stiff was discovered too early, the cell house would be swarming with pigs—even apparent suicides were thoroughly investigated by overly suspicious prison staff members.

"Okay," Frenchy said, "get your ass back inside when they call the eight-thirty voluntary lock-up. Keep everyone away from the kid's cell, but don't draw any heat. Steve's gonna need you when the time comes."

Walking back to the weight pile, the gang leader began to wonder about the wisdom of allowing Whitey to take part in the escape. Christ! If a little thing like the suicide of a punk got him down, maybe Whitey was too flakey.

Larry and Frank were among the men clustered about the body-building equipment, working out their regimens during the morning yard release when it was still possible to build up a sweat without keeling over. The afternoons were just too hot to be out-side. Larry had been doing a lot of thinking about his inability to contribute to the financial aspects of his relationship with Frank.

Earlier, he had overheard part of the conversation between Frenchy and Shotgun, wherein he had picked up the word "mule." He vaguely knew what the term meant; he wondered whether or not he himself could become a mule. There were risks, of course, but Larry knew that he could be extremely cautious when it was necessary. The only way to answer his question was to talk to Frenchy about it. As soon as he and Frank completed their workout, he would do so.

Although one day was much like the next, and only a few men could tell you that it was Friday, not Saturday or Thursday or

Monday, Rhonda was one of those who always knew. She knew that the inmate store was closed on Fridays and Saturdays, and she also knew about the upcoming riot. She had stocked up yesterday on such necessities as coffee, cigarettes, shampoo, and candy bars. It was well known that after any sort of prison disturbance, the first privilege to be suspended was access to the inmate store. Rhonda knew that it would be another three to six weeks before she could buy cigarettes or coffee.

She and Stella had become close friends. Rhonda could remember the time when all of the sissies on the yard stuck together; but times had changed. Brandy never came out of her cell, except in the company of her old-man, Baby Jim; Frank had given up cell-hopping and was never seen anywhere without Larry in tow; old Patty had her stable of young men on the second floor (most of the ugly ones, Rhonda felt); and the fourth floor, where Protective Custody cells were located, was now filled with the weaker queens who couldn't handle the pressures. Once, Rhonda had been the *Grande Dame* of the joint. Now she was just one of many, just a tip bitch, servicing her old-man Frenchy and his Nazi Brothers. In a way, she was glad that Frenchy and some of the others were going to break out. Things had changed, were still changing, and would probably change radically after the riot. Zapper would become Frenchy's replacement as Leader; but Rhonda knew that Zapper didn't really have what it takes to keep the gang together under tight control. Who knows, she thought, things might eventually come full circle, and she herself might again reign as the Dowager Queen Mother of the joint.

All these thoughts were running through her mind as she and Stella walked around the yard, taking several laps, cruising the semi-naked bodies on the weight pile, and even stopping briefly to chat with friends and acquaintances. It was such a peaceful morning that she almost wished the beauty and tranquility were not going to be shattered so violently at ten-thirty. She also wished that she could talk to Stella about it, but Stella had not been privileged with advance information because of her association with Weasel.

When they passed the inmate store, both of the sissies waved a casual "hello" to Whitey. Instead of returning the greeting, the young blond motioned for them to come over to him.

From his vantage point on the weight pile, Frenchy watched as the two sissies approached Whitey. He also saw that the young blond was doing most of the talking. It didn't take a genius to figure out the topic of conversation. If Rhonda had been alone, Frenchy would have given it no more thought; but he didn't like the idea of letting Stella know too much. He had always considered Stella to be okay until recently. Lately, she had been spending too much time with that snitch, Weasel. Stella could be trusted, but she did not know that Weasel could *not* be trusted. It had strictly been a precautionary measure to exclude Stella from any knowledge of the riot and of other things. And Whitey knew it as well as anyone.

He turned to Shotgun. "Who've we got out here this morning that lives on the second floor? Someone we can trust to give Steve a hand when the shit hits the fan?"

Shotgun looked around. He, too, quickly assessed the situation with Whitey. He scanned the faces closest to him. "There's Dakota. No, he lives on the first floor. I've got it. Daniels."

"Yeah, Daniels." Frenchy walked over to a bronzed, powerfully built man in his late twenties. He was doing curls with a 35-pound dumbell, the tattoo of SS-lightning bolts showing boldly on his left-arm bicep. "Hey, now, Rick," Frenchy greeted his brother. "I've got a favor to ask . . ."

From high in his tower in the southwest corner, Officer Reynolds surveyed the activity on the yard with mild interest. The towers were shaded, but not air-conditioned, and he knew it was going to be one helluva hot day. The inmates on the yard would wilt under the blazing sun. He could expect no excitement, nothing unusual would happen. Not today, that's for damned sure.

The phone rang; he answered it, listened, and hung up. The only relief he got from the boredom of tower duty came from the P.A. system; the microphone was located in his tower. He reached for the mike.

"ATTENTION ON THE YARD. VOLUNTARY LOCK-UP. LOCK-UP NOW OR STAY ON THE YARD 'TIL TEN-THIRTY RECALL. VOLUNTARY LOCK-UP. LAST CALL."

Shotgun intercepted Whitey and told him that Frenchy had changed his mind. "Frenchy wants Daniels to work with Brackman. He decided that since you're splitting with us, you should take part in the takeover of the sergeant's office."

Whitey shrugged and said, "Okay with me." Actually, he was relieved that he didn't have to go back to the second floor. He wanted to stay as far away as possible from the dead body of the kid he had fucked yesterday. It gave him a creepy feeling to realize that the kid's hot, sweet body was getting colder by the minute and would soon become putrid. Despite the increasing heat from the sun, already beginning to bake the yard, he felt a chill race through his body. Tommy was so young. How terrible for life to be cut so short when there was so much to live for.

He felt that he must get Tommy out of his mind. So even though he hadn't planned to work out that morning, he wandered over to the weight pile.

Larry had waited until he saw Frenchy take a break from his work-out, then approached the gang leader. "I don't think you know me, Frenchy," he began slowly, awed by the power wielded by this formidable convict, "but my name is Larry Jonas. I'm Frank's new old-man . . ."

"I know who you are," Frenchy answered, looking the other man in the eyes. "I make it a point to know a little bit about everyone."

"I've been told that a man can come to you with a problem. I've got one. It's called chronic broke-itis."

Frenchy laughed. "Chronic broke-itis. I like that. Whatcha got in mind? I don't run no loan-shark operation, and I don't run no Welfare agency."

"I want a job . . ."

"And I don't run no employment service."

Larry smiled, trying to get on the man's good side. "But I've heard that you are an animal trainer."

Frenchy frowned. "What are you getting at?"

"I heard you're a mule trainer."

"A mule trainer." Frenchy laughed again. "I like that one, too. You got style, Jonas. Real style. So you wanna be a mule, huh? Okay. Tell ya what. You're on the first floor, right? Talk to Zapper. We're gonna be needing a new mule. If Zapper clears ya, you're in. But the Zapper is the first floor boss. See him." With that, Frenchy turned away. He began to search the faces on the yard. It was still too early to corner Weasel, but he wanted to make sure that the sonuva-bitchin' punk rat snitch was on the yard. He spotted him near the Catholic Chapel doorway, talking to Rhonda and Stella. By now, he figured, word of that kid's suicide was getting all over the yard. Damn that Whitey and his big fucking mouth.

Suddenly, Frenchy realized that there were more people on the yard than he had anticipated. There were at least twenty White

Power Nazis, which was the correct number, insofar as he had planned it, and at least fifty non-gang members, which was one helluva lot more than he planned for. He had figured that the other cons would go inside to get out of the heat. He quickly reassessed his strategy. The entrance to the cell house, located twenty feet east of the northwest corner of the yard, was a tunnel-like alcove. At yard recall, the men filed into the tunnel to be pat-searched before passing into the cellhouse, where those who lived on the first floor simply walked directly onto their tier after turning left instead of going up the staircase. The sergeant's office was to the left. The storming of the cell house would begin in the tunnel and spread to the sergeant's office. It was necessary to have all non-brothers leave the yard first, otherwise a bottleneck would develop in the tunnel, impeding action. The original plan had been for the gang to be the first ones into the tunnel. Frenchy, like a field commander who made decisions according to the dictates of the changing situations, now decided that gang members would be the last ones to clear the yard and enter the tunnel.

He turned to Shotgun and said, "Pass the word along to all the brothers—hold back at recall; let the others go in first."

A few moments later, Frank approached Frenchy. "Did Baby Jim tell you that I want to lodge a complaint against Steve Brackman?"

"Yeah, Frankie. He told me. I'm gonna hold a Council this afternoon. Zapper will see to it that you're admitted. By the way, Baby Jim has already co-signed the complaint, so there shouldn't be any real problem. How're you and your new old-man getting along?"

"Great," Frank smiled. "Just great."

Slowly, the morning dragged on. The sun mounted in the sky, spilling its remorseless heat into the prison yard.

Weasel had wanted to talk to Frenchy early, in order to go inside at voluntary lock-up, but the gang leader had been too busy with other things. Weasel was curious about the new mule job. Being a mule had been a pretty good deal for Weasel. Two or three times a week he would get a visit from Julie, one of Frenchy's connections on the streets. Julie would hand over a pre-packaged roll of dope or grass, carefully wrapped for easy insertion into the rectum. Weasel would go to the bathroom, insert the package while standing at the urinal (something he had had to practise in order to perfect the movements, which were monitored through a one-way mirror window), then quickly rejoin Julie. Taking a piss was a natural thing to do; inserting the suppository of dope had become a remarkably easy thing to accomplish; and the visits with Julie were delightful. In addition, the financial remuneration was more than agreeable.

Yes, it had been a profitable proposition for Weasel, because he also kept Lt. Ramos supplied with enough information about prison drug-trafficking that Weasel was positive he would get a release his first time before the Parole Board. And Frenchy was getting ready to set up a new connection, which meant that no one suspected Weasel of being an informer.

The morning had seemed interminably long while he waited for Frenchy to take the time to fill him in on the new details. For the twentieth time, he glanced at his watch.

10:15.

It was getting late. The shade of the eastern side of the yard was almost gone, no more than fourteen to sixteen inches out from the building. He had noticed Whitey standing or crouching in that shade all morning long and idly wondered why the blond had bothered to come to the yard if he wasn't going to do anything but stand there. As these thoughts crossed his mind, he saw Whitey move away from the building and walk toward the weight pile.

Frenchy had caught Whitey's attention and motioned for him to come to the center of the yard. When the blond arrived, Frenchy gave him a stern look. "I'm gonna tell ya the truth, Whitey; you're makin' me nervous. You're supposed to be a Nazi, but you fell apart the first time you saw a stiff."

Whitey started to protest, but Frenchy waved him into silence.

"That's not what's botherin' me. Anyone can come unglued the first time he's got to handle a dead body. But a brother has to keep his lips shut about it. You blabbed it all over the fuckin' yard." He again waved off Whitey's attempt to defend himself.

"It's okay. You're young. You got a lot to learn. And believe me, today's the day you're gonna learn it. It's almost yard recall. Any minute now, things'll cut loose. We're gonna stick Weasel, right where you're standing. And you're gonna watch. Got it? He's standin' right over there near the Chapel. Go get him; tell him I'm ready to talk to him. But, be cool. Don't scare him."

Whitey turned slowly and began to walk toward Weasel. A thousand thoughts raced through his mind. He himself had voted to dust him. At the time, it had seemed so impersonal—like part of some movie script or a line from a gangster novel. Yet now, the reality of it was closing in on him. The horrible violence and finality of death had hit him in the face when he and Steve had cut Tommy down. Now, less than five hours later, he was approaching a very much alive young man who would be a very dead young man in a matter of minutes.

Judas Goat. The words flashed across his brain unexpectedly. How long had it been since he had heard that phrase? Isn't that what they called it? The goat that leads the lamb to slaughter . . .

Officer Reynolds looked down from his tower and stifled a yawn as he glanced at his watch. Seven minutes 'til recall. He reached for the 30-06 in its gun rack. As soon as he made the announcement on the P. A., he would step out of the tower and walk to the center of the chow hall roof, a meaningless ritual since nothing ever happened at recall to require the use of the powerful rifle.

He noticed that most of the inmates had drifted over to the cell house entrance. Only fifteen or twenty men remained in the center of the yard, and two men were moving away from the Chapel toward the weight pile.

As Weasel approached, Frenchy and Shotgun took up their positions near the incline bench, a six-foot slab of padded wood that angled at approximately 60° up from the ground—Frenchy facing south and Shotgun facing north. Weasel was ushered into their presence in between them. Whitey stood to Weasel's right. The incline bench was on Weasel's left.

"I want to talk to you about a very special mule job," Frenchy began. "The brothers had to approve of it ahead of time, but we figured that you was the only one for the job. The man we want is gonna pack some steel."

Weasel developed a weird feeling in the pit of his stomach. The words Frenchy spoke were not unusual; it was the way he spoke them—the sound of his voice and the look of cold hatred in his eyes. All of a sudden, he wanted to bolt and run, but he realized he was boxed in.

"Did I say *man?*" Frenchy asked. "I meant to say *snitch.*"

The blood drained from Weasel's face, and a shiver of stark terror shot up his spine. He knew he should try to get away, but it was too late.

"And the steel we want you to carry, you punk rat, is *this!*"

The shock of the homemade blade being shoved into his right

kidney was the last sensation to register in his brain. Merciful blackness enveloped him, while Shotgun twisted and turned the blade for the two seconds that Weasel remained standing.

Shotgun pulled out the blade, tilting Weasel's fall backward. He and Frenchy swiftly positioned the dying man on the incline bench.

Whitey watched in fascinated horror, frozen by the sight of cold-blooded murder. His mind went into a different kind of shock. He was aware of everything, but nothing seemed real. He himself was not real; he was detached, disembodied, unable to move.

"CLEAR THE YARD. YARD RECALL. ALL MEN RETURN TO YOUR CELLS." Reynolds repeated the announcement, grabbed the rifle, and moved to the chow hall roof. Men were running toward the cell house. He returned to his tower.

"NO RUNNING!" he ordered. He then saw two figures in the center of the yard, neither of them moving. "YOU MEN ON THE WEIGHT PILE—CLEAR THE YARD!"

He saw the other three guards emerge from their towers onto the various roofs. Something was wrong. His eyes were drawn to the weight pile. The man on the incline board was moving.

No. He was falling. He hit the sandy ground with a dull, lifeless impact, as if he were dead. Reynolds rushed onto the roof. The last of the inmates had disappeared into the tunnel, except for the. . . . Was it a dead body? And why was that blond inmate just standing there? *What the fuck's going on?*

His every instinct told him something bad was going on. Without further hesitation, he fired his rifle into the air. "You! On the yard! Stand where you are! Do not move!" Then he yelled to one of his fellow officers, "Stan, call Control. That looks like a dead body down there."

Whitey had heard Frenchy and Shotgun yelling at him, urging him to run, but he had been powerless to move. His legs would not respond. He had heard the announcements on the P.A., had even watched Weasel's body slump and fall off the incline board; yet, still he could not move. It was like a nightmare when you know you've got to move but can't.

The report of the rifle shot jarred him out of his stupor. He looked up toward its source, then looked around him. The yard was deserted. He had to get into the cell house. His legs responded slowly at first; then suddenly he was sprinting across the yard.

He saw dust kick up in front of him a split second before he heard the shot. Reynold's order to stop was meaningless. He couldn't stop now. He had to get to the tunnel.

He was almost there when he tripped.

No. He didn't trip; someone pushed him. The ground flew up and hit him in the face. At that same instant, he realized that he hadn't been pushed from behind—he had been shot. The pain flared through his back and his chest. He was breathing dirt, but he couldn't move his face. *I'm dying! I'm dying! I'm dying!* The thought ricocheted through his brain, repeating itself over and over again.

It's better this way, he decided. *It's better this way. It's better . . .*

Reynolds lowered his rifle and stared at the lifeless form of the blond inmate. "Stupid sonuvabitch should've stopped." He returned to his tower, reached for the phone and dialed.

"Watch Commander's Officer. Lieutenant Seaton."

"Reynolds, Tower Three," he said into the mouthpiece. "We've got an incident on the yard. Looks like two men dead, Lieutenant."

XIV. IN THE CELL HOUSE

Rick Daniels had returned to his cell on the second floor after telling Steve about Frenchy's change of plans regarding Whitey. Having two hours to kill before the riot broke loose, he decided to have a nice shower, after which he would discuss in detail with Steve their plans for the take-over of the second floor. It would probably be easy to take the guard as a hostage. There was only one guard on each floor, and that one guard had nothing to do but turn keys. He would key open the two grillgates at 10:30, then stand back while the inmates filed in from the yard. Today, there would be a slight change in his routine: He would not be around to key the doors shut again.

There were fourteen brothers on the second floor: Eight of them were on the yard and would help take over the sergeant's office; the other six would assist Steve and Rick in subduing the guard and in organizing the efforts of the cons housed on the second floor.

The guard was a fish officer named Cobb: a little guy who could probably be scared into giving up without a struggle, especially when surrounded by eight toughened cons.

Rick knew that the riot wouldn't be much of a show. There was no way for the inmates to take over anything but the cell house because there were no openings to other parts of the prison from the living quarters. The only entrance or exit was the tunnel. They would take a few hostages, make a little noise, give Staff an ultimatum, outline a few demands, then the stand-off would take place while the cons grew hungry without any food. Eventually, Staff would concede a few of the demands, the men would then return to their cells and lock up. Staff would then renege on their concessions, and a month from now things would be the way they were before the riot. The only things that would have been accomplished, Rick knew, were that one snitch would be dead and five cons would make good their escapes. The riot was nothing but a large scale cover-up and diversionary tactic. In the long run, the only winners would be the ones who got away.

On the first floor, Zapper and Baby Jim were also whiling away the time until the moment to strike. Zapper was deeply engrossed in an informative conversation with Pawnshop. The old man was relaying some very enlightening information.

Baby Jim, on the other hand, had decided that he wanted to have one last fling with Brandy, because, after 10:30, the two of them would never see each other again. After taking a shower, he lay on his bunk, face down. Brandy sat on the edge of the bunk and gently massaged his tense muscles.

He loved it when she did that. Her hands were soft, yet strong as they plied his muscles, kneading them, rubbing them, soothing them. He especially liked it when she worked on his buns; they were large, full, firm, amazingly sensitive, and erogenous. By the time he turned over, he was stimulated: His thick cock stuck straight up, the head of it large and swollen.

After massaging his chest, massive and muscular for one his age, she let her hands tease his balls and thighs. Baby Jim squirmed in delight; his cock throbbed in eager anticipation. Brandy sure knew how to make a guy's cock beg for action.

Suddenly, there was a moistness right on the tip of his cock. He looked down and saw Brandy's tongue licking across the reddish bulb of excited flesh. His cock wasn't long, but it was thick and huge when flooded with blood. Slowly, his proud organ disappeared into Brandy's mouth. He closed his eyes, allowed the euphoria of sexual arousal to inundate his entire body, and then began to move his pelvis back and forth, up and down, gliding in and out of Brandy's greedy mouth, feeling her tongue and lips working their expert technique—milking him, sucking him, urging him toward release. Her right hand cupped his nutsac, gently prodding, while her left hand glided up his body to feel and lovingly caress his wonderfully soft chest.

Baby Jim loved having his body felt up. When Brandy pinched one of his nipples, almost painfully, he thrust his cock deeper and began to hammer away at Brandy's tightening mouth. His pelvis left the bunk as he fucked her face, twisting from side to side, round and round, up and down, backward and forward, bucking and thrashing like a wild mustang trying to rid itself of an unwanted rider.

He was vibrantly aware of his total nudity. His entire body tingled with the flush of sexual excitement. Then he was erupting into Brandy's mouth. He could hear her avaricious gulping as she continued to milk his dick, even after he seemed to be finished. There was always more—slower in coming, but there, nonetheless, waiting to be coaxed.

His cock never went fully soft as long as Brandy continued to worship it with her lips and tongue. It lost a little of its rigidity, but in no time at all it began again to stiffen into granite-like hardness. A few times, during their relationship, Brandy had skillfully succeeded in causing him to reach three or four orgasms without having taken her mouth away. Baby Jim realized that this was going to be one of those Marathon bouts. What the hell. He couldn't think of any better way to pass the time until the riot.

On the third floor, where most of the White Power Nazis lived, Moose and Carver were passing the time smoking some grass and listening to music. A sissy named Buffy (so named because, like Frank, she was a body-builder and had a buffed-up, hairless chest) was being sandwiched by two men. Chuck was sitting on an upper bunk, legs dangling over the side. Buffy was greedily "goober-gobbling" between his legs, and Mitch was "punching her buns" from behind.

By the time 10:30 finally dragged around, all the White Power brothers were in place. Acting casual and talking idly, they loitered near their respective grillgates, waiting for the floor officers to open them. They acted as though nothing unusual was in the air. At yard recall, there was always five to ten minutes of general, chaotic confusion.

As a safety precaution, no weapons of any sort were allowed in the cell house (except in states of emergency). The guards would be unarmed and vastly outnumbered. More than likely, the guards would give up without a fight. They would be relieved of the sets of handcuffs carried on their utility belts. Handcuffed behind their backs, they would be taken to the sergeant's office to join the other hostages.

On the second floor, Officer Cobb unhooked his key ring from his utility belt, in response to the announcement received on his portable transceiver set, and moved away from his cubby hole beneath the stairwell. Approaching the northern grillgate first, he was only subliminally aware of the larger than usual number of inmates milling around.

Cobb had worked at the prison for five and a half months. He was still nervous around the tougher cons, but the fears he had experienced when first coming to work for the Department of Prisons had dissipated over the months. It was a tight security prison, and incidents of violence were always directed towards inmates by their fellow inmates. It was an oft-repeated maxim, openly propounded in the officer's muster room, that as long as the inmates fought among themselves, they would never form any sort of alliance strong enough to be a threat to the security of the prison or to the safety of its staff. It was an unwritten but, nevertheless, very official policy that members of the staff were to create dissension among the inmates whenever and wherever possible.

"Let them kill each other all they want," Cobb had heard Captain Fowler say often enough. And sure enough, in the short time he had worked there, two inmates had been killed by other inmates, but he knew of no incident wherein any guard or other "free-man" had been harmed. He thus gave it no thought when he keyed open the northern grillgate and noticed that there were far too many loiterers. He spoke casually to them and joked with them, as usual. Moving to the southern grillgate, he heard the noise of men in the stairwell returning from the yard. By the time he opened the southern grill-gate, he was surrounded by a couple of dozen cons, but that, in itself, was not unusual. Once the gate was open, the men would straggle into the tier.

Swinging the gate wide, he suddenly noticed that several of the shirtless cons were coming out through the gate. "Okay, you guys," he said, trying to sound forceful, "back inside. Lock up for count."

But they were not obeying his order. They were swarming around him, cutting him off from his cubby hole and his walkie-talkie.

Fear shot up his spine, but he tried to remain calm. "Come on, you guys, lock up."

Suddenly, dozens of hands were grabbing him, rendering his arms useless. Inmate Steve Brackman was directly in front of him.

"Shut up and you won't get hurt," Brackman told him. "We're taking over. Make it easy on yourself. Turn around and face the bars, unless you want to be a hero, that is. A *dead* hero."

Cobb was forcefully turned around.

"Rick, take his handcuffs," Steve ordered. "Mark, get his keys. Okay, let's get him into a cell..."

Rick Daniels interrupted. "We're supposed to take him downstairs."

"I'm in charge of the second floor," Steve growled. "Until we know for sure that Frenchy's got things under control down there, we put Cobb in a cell."

At that instant, the men gathered around Cobb heard the report of a rifle shot coming from the yard. Two more shots followed in rapid succession. A man near a window called out, "Jesus! It's Whitey! They got him!"

"See what I mean?" Steve asked with a degree of cockiness. "Until we know for sure, Cobb stays here." He tapped the young officer on the shoulder. "Move." He didn't bother to ask what had happened to Whitey.

With several men hanging on to each arm and blocking off any potential avenue of escape, Cobb was led through the grillgate into the cell area. "Take him all the way to the end cell," Steve ordered.

The other men in the prison, who had not been forewarned that a riot was going to take place, looked on with curiosity. They had heard the gunshots, and they were seeing an officer being taken hostage before their eyes; but so far no one had said anything about a riot, nor had anyone yet issued orders. They stood around in clusters, waiting to see what would transpire.

When they reached the last cell on the southern side, the men released Cobb's arms, and he was ordered into the cell. Steve looked around at his fellow Nazis. "How many times have you guys been forced to strip naked so that a pig could look at your naked body while he supposedly searched for contraband? Well, I've always wanted to put that shoe on the other foot." He glared at Cobb, hiding his inward satisfaction. "You know the routine better than we do, pig. Take 'em off, one piece at a time! And hand 'em out slow."

Steve could see that the fish officer was scared shitless. He made the cop jump as he yelled at him, "Strip!"

In the tunnel, on the first floor, a fist-fight had broken out between the four guards doing the pat-down searches and the Nazis who had swarmed the cell house after Weasel had been killed. The four guards, mostly out-of-shape and unprepared, were quickly and easily taken down. Frenchy, Shotgun, and several others raced past them into the sergeant's office.

"Control! This is Three-Post! Something's broken out down here. We don't know what the fuck's going on . . ." That was all that Sergeant Moreland was able to transmit before Shotgun wrenched the portable unit from his hand. He had been standing behind his desk and was now forcibly propelled backward into his old wooden swivel chair. He glowered at the men storming into his office. "What the fuck's going on here? Just what the hell do you think you're doing, Lefebvre?" he barked at Frenchy. Moreland was accustomed to being in complete charge; he was furious at this outrage against his authority. "I'll see to it that every man-jack one o' you punks gets thrown so far into the hole they'll have to pump daylight to you in plastic bags." His face turned bright red as his indignation began to feed on his own words.

"Oh, shut the fuck up, you old windbag!" Shotgun shouted as he slapped the aging sergeant's face.

At that moment, the four tunnel guards were unceremoniously ushered into the office, their hands cuffed behind their backs.

"Three-Post: This is Control," the disembodied voice crackled through the walkie-talkie. "What's going on, Brian?"

Frenchy grabbed the unit out of Shotgun's hand and depressed the transmit button. "Control, this is Three-Post, but this ain't Brian. This is Convict Lefebvre. We've taken over the cell house, and I ain't gonna talk to no one but the Warden, got it? We got ourselves eight hostages, and we ain't fuckin' around. So get the Warden and make it fast." He released the transmit button.

"Three-Post," the voice came immediately, "The warden's already gone for the weekend . . ."

Frenchy interrupted the message. "I don't give a fuck if he flew to France. Get him!" He slammed the unit on the desk. He looked at

Shotgun and nodded toward the sergeant. "Cuff him. Then get all these pigs into that storage room. Ray, get upstairs and get those other pigs down here to join their friends. Pass the word: Make a lotta noise and break a lotta windows. Let's let 'em know out there that we got a riot goin' on in here."

As Ray was leaving, Baby Jim and Zapper came in behind their hostage. A bruise mark on his left cheek testified to the fact that the first floor officer had put up a token resistance. Frenchy nodded in the direction of the adjacent storeroom. "In there."

In the meantime, Shotgun had handcuffed the sergeant, had removed his key-ring, and had pushed the heavy-set man into the storeroom. Turning to Frenchy, jangling the keys, he broke into a wide grin. "The keys to freedom, old buddy."

Frenchy bored a hole into his lieutenant with his eyes. Only then did Shotgun realize his faux-pas: Very few men knew about the plans for an escape.

To cover up the blooper, Frenchy grabbed the transceiver.

"Control, this is Three-Post. Listen up and listen good. You've got exactly forty-five minutes to get the food supervisor off his dead ass and make up one thousand sandwiches for the cell house. No. Make that *two* thousand sandwiches. Two apiece ain't enough. And we want fifteen five-gallon containers of milk."

Shotgun interrupted. "They're supposed to have cake for supper tonight. Make 'em send over that cake, too."

"And cake," Frenchy continued, "every sheet pan they got of it. You got inmates workin' in the kitchen; those inmates will deliver the food to the cell house, then they'll go back to the kitchen and get busy workin' on supper. We're gonna be watchin' real close."

During this tirade, Frenchy had not released the transmit button. The man at Control was given no opportunity to argue.

"Now listen real good. Any funny stuff—any tricks at all or any bullshit about not being able to do what I'm telling you to do—and one of these hostages gets dusted, you got that? You know and I know that what I'm askin' ain't no big deal, so just do it. If you fuck it off, we start with the sarge. We'll make the rest of our demands to the Warden. Right now we want food and plenty of it. If we don't get it by 11:30, we throw Moreland's head into the yard to prove we ain't joking. If you think we're bluffing, Moreland's the one who will call the bluff—with his fat fuckin' head."

He searched through the desk and found some cellophane tape. He

--

taped the transmit button in place. Control could not transmit to Three-Post while that button was held in the depressed position. Frenchy was not about to allow Control to argue with him or to come up with delaying tactics. He spoke now to Shotgun, fully aware that his words were being overheard at Control.

"I want a couple of lookouts on each floor. If anyone but a con comes across the yard or even sneezes in the direction of the cell house, have Carver go to work on Moreland."

At that point, Ray came back into the room preceding the third floor officer, Moose, and Carver.

Frenchy looked at Ray. "Where's Brackman and Daniels?"

Ray smiled. "They're having a little fun with their hostage."

XV. STEVE

As Cobb removed his shoes and socks, the inmates gathered around the outside of the cell and began to hoot and holler and laugh and tease. Steve stood silently watching amid the cacophony of sound. An idea was forming, taking shape as the guard was taking off his clothes.

When Cobb's t-shirt came off, Steve was reminded of Tommy. The guard was easily four or five years older than the young con who had hanged himself, but his chest was smooth and only slightly developed. In uniform, Cobb wasn't exactly an imposing or authoritative personality; out of uniform, he looked frail, defenseless, and boyish—the way Steve liked 'em.

Off came the uniform trousers, and Steve's cock began to stir. Cobb's legs were slender, boyish, hairless. The men were whistling and taunting, driving the fish officer to the verge of tears at being made a laughing spectacle. He gulped, breathed deep, then resolutely pulled off his jockey shorts. Every eye was suddenly rivited to the man's dick.

"Dick of death!" screamed Stella, who had joined the crowd. "Lunch for a party of four," she continued, as the men laughed at her antics.

To his credit, Cobb regained his composure. He had known for most of his life that his cock was above average in length. In both high school and college, he had always drawn admiring glances and envious leers in the showers and locker rooms. In early adolescence, it had been an embarrassment. As he grew older, it had become a source of pride.

"Okay, knock it off," Steve said to the mob of men around the cell. Then to the young officer he said, "Turn around. I'm gonna put cuffs on you. No funny stuff. Play it cool, and we won't hurt you."

When Cobb obeyed the order, another appreciative cry rose up from the crowd. His buns were nothing spectacular, but the buns of fat old Moreland would have received the same type of derisive response. The man was a Correctional Officer, a guard, a pig, a screw, and he was naked, and he was under their control.

Clicking the handcuffs into place, Steve let his right hand slide lasciviously over the naked buns, drawing a loud ovation from the cons. He backed away, then spoke. "Lie down on the bunk. We're gonna cover the cell door, but I'm gonna keep checkin' up on you. If I catch you off the bunk, we'll beat the shit out of you. Mark, cover the bars with a blanket. The rest of you, leave him alone until I say otherwise."

Outside the cell, he spoke to Rick. "Let's get some noise going and let's get some windows broken out. You and the other guys keep things happening. I've got a couple of things to take care of."

He followed the tier corridor around the end of the last cell on the southern side and walked to the northern side, where his own cell was located. He covered his cell with a blanket, then went looking for Donald Stuart, the sexy little redhead. He found him on the south side, helping to break windows. He pulled him aside.

"Hey, Don," he said in a friendly voice, "come by my cell in about three or four minutes. I'd like to talk to you."

Back in his cell, he found his shank and placed it strategically under the blanket at the foot of his bunk. He stripped to his shorts. A few minutes later, the blanket parted, and the unsuspecting redhead peeked in.

"You wanted to see me, Steve?"

"Yeah, Don. Come on in. Sit down." He acted casual, but his voice was authoritative, as if he fully expected to be obeyed in even the simplest of matters. "How much time you done, kid?"

"About a year."

"Have you ever had any problems? Like people trying to take advantage of you?" Steve stood up and casually positioned himself between Don and the cell door.

"No, not really."

"Well, you've got one now."

"What do you mean? Is someone after me?" Don was still unaware of Steve's design and was still naively certain that Steve was a friend.

"Yeah, kid." Steve towered over him menacingly. "You've got a problem. Me. I want to fuck you."

"Hey, wait a minute, Steve, I don't play that shit." He started to stand, but Steve pushed him back to a sitting position.

"You'll play whatever I tell you to play, punk." Steve's face contorted into an ugly grimace. "There ain't no one around to help you, and you sure as hell can't go running to the pigs. I'm gonna fuck those sweet buns of yours."

The redhead glared at Steve with hatred blazing in his blue eyes. "You might be bigger than me, but I ain't giving up without a fight."

An ugly smile crept across Steve's face. "Good. I like that. I like a guy to struggle; all that wild movement just makes me hornier." He moved to the foot of his bunk (which was nearest the cell bars) and withdrew his shank, making sure that Don got a good look at it. "Do you want to take your clothes off voluntarily? Or do you want me to cut 'em off? That could add a lot of fun to the game. But make no mistake: I'm gonna fuck you, kid. A little bloodshed'll just make it that much more exciting."

He approached Don and pressed the point of the blade against the kid's right arm to impress him with the sharpness of the point. "Take off your t-shirt or else we'll see whether or not my little toy is sharp enough to cut it off."

Don was frozen to the spot. His mind raced furiously for some avenue of escape. The cellhouse, in the hands of rowdy convicts, was so noisy that no cry for help would be heard, nor would anyone come to the aid of a non-Nazi against a Nazi leader.

Impatiently, Steve slipped the knife into the short sleeve of the t-shirt and ripped it savagely. "It's not as sharp as a razor blade," Steve commented, noting the look of fear that had crossed Don's face, "but it'll do the trick. Take it off!"

Slowly, Don drew the t-shirt up over his head and pulled his arms through the sleeves.

Grabbing the shirt, Steve ordered, "Now your shoes and socks."

He watched with mounting excitement as Don leaned forward and reached down to untie his shoes. Absent-mindedly, Steve lifted the t-shirt to his nose and smelled it while his eyes drank in the sight of Don's shoulders and back. The youth's skin was smooth, had a ruddy complexion and appeared to be invitingly soft.

"If you try to get brave," Steve said, as soon as Don was barefoot, "I'll use this to carve you up, you hear? I'll be sure not to kill you, but I'll carve the words 'Nazi Property' on your chest. Now, stand up and take off your pants and underwear."

When Don at last stood naked in front of him, Steve found himself staring at the patch of reddish-gold hair framing the kid's elegantly sculptured cock. He switched hs shank from his right hand to his left, then instructed Don to turn around slowly.

Don stood up. The look of hatred in his eyes had given way to fear. He was afraid to turn around and afraid not to. He backed up to the basin, then slowly turned around.

The sight of soft, plump buns greeted Steve's eyes as Don slowly turned around, sending a thrill of expectant delight racing to the head of his cock.

Nudging his shorts from his hips with his free hand, he quickly took them off. Stepping out of them, he approached Don from the rear, his cock sticking out: thick, swollen, throbbing.

"Don't move," he commanded, as he slipped the hand holding the shank between Don's left arm and his body. He positioned the point of the blade in the patch of curly hair just above Don's dick. "Any false moves, and the blade cuts your meat off."

His right hand began to feel the boy's delicately soft body, and Steve couldn't help but notice that Don was trembling. "Reach forward and grip the edge of the sink," Steve commanded. As Don complied, Steve spit on his right hand, stroked the head of his pulsating tool, then ran his hand along the crack of Don's ass. Finding the knot of muscles, he forced a finger into the youth's orifice. "Relax. Believe me, it'll be easier if you relax."

He guided his cock toward the opening, removed his finger, then began to press. "God, you're tight! Relax, dammit!" Steve had been fucked, himself, too many times to count, and he knew that Don could ease up if he wanted to. "Fuck it," he murmured. "If he wants it to be rough, I'll make it rough on him."

His cock was rock-hard. No ass, no matter how tight, could successfully refuse entrance to Steve's steel shaft. It might cause a lot of pain going in, but it was going in.

The redhead moaned, then gasped in pain as Steve's cock brutally forced itself past the reluctant ass muscles, gaining entry.

"Oh, God, you're good," Steve groaned. "Oh, Baby! Jesus, that's sweet!" His right arm wrapped around Don's slender chest, and his hand began to fondle spongy nipples.

He drove his cock deep into Don's ass and heard the kid cry out in agony. The kid's ass was so tight around his thick peter that it hurt like hell, but it was fantastically pleasurable at the same time. He slowly retracted his shaft, being careful to leave the head of it firmly embedded; then just as slowly, he repenetrated, gliding and shoving it all the way in.

Suddenly, a searing, blinding, flashing bolt of pain shot into his back, left of center between his shoulder blades. He let out a blood-curdling cry as his cock rapidly retreated pulled out of Don's ass. In shock, his left hand jabbed into Don's pubic area, the knife breaking skin just deeply enough to draw blood, then the knive dropped from his hand. He slumped forward, all of his weight resting on top of the redhead.

Dully, he realized he had been stabbed. But who? Why? He struggled to turn around, to face his assailant. He could feel the blade, still lodged in his back. He could almost see it, scraping against bones, ripping into his lungs, tearing at the edge of his heart.

Summoning all of his strength, he twisted his body around, but an angry red haze blurred his vision and intolerable pain and agony gripped his body. Then the red gave way to purple, then to blue, then to gray, then to black, then to—nothingness.

His nude body slid off Don's and crumpled to the floor.

Amazed, and partially in shock, Don Stuart turned away from the basin, unaware of what had happened, unaware of what had made Steve cry out. He looked down at Steve's dead body, then up into the eyes of the old man whom he knew only as Pawnshop.

The old man was breathing heavily. "Don't worry about me, kid. I didn't come here to hurt you; I came to get him."

Don was stunned. Like an idiot he said, "Thank you. I mean . . . I don't know what I mean. It's just that he was . . . well, I mean . . ."

"Thank me?" Pawnshop looked perplexed.

Don swallowed hard. "He was . . . raping me."

"Oh? I couldn't tell. From my angle, it looked like you was both enjoying it. But now I can see where he cut you with his shank. I tell you what, kid; we'll just tell ever'body that he forced you into lettin' him suck your dick. No one needs to know he was fuckin' you. And don't worry about keepin' your mouth shut. I intend to let ever'body know that it was me what killed him. In fact, when the time comes, I want you to be sure to tell ever'body what I just said. The punk was suckin' your dick."

All of a sudden, Don felt faint. He slumped onto the bunk.

Pawnshop looked at him sympathetically. "It's like I always said," he muttered, walking out of the cell, "no one ever wins in a riot. Losers. We're all losers. Ain't never any winners in prison."

XVI. WARDEN BARSTOW

By the time the sandwiches, cakes, and milk were being delivered to the cell house, Lt. Seaton had reached the warden at his home only eight miles from the prison, and Warden Barstow had hurriedly returned to take control of the situation.

Before going to Control, he met with Captain Fowler and Lieutenant Seaton. They briefed him on the events of that morning and told him as much as they knew about the situation in the cell house. Barstow took the time to call the governor. He, too, was out of his office, and a blustery Barstow demanded that he be located.

"So far," Fowler commented, when the warden slammed down the phone, "they've made no demands other than food. We really don't know what they want or what they have in mind, Warden."

"It's them goddamn Nazis, ain't it!" the warden spluttered.

"Yes, sir, we believe so. The man on the portable radio unit gave his name as Lefebvre; we know that he's the leader . . ."

"When this is over," the warden interrupted, "I want every cocksucking one of those shits locked up so tight they'll *never* see daylight again. And I want you to work with the Attorney General's office to pin a murder rap on every single one of 'em, and if we can't make First Degree Murder stick, I want every one of them to be charged as accomplices or at least make Conspiracy stick. Get Ramos on this right away. I want him to grill his informants as soon as we regain the cell house."

Seaton picked up the phone on the warden's desk and relayed the message to Lt. Ramos, Chief of Investigations.

Barstow continued to harangue Fowler. "Give 'em anything they ask for. Uh, no weapons, of course, but we'll meet all of their demands, got it? Once we're back in control, they can shove their demands up their asses! Do *anything,* but let's get our men out of there safely, and let's get that scum locked up."

He looked out of his second floor office window, which overlooked the prison yard. "Do we know who those two men are? The dead ones, I mean."

"No, sir, not exactly. They're both lying face down. But Lt. Ramos thinks that the one near the weight pile might be one of his informers. He figures the Nazis might have found out about him. The blond man near the cell house could be one of a dozen different inmates. Officer Reynolds, by the way, is exonerated in the man's death. We've got several witnesses that Reynolds fired two warning shots. The inmate not only failed to obey several orders, he was obviously taking flight from the scene of a murder."

The warden turned from the window. "How many ways are there to get into that cell house, John?"

"Just the tunnel, Warden."

Barstow shook his head. "I can't believe they built this place with only one entrance or exit to that goddamn cell house . . ."

"For security reasons, Warden. There ain't no way to escape . . ."
He thought for a moment, then said, "Just a minute, now. We've had a couple of escapes from here in the past. The escapes took place through the sewer. Yep, Warden, there is one other way into the cell house, come to think of it."

The phone on the warden's desk rang. Barstow answered, listened for a few moments, then said, "Yes, sir, that's right. At the moment things are pretty much up in the air, Governor; but this much is certain: they've taken eight hostages, all uniformed. I want the National Guard called out, and the State Troopers. I want them cons to know that if they harm any of my men . . ."

Barstow was silent for a moment, then said into the telephone, "I quite agree, Governor. You get me the troops, and I'll return this prison to normal. Captain Fowler, here, has an idea about how to get into the cell house. . . . Yes, sir, I'll stay in touch with you."

XVII. THE COUNCIL

The sandwiches, the cake, and the milk had been delivered to the cell house in accordance with Frenchy's directive. The Nazis had seen to it that each man got his issue—all the extras, of course, went to the brothers.

After everyone had eaten, Frenchy gave orders to clear the third floor. Some lesser ranking brothers were left to guard the hostages and to keep up the semblance of a riot on the lower floors. On the third floor landing, Frenchy convened the Council.

The first order of business had not been planned. Pawnshop told Zapper that he had killed Steve Brackman; the murder of a brother demanded the attention of the Council. Frenchy spoke first.

"Old man Pawnshop has admitted to killing Brackman. If the old man can prove that he was in the right, nothing'll happen to him. If we decide that he was in the wrong, he gets the same thing he gave Steve. Okay, Pawnshop, tell your story."

An old-time con, who had been around, Pawnshop knew his ground. He got straight to the point, "Brackman was a punk and a snitch."

Several of the brothers who had known and liked Steve began to object. Frenchy silenced them. "Hear the old man out. You'll have your turn."

"We did time together in North Carolina—five, six, seven years back—I'm not sure now. For the longest time, I didn't connect the name or the face. He was just a punk kid; couldn't take care o' hisself—so he got turned-out into a punk. I mean a real punk! Eye shadow, lipstick, makeup, the whole works. No wonder I didn't recognize him. What made me remember was when Zapper told me we was gonna have a riot today. I'm too old to play the games you youngsters play, but back then, just like right now, I got along real good with the cons that run the joint. They had planned a riot, too, but they wasn't as smart as you guys—they made the mistake of telling too many people about it. Sweet Stevie—that's what they called him—knew all about it.

"I overheard him telling one of the screws, droppin' names, dates, and places. I hurried on to tell some of the guys what Stevie was up to. We was gonna way-lay his snitchin' ass when he come back to his cell, but he never come back. Next thing we knew, all the big-guns back there got taken to the hole. Stevie might've been a Nazi, this time around the block, but he was a snitch and a faggot last time around. Once a snitch, always a snitch. Zapper's been good to me, and I wasn't gonna take no chances of this Stevie character snitchin' on my only true friend. And even if he didn't plan to snitch this time, he deserved to die for what he did to them guys back then."

Rick Daniels spoke up. "That don't prove nothing. This old man's just talking. He could be makin' it up as he goes along." Several others joined in, agreeing with Rick.

Don Stuart was brought up from the second floor. He told the Council what Pawnshop had told him to say, then dropped his jeans to his knees, exposing the still-fresh stab-wound.

"How do we know that this kid wasn't being fucked by Steve? We all know that Steve was a booty-bandit," Rick pointed out.

The argument raged back and forth, consuming precious time. Frenchy kept looking at his watch. Zapper finally came to his aid.

"Hey, look. I've known Pawnshop a very long time. I say he would not lie about a thing like this."

"I say this: Bring Frank up here," Rick insisted. "Steve and Frank were as tight as any jock-and-sissy combo at this prison. If Steve had tendencies, Frank would know."

"Okay," Frenchy interrupted. "But let's get this resolved."

Frank was called as the next witness. Rick asked the questions. "How long did you and Steve Brackman share the same cell?"

Frank shrugged his shoulders. "A little over a year, I guess."

"He was your jock? You were his old-lady?"

"Yes."

"Did you and him ever flip-flop?"

Frank hesitated. "If you know anything about me at all, you know that I do not discuss who does what with who when we're in bed . . ."

Frenchy cut in. "Frank! We know you don't kiss-and-tell, but you might as well know that Steve is dead and that we've got our reasons for asking these questions. So cut out the horse-shit and tell us. Was Brackman queer?"

Frank took a deep breath, then answered, "Yes."

"Okay! That settles it," Frenchy said with finality. He faced the assembly of Nazis and made an announcement. "Listen up. Zapper's gonna take over. There's still a lot of unfinished business, but me, Moose, Shotgun, and Baby Jim got things to take care of downstairs. I belong in the sergeant's office. Zapper has full powers in my absence. Take over, Zapper."

Frenchy motioned for Frank to go down the stairs ahead of him. "By the way, Frank, with Steve dead you can forget about your watch. But tell me, for real—you and Steve, you really did . . . you know . . . you guys really flip-flopped, huh?"

"Why not," Frank said with a smile. "Try it! You might like it."

"Get outta here," Frenchy laughed. He, Shotgun, Moose, and Baby Jim started down the stairs. Frenchy turned to the group of Nazis. "See you guys later," he lied.

XVIII. THE PLUMBING CHASE

Arriving at the sergeant's office, Frenchy immediately dismissed the men who had been appointed to guard the hostages, telling them to take a tour of the cell house to find any malingerers. "If any man is caught inside his cell, kicking-back, take him upstairs to the Council. Zapper knows what to do with them."

As soon as he and the three other Nazis were alone, Frenchy said, "Now here's what's happening. Zapper knows to hold out until at least midnight and even longer if possible. If they fire tear gas through the broken windows, this place'll give in real fast; these punks ain't got the stomach for a little pepper gas. It's two forty-five right now; that gives us nine hours, which should be plenty of time. Just in case we get split up, I'll divvy-up the money right now. With Whitey gone, that gives us one-and-a-quarter apiece."

He counted out the money into four equal stacks. Each man took a stack of bills and pocketed them. "Okay, let's go."

The plumbing chase ran through the center of the cell house. On each of the floors above ground, the plumbing chase separated the northern from the southern tiers. It was six-feet wide, allowing access to workmen, and contained all the necessary pipes and drains for each of the cells. There was a walkway on each floor, but the drains went all the way to the subterranean sewer. The door to the underground access opened off the sergeant's office, directly adjacent to the cell house tunnel. Frenchy found the proper key and the four men filed into the dark, gloomy interior. They found themselves on a narrow landing, stone steps on the right leading down into the foul-smelling cavern, twenty feet below.

Frenchy's imagination took hold of him. It was like entering the set of an old horror movie, *The Phantom of the Opera,* or whatever the hell that movie was. The sounds of their boots and shoes echoed throughout the subterranean chamber. The deeper they descended, the wetter the air and the stones and the walls became. The dampness and the quiet seeped into the bones of the four men.

Halfway down, there was a second landing; the stairs took a left turn to cross over the open sewer, ending at the old stone walkway which apparently followed the sewer the three-and-a-half miles out to the sewage treatment plant. No light shone in the cavern. Once Frenchy closed the door behind him, the men had to take several minutes to let their eyes become accustomed to the dark. Their progress was painfully slow, as they had to feel their way into the depths, one cautious step at a time.

"Did anyone bring a book of matches?" asked Baby Jim as he stopped on the mid-point landing.

"I did," Moose's voice came out of the darkness. There was a brief scratching sound, then a brilliant flare of light as Moose struck a match. "We should've taken one of the pigs' flashlights."

"Good idea," Frenchy said. "You guys wait for me at the bottom of the stairs." He turned and hurried back up the stairs. When he reopened the door, light spilled into the underground chamber. Moments later, he reappeared, locked the door behind him, and switched on the flashlight. Arriving at the bottom of the stairs, he said, "I left the other keys there for Zapper to use. I kept the key to the plumbing chase door." He paused, then said, "Are we ready?"

Shotgun answered for all of them. "We've never been readier. Let's get the fuck outta this shit hole. I want to be free, baby."

Frenchy led the way, keeping the light beam aimed at the floor. A minute later, they discovered ten steel doors on their left. The doors were ancient, rusted, corroded, and streaked with slime. "These are the old isolation cells that Moose was telling us about, Baby Jim." He shined the light on the first door. "See that six-inch space at the bottom?"

"That's where they slid the food trays, right?" Baby Jim ventured. "Those peep-holes sure look small; I wonder if they still open." He pulled on a piece of hinged metal at the upper center of the door. The creaking sound of the tiny door being opened echoed around them.

Moose then said, "I wonder if these old doors still come open." He pulled on the large metal handle and the door squeaked open, slowly yielding to Moose's strength.

"Let's get the fuck outta here," Shotgun insisted.

Silently, the other three agreed, and Frenchy again led the way. Suddenly a rat scurried out from beneath one of the old doors, racing across their path and over the edge of the walkway to disappear into the darkness of the sewer.

The stench became increasingly overwhelming as they put the prison farther and farther behind them. There was no way for fresh air to circulate, and the putrid odors from the river of filth had been accumulating for countless years. Breathing became more and more difficult. The four of them were desperate, determined men, however. A successful escape was mandatory. Failure now meant failure forever. Eventually, the riot would be suppressed. If they did not make good their escape, they would be held accountable—for rioting, for kidnapping, and for murder.

In order for Zapper and the other Nazis to clear themselves, Frenchy had left instructions that everything was to be blamed on the guys getting away. A soft spot in his heart for Baby Jim had led him to emphasize to Zapper that Jim's name was not to be linked to any of the crimes.

Frenchy was certain that, once he got out, he was never coming back. Before he would ever let himself be taken, they would have to kill him. "We'll hold Court in the streets," he was fond of saying, "with rifles, and guns, and knives; but they'll never take me alive."

Moose intended to go to Canada—the Yukon or the Northwest Territory. Hell would freeze over before they would ever find him. He would hunt deer, elk, bear—stake out a homestead, and live the rest of his life as free as the great outdoors.

Shotgun had decided that Mexico or South America was the place for him. In the jungles of Venezuela he could make a small fortune growing marijuana, perhaps even get into cocaine.

Baby Jim had come to the conclusion that, given his boyish good looks and his gorgeous physique, he could easily become a hustler in New York City or Los Angeles. He would be just one person in a city of millions. They would never find him.

They had been walking in silence, each lost in his own private world beyond fences, guard towers, and smelly living quarters, beyond the fetid odor of the sewer, beyond the precarious first few moments of freedom. When the cavern took a sharp turn to the left, Frenchy estimated that they had come at least two miles.

Abruptly, Frenchy stopped, rudely drawing the others out of their reveries. "Shhh," he whispered. "Listen." He switched off the flashlight, and in the distance they could see light—the sewage treatment plant. But there were shadows moving across that light, and voices could be heard reverberating into the tunnel.

Shotgun swore in a coarse whisper. "Goddamn you and your fuckin' Council. Them's cops up there. I'll bet my ass on it. I *knew* we should've split the second we got ahold of those keys."

"Oh, shit!" Frenchy exclaimed. "They're starting to move this way. Let's get the fuck outta here." He turned and started walking rapidly in the direction from which they had come.

"And just where the fuck are we gonna go?" Shotgun demanded.

"Just come on," Frenchy called back to the three others. "I'll show ya when we get there."

All three men rushed to catch up with Frenchy, who had already ducked back beyond the sharp turn. The tunnel was dark, and Frenchy's flashlight was moving away from them. "Come on," they heard again.

Moose and Shotgun hurried to catch up. Unseen by the rest of them, Baby Jim held back. Remembering Frenchy's words of last night, he smirked derisively. "I would wade up to my neck in shit to get out of here," Frenchy had vowed. And now, Frenchy and the others were running like scared rabbits. Baby Jim had a better idea, and it involved swimming in urine and feces. What Frenchy had only given lip-service to, Baby Jim was ready to put into action. He crept back to the bend in the tunnel and watched the slow-paced approach of what he assumed were National Guardsmen. He waited until the last moment, then slipped over the edge of the walkway, lowering himself into the slow-moving waters and filth of the sewer. He had gambled on finding a hand-hold and the gamble paid off. The sewer canal was approximately three feet deep. The drains from more than three hundred cells and from the rest of the prison's plumbing facilities kept the channel close to full. He was confident that he would not be seen in the gloom.

When the Guardsmen, or whatever they were, passed by above him, he assessed their number at about thirty, maybe more. As soon as he was sure that no more were coming, he slipped away from his hand hold and glided along with the lazy stream of filth. Keeping his body submerged, but his head above water, he executed a silent breast stroke to propel himself forward.

As the end of the sewage chase approached, he saw that the light came from a portal-like opening at the end of the walkway. The sewer itself disappeared into what looked like a stone wall. He had to decide quickly what to do. He made his decision and glided toward the edge of the channel. Finding a similar lip-type hand-hold, he held on, breathed fresh air coming through the opening above him, and set his mind to the long wait ahead. He would not come out of the sewer 'til late that night. He would not gamble on being seen; therefore, he would not allow himself the luxury of climbing out of the cesspool for even the briefest of reconnoitres. By nightfall, he reasoned, the force that had gone into the prison through the plumbing chase would have quelled the riot and would have regained control. If any members of that same force remained just beyond the portal, they should have been recalled by dusk.

With the maturity of a man twice his age, Baby Jim realized that his biggest enemy, now, was impatience. *Wait it out,* he commanded himself, *don't fuck up this close to freedom!*

In the meantime, Frenchy, Moose, and Shotgun had found their way back to the isolation cells. "You see?" Frenchy asked, the beam of the flashlight playing over the surfaces of the ten doors. "They appear to be shut and unused. We'll hideout in one of them until we're certain it's safe to leave. Those troops won't stay in the plumbing chase once they've secured the cell house."

There was no time to debate the issue; the sounds of the approaching troops were getting louder rapidly. Moose set his powerful muscles to the task of pulling open the rusted old door, opening it just wide enough for the three of them to get inside.

Having slightly loosened the ancient hinges, Moose was able to pull it shut with greater ease. A dull click echoed in the small cell.

"What the fuck was that?" Shotgun asked quickly, his voice booming in the narrow confines of the tiny cubicle.

"Shhh!" Frenchy cautioned. "Those troops will be on top of us any minute now." He wondered where Baby Jim had disappeared to.

They waited in silence. Soon, the troops were filing past their cell, unconcerned or unaware; they had a different objective: the retaking of the cell house.

A moment later, the troops were quiet. Frenchy assumed that they had arrived at the staircase to the sergeant's office. For a while, he could hear only muffled noises and indistinct whispers. The sound of a key being turned in a lock, however, resounded loud and clear and was followed by a noisy commotion. One rifle shot reverberated through the chamber; more noise; then the sound of the sergeant's door being closed and locked; then silence.

Still Frenchy waited. At length, he said, "Okay. Let's try again. I can't help but believe that Baby Jim made it, somehow. Maybe we'll all be lucky."

Moose struggled against the door without success. "Give me a hand, Shotgun. Let's both of us push."

The two men bent their shoulders into the door, exerting every ounce of strength they possessed. It wouldn't budge.

"It's locked," Shotgun whispered. Then, as the full impact of the meaning of his words crept over him, he cried out in a voice bordering on primitive savagery. "It's locked! Goddamn you to Hell, Frenchy! I'll kill you, you son of a bitch! I'll kill you!"

XIX. THE AFTERMATH

"It's been a long weekend, John," the warden said to Captain Fowler the Monday morning following the riot. "Do you have all the reports I've asked for?"

The captain handed the warden a thick sheaf of papers. "Yes, Warden. It's all in here. Lt. Ramos' report is on top. I'm sure you'll want to read each of them, one at a time, but I'd be happy to give you the highlights, if you'd like me to."

"Good idea. Go ahead."

"Five men dead. Michael Weaver, alias the Weasel, was fatally stabbed by inmate Robert Willis, alias Shotgun. Willis was assisted by inmates Lefebvre and Janssen, aliases Frenchy and Whitey.

"Inmate Rodney Janssen, *a.k.a.* Whitey, was shot and killed by Officer Curtis Reynolds in the line of duty.

"Inmate Alois Lefebvre, *a.k.a.* Frenchy, was strangled to death by inmate Willis, known as Shotgun.

"Inmate Thomas Jordan died from strangulation. The man was probably hanged in his cell by persons unknown. So far, the investigations have failed to shed any light on Jordan's death. Hopefully, the autopsy will give us more to go on.

"Inmate Stephen Brackman was stabbed to death by inmate Hiram Little, alias Pawnshop. The man confessed to the murder, stating that it was an act of revenge going back seven years.

"Fortunately, no member of the staff suffered any harm. Officers Reynolds and Cobb have been granted thirty days paid leave for emotional trauma arising out of incidents which occurred during the riot. Reynolds was forced to take a man's life; Cobb was subjected to sexual molestation, harrassment, and ridicule. Cobb was not sexually abused, Warden, merely stripped naked in front of a crowd of inmates.

"Four escapes were attempted: one was apparently successful, three were aborted when our off-duty officers, called up for emergency duty, breached the cell house via the plumbing chase. The three inmates got themselves locked in one of the old isolation cells. A quarrel erupted. The man called Shotgun vented his frustration by killing the former leader of the White Power Nazi gang . . ."

Barstow interrupted. "I want that gang abolished. I mean totally wiped out, John. But go on; we'll discuss that issue at a later date."

"Yes, sir. One man only is unaccounted for, and it must be assumed that he made good his escape. Inmate James Ercolini, alias Baby Jim, was last seen in the company of the three men whose escapes were thwarted. It is not yet known how or why he got separated. A thorough search of the prison, the grounds, the plumbing chase, and the immediate vicinity of the sewage treatment plant has failed to give us any leads as to Ercolini's whereabouts."

Captain Fowler paused, then continued. "Damage assessments reveal that broken windows account for ninety-five percent of the damage done. And that, Warden, is what all those reports will boil down to."

"Thank you, John." Barstow sipped his coffee, then said, "Let's keep the joint locked-down for about three weeks or so; give the men time to cool off a little. We'll continue to milk this in the press and see if we can't get a bigger chunk of money out of those cheapskates in the legislature."

After another sip of coffee, Barstow stood up. "We'll tell the press that we've found dozens of shanks, several pounds of marijuana, and heaps of other dope and paraphernalia. We'll offer overtime to any officer who wants to work it. I'm just glad that no one got hurt."

When the warden saw the questioning look on Fowler's face, he emended his remark. "I'm talking about *my* men, Captain. I don't give a damn how many inmates got themselves killed. But come to think of it, John, I'm going to let you talk to the relatives. You handle the public better than I do."

He walked to his window overlooking the yard. "Looks nice out there, don't it. Ya'in't got the scum of the earth fouling up the air. Yes, I do believe we'll keep 'em locked down for maybe six weeks, instead of three. And as for them Nazis, we'll just have to make a little room for 'em somewhere. I'd bet that half the guys on P.C. could walk the yard if the Nazis was locked up. Let's get with Ramos and see if we can't turn the fourth floor back into a lock-down unit instead of a snitch unit. We'll feed them Nazis dry sandwiches for about six months and keep 'em locked down tighter than a drum."

He turned to look at his captain. "Well, now! Let's see if we can't get this joint back to normal, huh?"

BOOKS FROM LEYLAND PUBLICATIONS / G.S PRESS

☐ **KISS FOOT, LICK BOOT**. Foot, Sox, Sneaker & Boot Worship/Domination Stories. Edited by Doug Gaines/The Foot Fraternity. $16.95.

☐ **MUSCLESEX A collection of erotic stories** by Greg Nero. $16.95.

☐ **CRYSTAL BOYS** The first modern Asian gay novel by Pai Hsien-yung $16.95.

☐ **PARTINGS AT DAWN: Anthology of Japanese Gay Literature.** Edited by Stephen Miller. Brilliant collection covering 800 years of Japanese culture. $17.95.

☐ **MEN LOVING MEN: A Gay Sex Guide & Consciousness Book** by Mitch Walker. New revised edition. 40+ photos. $16.95.

☐ **MEATMEN Anthology of Gay Male Comics.** Tom of Finland, Donelan, etc. Large sized books / $17.95 each. Circle books wanted. Volumes 1, 3, 4, 5, 6, 7, 8, 9, 10, 11, 12, 13, 14, 15, 16, 17, 18.

☐ **ENLISTED MEAT / WARRIORS & LOVERS / MILITARY SEX / MARINE BIOLOGY / BASIC TRAINING: True Homosexual Military Stories.** $15.95 each. Circle books wanted. Soldiers / sailors / marines tell all about their sex lives.

☐ **SEX BEHIND BARS / BOYS BEHIND BARS / THE BOYS OF VASELINE ALLEY** (3 Vols.) by Robert N. Boyd. True stories of male-male prison sex, and street hustling. $16.95 each. Circle books wanted.

☐ **MANPLAY / YOUNG NUMBERS / 10½ INCHES / BOYS BOYS BOYS! / STUDFLESH / BOYS WILL BE BOYS / EIGHTEEN & OVER:** True Gay Encounters. Circle books wanted. Hot male-male sex stories. $12.95 each.

☐ **LUST** and **HUMONGOUS** True Gay Encounters. Vols. 1 & 5 $16.95 ea.

☐ **LEATHERMEN SPEAK OUT** Vols. 1 & 2. Ed. Jack Ricardo. 50 leather dads & sons, slaves & masters reveal their S&M sex encounters. $16.95 ea.

☐ **SIR! MORE SIR! The Joy of S&M** by Master Jackson. Complete guide to S&M / leather sex with sections on bondage, spanking, etc. $16.95.

☐ **THE KISS OF THE WHIP: Explorations in SM** by Jim Prezwalski $17.95.

☐ **TRASH / TRUCKER / SEXSTOP / HEADSTOPS / HOT TRICKS / MEAT RACK: True Revelations from 18 Wheeler** Vols. 1 to 6. Ed. by John Dagion. True sex stories. Circle books wanted. $12.95 each.

☐ **ROUGH TRADE: True Revelations** Vol. 7. Hot sex stories. $16.95

☐ **ROCK ON THE WILD SIDE: Gay Male Images in Popular Music of the Rock Era** by Wayne Studer. Illustrated. $17.95.

☐ **GAY ROOTS: Anthology of Gay History, Sex, Politics & Culture.** Vols. 1 & 2. Edited by Winston Leyland. More than 100+ writers. Illustrated. More than 1000 pages total. Vol. 1: $25.95; Vol. 2 $22.95.

☐ **HIGH CAMP: A Guide to Gay Cult & Camp Films** by Paul Roen. $17.95.

☐ **AUSSIE BOYS / AUSSIE HOT** by Rusty Winter. $16.95 each.

☐ **MEAT / CUM / JUICE / WADS / CREAM True Homosexual Experiences from S.T.H.** Boyd McDonald $14.95 each (5 vols.). Circle books wanted.

☐ **MILKIN' THE BULLS and other Hot Hazing Stories** by John Barton. Stories of military school, sexual hazing, etc. $16.95.

☐ **ORGASMS / HOT STUDS / SINGLEHANDED:** Homosexual Encounters from *First Hand*. $12.95 each (3 vols.). Circle books wanted.

☐ **GHOST KISSES Gothic Gay Romance Stories** by Gregory Norris $14.95.

TO ORDER: Check book(s) wanted (or list them on a separate sheet) and send check / money order to Leyland Publications, PO Box 410690, San Francisco, CA 94141. **Postage included in prices quoted.** Calif. residents add 8¼ % sales tax. Mailed in unmarked book envelopes. Add $1 for complete catalogue.